SECOND EDITION

The Politics of Injustice

For our newly arrived children,
AnnaRose Beckett-Herbert
and
Asher Grant-Sasson

SECOND EDITION

The Politics of Injustice

Crime and Punishment in America

Katherine Beckett
University of Washington

Theodore Sasson
Middlebury College

SAGE Publications
International Educational and Professional Publisher
Thousand Oaks ■ London ■ New Delhi

For information:

Sage Publications, Inc.
2455 Teller Road
Thousand Oaks, California 91320
E-mail: order@sagepub.com

Sage Publications Ltd.
6 Bonhill Street
London EC2A 4PU
United Kingdom

Sage Publications India Pvt. Ltd.
B-42, Panchsheel Enclave
Post Box 4109
New Delhi 110 017 India

Printed in the United States of America

Library of Congress Cataloging-in-Publication Data

Beckett, Katherine, 1964–
The politics of injustice: Crime and punishment in America / Katherine Beckett, Theodore Sasson.—2nd ed.
    p. cm.
Originally published: Pine Forge, 2000.
Includes bibliographical references and index.
ISBN 0-7619-2994-0 (pbk.: alk. paper)
    1. Crime—United States. 2. Crime prevention—United States. 3. Criminal justice, Administration of—United States. I. Sasson, Theodore, 1965– II. Title.
HV6789.B38 2004
364.973—dc21

                                2003013109

This book is printed on acid-free paper.

05 06 10 9 8 7 6 5 4 3

Acquisitions Editor:	Jerry Westby
Editorial Assistant:	Vonessa Vondera
Production Editor:	Denise Santoyo
Copy Editor:	Liann Lech
Typesetter:	C&M Digitals (P) Ltd.
Indexer:	Teri Greenberg
Cover Designer:	Janet Foulger

Contents

Preface

Over the past 35 years, crime has played an increasingly pivotal role in U.S. politics and culture. Many politicians go to great lengths to define themselves as tough on criminals and drug addicts. Journalists cover crime more extensively than any other issue. Television networks launch new "reality-based" shows that glamorize law enforcement and blur the line between entertainment and news. And victims' rights activists clamor for more aggressive policing and harsher penalties. In this context, lawmakers have adopted a wide range of anticrime policies aimed at "getting tough" on offenders. As a result of these policies, the rate of incarceration in the United States is now the highest in the world, and one out of three young black males is under the supervision of the criminal justice system.

Throughout this period, most criminologists have devoted their attention to investigating the causes of crime and analyzing criminal justice processes. At the margins of the discipline, however, a growing number of scholars have pursued a different line of inquiry, one that focuses on the role of the crime issue in U.S. politics and culture and the way in which the construction (or framing) of the crime issue in these spheres has affected the policy-making process. In spite of widespread interest in these issues, almost none of this new work is discussed in standard sociology, criminology, and criminal justice texts.

The Politics of Injustice is the first book to communicate this new research to nonspecialists and specialists alike. In it, we examine crime as a political and cultural issue, as well as the policies that have resulted in the dramatic expansion of the penal system. In so doing, we draw on a wide range of scholarship, including research on crime, its representation in political discourse and the mass media, public opinion, crime-related activism, and public policy. Our review of these literatures is thorough yet focused on the development of our central argument: The punitive turn in crime policy is not primarily the result of a worsening crime problem or an increasingly fearful and vengeful public. Rather, above all else, the war on crime and drugs is the consequence of political efforts to shift perceptions of and policy regarding a variety of social problems—including crime, addiction, and poverty—toward harsher, more repressive solutions.

We hope the book will provide readers with a better understanding of the nature of crime and punishment in the United States, as well as the cultural and political contexts in which they occur. We further hope that the new material on activism and reform will inspire convinced readers to join the struggle for a more just and effective approach to crime.

Acknowledgments for the Second Edition

The book reflects our efforts over several years, together and separately, to understand the political and cultural determinants of crime policy. Parts of Chapter 4 appeared in Katherine's *Making Crime Pay* (1997). Parts of Chapter 5 originally appeared in our contribution to *The New War on Drugs*, edited by Eric Jensen and Jurg Gerber (Beckett & Sasson, 1998). Material borrowed from these earlier publications has been revised and updated.

We would like to thank Jerry Westby, Senior Acquisitions Editor at Sage/Pine Forge Press, for encouraging the second edition of the book and shepherding it to completion. We would also like to thank Liann Lech for her expert copyediting and Erik Carleton for research assistance.

We are grateful to the following individuals for reviewing the first and second editions of the manuscript: Gray Cavender, Vincent F. Sacco, Raymond Surette, David Forde, Barbara Belbot, Rebecca Petersen, Roland Chilton, Karen Heimer, Jim Thomas.

Last, but always first and foremost, we want to thank our partners, Steve Herbert and Deborah Grant, for their intellectual and emotional support. This project would not have been possible without it.

—Katherine Beckett
—Theodore Sasson

1

Criminal Justice Expansion

Sabrina Branch, a 10-year-old Baltimore resident, sounds a lot like other children her age. She likes pizza and Cherry Pepsi slushes, playing basketball, and reading *Goosebumps* mystery books. When she grows up, she would like to be a lawyer or a basketball player. And like a growing number of children, Sabrina's life, described in a recent newspaper article (Kaufman, 1998, p. 10), has been turned upside down by the dramatic growth of the U.S. criminal justice system.[1]

Sabrina and her three brothers live with their grandmother. Her father, an Army veteran, has been arrested and jailed several times for selling drugs. After his most recent release, he concealed his criminal record and tried to find work. Unsuccessful, he began using drugs again, then unsuccessfully sought treatment for his drug habit (Baltimore has treatment beds for 15,000 of its estimated 60,000 addicts). Arrested again for selling drugs to support his habit, Vernon Branch was sent to the city jail before being sentenced to prison. Sabrina's mother, also addicted to drugs, has been locked up for petty theft. Sabrina's cousin, Tony, served 7 years for selling drugs and now wears an electronic monitor strapped to his ankle. One of Sabrina's aunts is serving 6 months for assault. Another aunt is nurturing a romantic relationship with a prison inmate.

Most of Sabrina's relatives have been incarcerated in the penal complex right down the street from her apartment. The complex—known as "Eager Street University" to distinguish it from Johns Hopkins University a mile away—includes the city jail, two new high-security prisons, and the state penitentiary that houses death row.

These institutions reach into the lives of Sabrina's schoolmates as well. Seven of the 15 students gathered in Sabrina's math class one afternoon had fathers who have been in prison. One boy's father died in prison. A girl said she regularly visits the local jail with her older sister to visit her boyfriend. Likewise, almost half of the players on a local youth basketball team have a relative in prison, and several have served time themselves.

One hot afternoon, a 20-year-old shoots baskets on an outdoor court. He is wearing long pants so no one will see the monitoring device strapped to his ankle. An 11-year-old tossing lay-ups is wearing a t-shirt from Courtside Bail Bonds featuring a silhouette of a man behind bars.

Upstairs in a meeting room, Harold Richard, 14, sits with some friends and calmly ticks off the people he knows who have served time. "My father," he begins in a soft monotone. "My mother. Both my uncles. My cousin." Around the table, other boys chime in—one has an uncle just imprisoned for theft; another visited his mother in prison last week.

Derrick Ross, 15, is waiting for his favorite uncle to be released in 2 weeks. His father and several cousins have also served time. Still, he declares, "I'm never going to prison." His twin brother, Eric, interrupts him: "Never say never."

On a trip to the courthouse with her grandmother to straighten out administrative issues relating to her guardianship, Sabrina witnesses a group of women prisoners being led away. "I saw all these women," she later told the reporter. "They were walking through the hallway with shackles. It made me think, is that going to be my mother? Or my aunt? It could be any one of my relatives. Who will be next?"

Sabrina's concern is well-founded. In Baltimore and nearby Washington, DC, more than half of all African American men between the ages of 18 and 35 are under the supervision of the justice system. The State of Maryland recently assigned probation officers to Baltimore schools, in which as many as 4 out of 10 students have served time. Sadly, Baltimore and Washington, DC, are not unique but are the leading edge of a national trend. Between 1980 and 2001, the number of people incarcerated grew by more than 300%, from half a million to just over 2 million. The proportion of the population imprisoned has also grown rapidly, as Exhibit 1.1 shows, and more than 4.6 million people are now on parole or probation. By 2001, 6.5 million people—more than 3% of the adult population—were under some form of correctional supervision (Bureau of Justice Statistics, 2001).

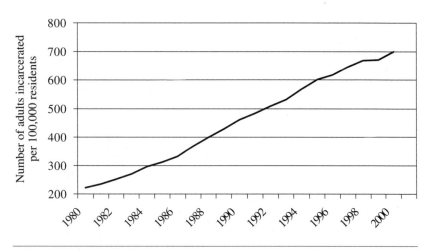

Exhibit 1.1   U.S. Incarceration Rate

SOURCE: Bureau of Justice Statistics (1995), Table 1.5; Bureau of Justice Statistics (2001), Table 1; Maguire and Pastore (1995), Table 6.21.

These developments have disproportionately affected young African Americans and Latinos (see Exhibit 1.2). In 2001, 10% of all African American males between the ages of 25 and 29 were incarcerated in a state or federal prison, and the lifetime likelihood of such incarceration for any given African American male was 28% (Bureau of Justice Statistics, 2002b). The number of Latino prisoners has more than quintupled since 1980; the lifetime likelihood of incarceration for Latino men is now 16% (Bureau of Justice Statistics, **1998b**; Currie, 1998, p. 14).[2]

These developments have also disproportionately affected women and juveniles. In 1980, 12,000 women were incarcerated in state or federal prisons (i.e., excluding the jail population), comprising 3.9% of the total population. Today, more than 94,000 women are behind prison bars, comprising 6.7% of the total inmate population (Chesney-Lind, 2002). Thus, over the past two decades, female prison incarceration actually grew at a faster rate than male incarceration.[3] Over the same period, the number of juveniles transferred for prosecution from juvenile to adult court increased from a yearly average of around 10,000 in the 1970s and 1980s to roughly 200,000 annually during the 1990s. Today, roughly 110,000 juveniles are living in locked residential facilities in the United States (Sentencing Project, n.d.-a).

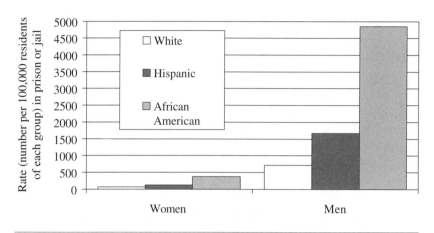

Exhibit 1.2   Incarceration Rate by Race and Sex, 2001

SOURCE: Bureau of Justice Statistics (2002a), Table 1.5.

Apprehending, processing, and warehousing this many people is quite expensive. Annual expenditures on law enforcement, for example, have increased from $15 billion to $65 billion over the past two decades (Maguire & Pastore, 2002). It costs approximately $30,000 to house a prisoner for a year—even with cuts in prison programs—so spending on correctional institutions has grown even more dramatically. Between 1980 and 2000, the cost of the nation's prisons increased from just under $7 billion annually to nearly $50 billion. As shown in Exhibit 1.3, the United States now spends nearly $150 billion annually fighting crime and drugs (Donziger, 1996; Maguire & Pastore, 2002).

Explaining the Expansion of the Penal System

The expansion of the criminal justice system is a consequence of two decades of "get-tough" policy making. New policies include those targeted at violent and repeat offenders, such as the death penalty and three-strikes laws. They also include new mandatory sentences and policing strategies that target nonviolent property and public order offenders, especially drug users.

Much of the growth of the prison and jail populations is a result of policies and practices that target these nonviolent offenders. Indeed, the U.S. now arrests and incarcerates a much larger proportion of those accused of property, public order, or drug offenses than do other industrialized countries, and it does so for significantly longer periods of time.

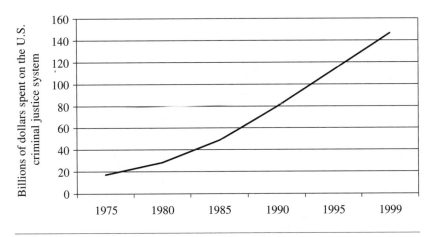

Exhibit 1.3   U.S. Criminal Justice Expenditures

SOURCE: Maguire and Pastore (1980), Table 1.2; *Justice Expenditure and Employment Extracts 1992-1999* (Table 1).

In 2000, police arrested more than 2 million individuals for such "consensual" or "victimless" crimes as curfew violations, prostitution, gambling, drug possession, vagrancy, and public drunkenness (see Maguire & Pastore, 2002, Table 4.1). Fewer than one in five of all arrests in that year involved people accused of the more serious "index" crimes (for an explanation of index crimes, see Chapter 2). And as Exhibit 1.4 shows, only about one quarter of these more serious index crimes involved violence.

As a result, our prisons and jails house many people whose most serious violation is the possession or sale of illicit drugs. In state prisons in 2001, 21% of inmates were serving time for a nonviolent drug offense, up from 9% in 1985. In the smaller federal system, 57% of inmates are serving time on drug charges (Bureau of Justice Statistics, 2002b). Most of those imprisoned for drug offenses are convicted of possession—rather than distribution—of drugs (Tonry, 1995).

How did we get to this point? How did get-tough policies come to be defined as the best solution to our crime and drug problems? Many popular and academic explanations of this pattern identify high or rising rates of crime and the popular outrage crime engenders as the key explanatory factor. As we will show, one difficulty with these explanations is that the most reliable data indicate that U.S. crime rates have been stable or in decline since the mid-1970s, and that they are

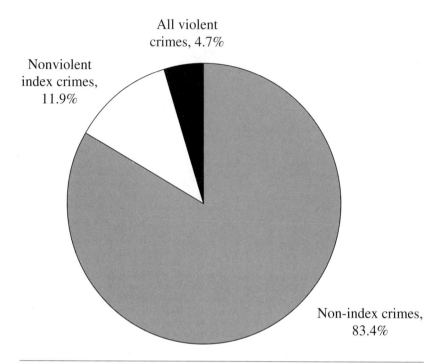

Exhibit 1.4   Arrests by Offense Type, 2000

SOURCE: Federal Bureau of Investigation (FBI) (2001).

comparable to those of other countries that incarcerate far fewer of their inhabitants. Another problem with these explanations is that expressions of popular outrage about crime are more closely related to shifts in the quantity and tone of crime-related media and political discourse about crime than to the volume of crime in society.

Our explanation for the punitive policies associated with the wars on crime and drugs therefore highlights the leading role of politicians and the mass media in transforming public discourse around a range of social problems, especially crime, drugs, and welfare. We argue that prominent politicians declared war on crime and drugs as part of a broader political and economic strategy aimed at rolling back the reforms of the 1960s. Their efforts in these areas were successful, in part, because of the media's receptivity to the tough-on-crime rhetoric and eagerness to amplify its core messages.

The capacity of politicians and media to shape popular policies, however, is not unlimited. Although not the driving force behind the new punitive policies, the public was, for the most part, receptive to the assumptions and images upon which they rest. We attribute this receptivity to a variety of factors, including the high homicide rate in the United States, but also, and more important, to a new and more subtle form of racism and the ongoing popularity of individualistic understandings of and solutions to complex social problems. Some elements of the public have taken a leading role in advocating get-tough policies, whereas others have actively opposed them. We examine the influence of this grassroots activism as well, paying particular attention to the emergence of increasingly organized and effective efforts to reverse some of the most punitive aspects of the wars on crime and drugs.

Outline of the Book

We begin by showing in Chapter 2 that the expansion of the criminal justice system in recent decades is not a consequence of a rising or unusually high crime rate. On the contrary, the best available data indicate that the level of criminal victimization was more or less stable in the 1980s and has been in decline since the 1990s. Comparative data also suggest that levels of criminal victimization in the United States, although somewhat high, are comparable to those in other industrialized countries.

There is one exception to this generalization: The United States has an exceptionally high rate of homicide. Indeed, despite recent declines in the murder rate, people in the United States are between 3 and 10 times more likely to be killed than in comparable countries.

In Chapter 3, we analyze why this is the case and argue that the United States' unusually high homicide rate results from the catastrophic interaction of a number of factors: the ubiquity of guns, high rates of economic and racial inequality (especially in the form of concentrated urban poverty), the trade in illegal drugs, and the emergence of a "code of the streets" that encourages the use of violence. This understanding of the pervasiveness of lethal violence in America has important policy implications and helps to understand the limited utility of the prevailing "lock-'em-up" strategy. But the fact that the United States has a higher homicide rate than comparable countries does not explain the growth in prison and jail populations: Homicide is a relatively rare crime, and most of today's offenders are incarcerated for crimes that are far less serious than murder.

Chapters 4-7 set out in detail our explanation for the adoption of punitive anticrime policies. In Chapter 4, we show that the politicization of crime began in earnest more than four decades ago. In response to the civil rights movement and the expansion of the War on Poverty programs of the 1960s, conservative politicians highlighted the problem of "street crime" and argued that this problem was caused by an excessively lenient welfare and justice system that encouraged bad people to make bad choices and rewarded them for doing so.

By emphasizing the severity and pervasiveness of "street crime" and framing the problem in terms of immoral individuals rather than criminogenic (crime-causing) social conditions, these politicians effectively redefined the poor—especially the minority poor—as dangerous and undeserving. In the process, these political leaders attracted socially conservative voters to the Republican Party and legitimated efforts to redirect state policy toward social control and away from social welfare. This reorientation of state policy around social control rather than social welfare now enjoys widespread, bipartisan support. In fact, the conservative ideological campaign was so successful that Democrats are now nearly as likely as Republicans to support welfare spending cuts and draconian anticrime initiatives.

The mass media were crucial to the success of these efforts to highlight crime-related problems—especially violent street crime—and frame them in ways that indicate the need for enhanced punishment. In Chapter 5, we examine the role of the news and entertainment media, arguing that media imagery of crime and drugs has tended to amplify rather than challenge the claims of national politicians. Indeed, surges in news media attention to crime have been tied more closely to the initiatives of politicians than to trends in officially reported crime. Additionally, the news has tended to frame the crime issue in terms of the alleged unwillingness of the criminal justice system to truly get tough on criminal offenders, and to focus on the most sensational types of violent crime, ignoring the less frightening and far more petty offenses for which an increasing number of Americans are incarcerated.

Americans are drawn to fictional as well as news accounts of crime, and these representations have also affected the way people think about the issue. The rate of violence in entertainment television and film has historically outstripped real-world rates, and this gap has grown wider in recent decades. Moreover, in film and television programming, police efforts to catch criminals are often thwarted by legal technicalities, liberal judges, and bureaucratic red tape. The thin blue line protecting citizens from criminals is thus patrolled by heroic cops who must operate outside the boundaries of the law to get the job done. Although complex and contradictory, these programs, like crime news, tend to echo conservative complaints about the alleged leniency of the criminal justice system. Reality-based police shows (*COPS*, *Real Stories of the Highway Patrol*) further amplify this theme and, by blurring the line between news and entertainment, do so in ways that are particularly dramatic and emotive.

Although the American public did not put the crime issue on the public agenda, many people have responded to political calls for a tougher justice system. In Chapter 6, we examine public opinion regarding crime and punishment and conclude that the tendency of many Americans to support the get-tough rhetoric of politicians—a tendency rooted deeply in American culture—has grown more pronounced. But this conclusion needs to be qualified in two important ways. First, we argue that the intensification of popular punitiveness is largely a consequence rather than a cause of political initiative on the crime issue; popular attitudes increasingly reflect the claims and narratives about crime that dominate political rhetoric and saturate the mass media. Second, we marshal evidence to show that although popular attitudes and beliefs have hardened, they remain ambivalent and contradictory. Even when the get-tough mood was at its peak, most Americans were still eager to see a greater emphasis placed on crime prevention and were willing to support a variety of alternatives to incarceration. Therefore, there is reason to suspect that politicians willing to challenge the prevailing get-tough approach to crime control might enjoy popular support for doing so, and recent developments, discussed in the following chapter, indicate that this is increasingly the case.

In Chapter 7, we continue our discussion of popular responses to crime, this time analyzing a range of crime-related grassroots activities. These include neighborhood anticrime efforts; the victim's rights movement; and human rights activism against the death penalty, mandatory drug sentences, and police brutality. Some of these movements have been able to influence the direction of crime control policy; others have not. In this chapter, we analyze why this is so and, in particular, explain why the victim's rights movement has received more attention and more successfully affected policy (at least until recently) than have groups that challenge the logic of the war on crime.

Our theoretical argument in Chapters 4-7 is summed up in Exhibit 1.5. In our view, the initiatives of conservative and, more recently, moderate politicians are the key factor, the driving force behind the policies that have resulted in criminal justice expansion. Other factors, including

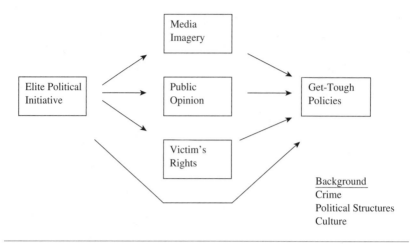

Exhibit 1.5   A Theoretical Model of Criminal Justice Expansion

media imagery, public opinion, and the victim's rights movement, have amplified the effects of politics while also exercising their own, more modest influence. Finally, we have placed several factors, including crime, political structures, and culture, in the background to indicate that these are important but indirect sources of support for the policies that produce mass incarceration.

The initiatives of politicians, amplified through the mass media and victim's rights movement, and resonant with many Americans, have prompted lawmakers at the state and federal levels of government to adopt many new laws and practices. In Chapter 8, we take a closer look at the policy changes that have contributed most directly to the growth of the criminal justice system, including harsh mandatory minimum and three-strikes sentencing laws, the revival of the death penalty, and intensification of surveillance in the community. We argue that these and other get-tough policy initiatives have done little to suppress crime. In fact, by breaking up families, disrupting communities, reducing the job prospects of hundreds of thousands of ex-cons, and consuming resources that might otherwise be directed toward drug abuse and crime prevention, these new policies are increasingly important causes of contemporary urban problems, including crime. Furthermore, these policies are corrosive of democratic institutions and values, and they reflect a disturbing tendency to scapegoat and discard those citizens now considered to be part of an "urban underclass."

Finally, in Chapter 9, we suggest that political activism is needed to induce politicians to reconsider the policies associated with the war on crime. In the hope of furthering this cause, we sketch out an alternative policy agenda, much of which has been taken up by an increasingly active network of grassroots opponents of the wars on crime and drugs. These proposals emphasize the need to scale back the reach of the justice system and to shift the balance in crime control from punishment to prevention. Toward that end, we recommend decriminalizing drugs, reducing the number of guns in circulation, investing in social welfare and social justice initiatives, and improving the quality of life and opportunities of the poor.

2

Crime in the United States

The extraordinary expansion of the penal system—especially the prison and jail populations—cries out for explanation. Many have assumed that the criminal justice system has grown so rapidly because U.S. crime rates are unusually high and getting higher. According to this argument, the worsening of the U.S. crime problem generated much fear and concern among the public, and politicians responded by enacting tough criminal justice measures. In this chapter, we analyze the available evidence to assess whether the crime problem has, in fact, worsened. Is the U.S. crime rate really higher than ever? Is crime a far more serious problem in the United States than in other industrialized countries? If so, the growth of the U.S. prison and jail populations could be seen as a response to a worsening or particularly severe crime problem and the fear it engenders. But if the U.S. crime rate is neither increasing nor unusually high, the unprecedented expansion of the penal system remains mysterious.

Crime in Historical Perspective

It is commonly asserted that crime, especially violent crime, is a much more serious problem than in the past. In fact, historical research suggests that modern industrialized societies—including our own—are significantly *less* violent than the predominantly rural societies of previous centuries. In Europe, for example, rates of crime and violence declined steadily from the 13th century through the mid-20th century. In fact, levels of homicide were between 10 and 20 times higher in the medieval and early modern periods than in the 20th century. In the United States, too, urbanization and industrialization were associated with declining levels of violence (Hagan, 1994). Contrary to popular perceptions, then, it appears that Western society has become less rather than more violent over time.

The incidence of violence continued to decline through the 1940s in most industrialized countries, although the U.S. homicide rate did increase under Prohibition in the 1920s (Gurr, 1989; Haller, 1989; Monkkonen, 1981). After World War II, reported rates of crime in the United States (and most European countries) began an upward trend that continued for some time. The Uniform Crime Reports, which we will discuss momentarily, indicate that this increase continued through the 1980s. Despite this upward trend, homicide was far less common in 1981 (a peak year for murder in the 20th-century United States) than it had been at several points in the 19th century (Lane, 1989).

Whether or not the incidence of crime has increased in the more recent past is hotly debated. The uncertainty stems from the fact that different data sources generate quite varied assessments of crime trends. For most of the 20th century, the Federal Bureau of Investigation's Uniform Crime Report (UCR) served as the main source of information about crime. The UCR measures how frequently seven so-called index crimes— homicide, robbery, rape, assault, larceny, burglary, and arson—are reported to the police. According to the UCR, both violent and property crime rates increased fairly steadily from the early 1960s through the early 1990s but dropped considerably over the course of the 1990s. Thus, the overall picture provided by the UCR suggests that crime rates rose throughout the 1960s, 1970s and 1980s but declined noticeably in the 1990s (see Exhibit 2.1). The problem is that these data are quite inconsistent with the results of other measures of crime rates for all but the 1990s. In particular, criminal victimization surveys tell quite a different story about U.S. crime patterns.

In the early 1970s, concern about the significant numbers of criminal victimizations that were not reported to police (and hence omitted from the UCR) led to the creation of the National Crime Survey (now called the National Crime Victimization Survey, or NCVS). The results of the NCVS are based on interviews with a random sample of 100,000 noninstitutionalized U.S. residents 12 years old and older. These NCVS respondents are asked by interviewers to describe their experiences with different types of crime. Because many people do not report such experiences to the police, but are willing to discuss them with telephone

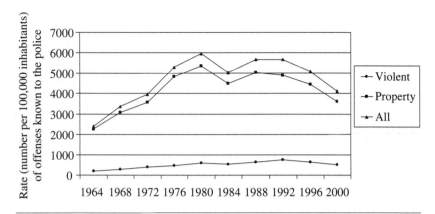

Exhibit 2.1   Crime Trends: Uniform Crime Report Data

SOURCE: Federal Bureau of Investigation (2001); Maguire and Pastore (1997), Table 3.11.

interviewers, the NCVS data show a much higher level of criminal victimization than do the UCR. (Many people also do not report their experiences to telephone interviewers, and those most likely to be victimized are less likely to be reached by telephone, so the victimization survey data still underestimate the incidence of criminal victimization).

Unlike the UCR data, the NCVS results suggest that rates of violent crime fluctuated (rather than increased) over the course of the 1970s and 1980s (see Exhibit 2.2). Also unlike the UCR estimates, the NCVS data indicate that rates of property crime declined sharply during this period. The two data sources are in agreement only with respect to the 1990s: Both suggest that violent and property crime rates dropped significantly during that time.

Why do the UCR and NCVS provide such contradictory assessments of trends in criminal victimization during the 1970s and 1980s? Answering this question is a bit more complicated than it may seem. For one thing, the UCR and NCVS do not measure exactly the same crimes or cover an identical time period.[1] Comparisons of the two data sources must take this and other methodological differences into account. Most researchers attempting to sort out these issues have concluded that much of the increase in crime reported in the UCR is a consequence of two main developments:

- Members of the public became more likely to report their victimization to the police.

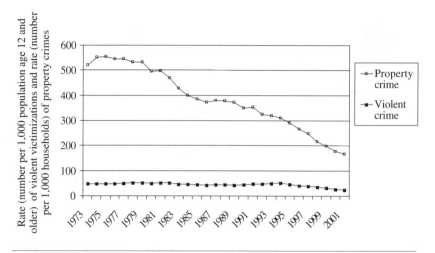

Exhibit 2.2   Crime Trends: National Criminal Victimization Survey Data

SOURCE: Bureau of Justice Statistics (1998a).

Note: The 1976-1991 data were adjusted to make them comparable to data following the 1992 redesign.

- The police became more likely to record these reports and to share their records with the FBI, the agency responsible for compiling the UCR (Boggess & Bound, 1997; O'Brien, 1996).

The fact that more victims of crime are choosing to report their victimization to the police appears to reflect growing awareness of and concern about crime.[2] Studies investigating the decision to report rape, for example, suggest that heightened concern about violence against women has increased the likelihood that rape victims will report their victimization to the police (O'Brien, 1996; Orcutt & Faison, 1994).

In addition, the police have become more likely to record these reports. For example, in 1973, about half of all aggravated assaults reported in the NCVS were recorded by the police; in 1988, the police recorded an estimated 97% of all such reports (Donahue, 1997; Miller, 1996, p. 27). Similarly, growing police awareness of the prevalence and seriousness of rape has increased the likelihood that police will "found" (i.e., judge to be reliable) reports of rape and include them in official records. In Indianapolis, for example, the number of rape reports founded and recorded by the police increased significantly following the establishment of a sex offender unit in that department (LaFree, 1989).

Police diligence in recording crime reports occurred largely at the behest of the federal government. In 1973, in an effort to improve crime statistics, the Justice Department began to assist local police departments with their record keeping and encouraged officers on the beat to spend more time on paperwork. As a result, the number of crimes recorded by police departments between 1973 and 1995 grew by 116%, although the number of victimizations reported to the police decreased 5% during this period (Rand, Lynch, & Cantor, 1997, p. 3). As one crime trend analyst concluded, "The 20 year period from 1973 [through] 1992 was not a period of ever-increasing rates of violent crime. Instead it was a period of increasing police productivity in terms of the recording of crimes that occurred" (O'Brien, 1996, p. 204). As a result, there is good reason to suspect that the NCVS data provide a more accurate picture of crime trends, and to conclude that levels of crime have not risen sharply over the past three decades.

But one type of crime measured in the UCR has been less affected by public reporting and police recording practices: homicide. Unlike other types of crime, homicide comes to the attention of the police in the vast majority of cases. Friends and relatives are unlikely to be able to cover up a murder, and the police rarely fail to record a crime as serious as homicide. Moreover, data from medical sources regarding the incidence of death by homicide closely parallel the homicide rate compiled by the FBI. For all of these reasons, UCR estimates of the murder rate are seen by most experts as fairly trustworthy.[3]

What do these data tell us about lethal violence in the United States? According to the UCR, the incidence of homicide doubled from the mid-1960s to the late 1970s, peaked in 1980, fluctuated for most of the 1980s, spiked again in 1991, and dropped throughout the 1990s (see Exhibit 2.3). This drop was quite dramatic, and murder rates at the dawn of the 21st century are lower than they have been for decades. In short, it appears that the United States did experience quite high levels of lethal violence in the late 1970s and 1980s, and again in the early 1990s. And as we shall see, homicide is a more serious problem in the United States than in other industrialized countries, even after the declines of the 1990s.

In sum, the upward trend in the crime rate between 1960 and 1990 suggested by the UCR appears to be largely a consequence of increased reporting and improved police recording practices. Although also

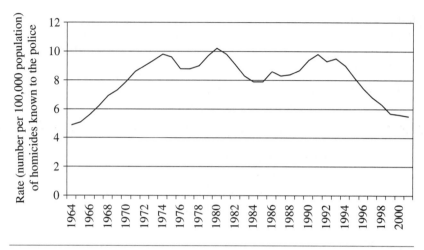

Exhibit 2.3   U.S. Homicide Rate

SOURCE: Federal Bureau of Investigation (1950-2001).

imperfect, the NCVS is considered to be a more reliable indicator of crime trends (Donahue, 1997; O'Brien, 1996).[4] The results of this survey indicate that rates of property crime have dropped steadily over the past two decades and that violent crime was less common in the year 2000 than it was two decades ago. Homicide data clearly indicate that lethal violence is a serious problem in the United States, but do not suggest that homicide has become evermore frequent in recent decades.

Together, these findings suggest that the expansion of prisons and jails is not a result of a worsening crime problem. Recent trends have made this even more evident. Both the NCVS and the Uniform Crime Reports indicate that crime levels dropped significantly during the 1990s. Despite this, the U.S. incarceration rate rose from 458 per 100,000 in 1990 to 699 per 100,000 in 2000 (Bureau of Justice Statistics, 2001, Table 1). Of course, the correlation between rising rates of incarceration and declining levels of crime raises the possibility that the growth of prisons and jails is an effective anticrime measure. We will have more to say about this possibility in subsequent chapters. For now, the point we wish to stress is that the massive expansion of the criminal justice system has not been primarily a consequence of rising levels of crime.

Crime in Comparative Perspective

Even if crime rates are stable or declining, it is possible that the crime problem is far worse in the United States than in other comparable countries. Indeed, many people believe that the United States has more crime than other industrialized countries. This difference, if it exists, could generate much anxiety and concern about crime and thus indirectly explain the United States' exceptionally high rate of incarceration. The impression that the United States is far more crime-ridden than other comparable countries is based largely on research that compares UCR data and European crime statistics. Such comparisons are unsound, for a number of reasons:

- As discussed earlier, the UCR data appear to misrepresent crime trends in recent decades; comparisons that rely on them are therefore misleading.

- Some European crime statistics are based on the number of people convicted, but the UCR data measure those crimes that are known to the police. Clearly, most crimes known to the police do not result in convictions. As a result, such comparisons overestimate the difference between crime rates in the United States and crime rates in other industrialized countries (Miller, 1996).

- Cross-national comparisons have been hampered by the fact that countries may define crimes differently. For example, what would be considered pickpocketting in one country might be classified as robbery in another and larceny in yet a third.

Recognition of these problems fueled the creation of the International Crime Surveys, first administered by the Dutch Ministry of Justice in 1988. These international surveys offer some advantages:

- Those administering the international survey use a single definition of each type of crime in every country in which the survey is conducted.

- Like the NCVS results, the findings of the international surveys do not depend on the actions of criminal justice officials but are based on the direct reports of surveyed individuals. (Although some survey respondents lie, we have no reason to suspect that Americans lie any more or any less than Belgians, Swedes, or Japanese.)

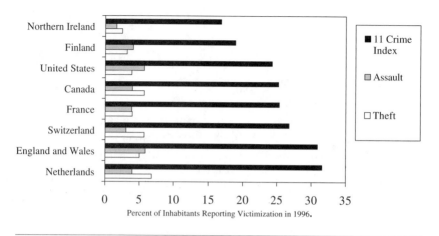

Exhibit 2.4   International Rates of Criminal Victimization

SOURCE: Mayhew and Van Dijk (1997).

The results of the International Crime Surveys cast doubt on the assumption that the United States is far more crime-ridden than other industrialized nations. The 1989 survey found that although rates of victimization in the United States were somewhat high, for no single crime were American rates the highest. For example, rates of auto theft were higher in England, Italy, Australia, New Zealand, and France than in the United States, and burglary was more common in New Zealand and Australia than in the United States (Van Dijk & Mayhew, 1991, p. 199; see also Donziger, 1996; Tonry, 1995, p. 198). Surveys administered by the United Nations in 1991 also found that U.S. rates of property crime were fairly average, and that the incidence of violent crime was on the high end, but not exceptionally so (see Zimring & Hawkins, 1997, chap. 3).

The 1996 International Crime Survey suggests that as a result of their recent declines, U.S. crime rates—including levels of violent crime—have become quite average. According to this survey, the overall victimization rate (weighted to reflect the seriousness of offenses) was lower in the United States than in six other industrialized countries and was actually slightly below the norm (see Exhibit 2.4).[5]

In sum, international survey data suggest that the United States does not have an unusually severe crime problem. Although U.S. rates of violent crime historically have been at the high end of the international distribution, this fact alone cannot account for a U.S. incarceration rate that

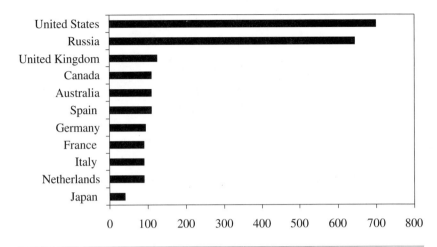

Exhibit 2.5   International Incarceration Rates, 2000

SOURCE: Sentencing Project (n.d.-i).

Note: Data for United States are for the year 2000. Data for other countries measure incarceration rates on varying dates between 1997–2000.

is *6 to 10 times greater* than that of other industrialized nations (see Exhibit 2.5). Furthermore, recent surveys suggest that the rate of violent crime is now actually lower in the United States than in many other developed countries.

Cross-national comparisons of crime that analyze all available data sources (police statistics as well as national and international survey data) reach similar conclusions. One such study sponsored by the National Institute of Justice found that England and Wales suffer higher levels of crime than does the United States (Bureau of Justice Statistics, 1998a). Another study concluded that U.S. rates of nonlethal violence are roughly similar to those in other English-speaking countries, but that rates of serious property crime are significantly lower than in many other industrialized countries, including Australia, Canada, Sweden, and the Netherlands. As the author of this study concludes, "The United States has higher levels of lethal violence than other nations but similar levels of minor [nonlethal] violence and property crime than other nations normally considered more civil" (Lynch, 1995, p. 11; see also Zimring & Hawkins, 1997).

Indeed, lethal violence is the exception to the rule that U.S. crime rates are unexceptional. (Homicide is not measured in the International

Crime Survey—or any other survey—because dead people cannot report their victimization.) According to police statistics, homicide is 3 to 5 times more common in the United States than in any other industrialized country, even after the recent decline (Zimring & Hawkins, 1997). Murder thus remains a significant problem in the United States, the causes of which will be explored in the following chapter.

But the high murder rate in the United States cannot explain why we have such large and growing prison and jail populations. Homicide convictions account for only a small proportion of those admitted to prison. In 1997, for example, only 2.7% of new court commitments to state prison involved people convicted of homicide. By contrast, more than 30% of those sentenced to state prison were convicted of drug offenses (Maguire & Pastore, 1995, Table 6.32). Jail inmates are even less likely to have been charged with homicide and more likely to be minor offenders (Bureau of Justice Statistics, 1997, Table 15). Similarly, homicide offenders account for 0.4% of the past decade's growth in the federal prison population; in contrast, drug offenders account for nearly 61% of that expansion (Maguire & Pastore, 1998, Table 6.29). In short, most of those incarcerated in the United States are doing time for crimes much less serious than homicide.

Conclusion

In this chapter, we have argued that the U.S. crime rate is neither rising nor (with the exception of homicide) unusually high in comparison to other industrialized countries. Thus, it is clear that the prison boom in the United States is not a consequence of a worsening or exceptional crime problem.

The fact that levels of crime dropped while rates of incarceration continued to rise in the 1990s and into the 21st century might be interpreted as evidence that incarceration is an effective anticrime strategy. According to this argument, crime rates are dropping in the United States—both absolutely and relatively—because we have incarcerated so many people.[6] Although this argument sounds plausible, there are many reasons to doubt that the incarceration boom is responsible for declining crime rates. In particular, the recent correlation between rising rates of incarceration and declining levels of crime is fairly unusual: Comparative research shows that states and countries that incarcerate at higher rates are not necessarily characterized by lower crime rates (Currie, 1998, pp. 56-57). This issue will be addressed in greater detail in Chapter 9.

Although crime in the United States has diminished over the past decade and is roughly comparable to the level experienced in other industrialized countries, the U.S. homicide rate continues to be exceptionally high. In the next chapter, we examine why this is so and consider the significance of this pattern for the recent expansion of the criminal justice system.

3

Murder, American Style

The United States does not have an unusually severe crime problem, but it does have an exceptionally high rate of homicide. This fact does not, by itself, directly explain our high rate of incarceration—the main focus of this book. It may, however, help to explain why many Americans worry a great deal about crime, and why so many responded positively to tough-on-crime political rhetoric during the years of the prison boom.

This chapter provides a comprehensive explanation for the United States' high homicide rate. Some might object that by focusing on conventional, interpersonal homicide, we are defining the concept of murder too narrowly. In the United States, thousands of people are killed every year by unsafe products, dangerous working conditions, and illegal hazardous waste disposal, and these irresponsible corporate actions are not usually understood to be "homicidal" in nature. By excluding these acts of corporate violence from our analysis, we may be reinforcing the erroneous impression that murder is something done mostly by the poor and powerless rather than by the rich and powerful.

We are, for the most part, sympathetic to this argument. However, our aim in this chapter is to set the stage for our critique of political and media claims about violence and the policies that derive from them. These claims and policies largely ignore corporate violence and focus instead on "street crime." In order to critique popular representations and explanations of this type of violence, we also focus on the problem of interpersonal homicide in this chapter.

In what follows, we suggest that four interrelated factors underlie the unusually high rate of interpersonal homicide in the United States:

1. A profusion of guns makes assaultive behavior much more likely to result in death than if guns were not so widely available.

2. High levels of economic and racial inequality, particularly in the form of concentrated urban poverty, create ecological contexts that encourage lethal violence.

3. The illegal drug trade generates a significant amount of deadly violence in the form of battles over turf and drug deals gone bad.

4. In the context of meager job opportunities, a "code of the streets" that prizes respect and regards violence as a necessary means of obtaining it governs conduct in many poor, urban communities.

These four factors are intertwined in complex ways. For example, the drug trade and the code of the streets are both related to the social and economic organization of inner-city neighborhoods, especially the high concentration of poverty and increased family disruption. Therefore, one dominant theme in our discussion of contemporary patterns of homicide will be the significance of the social transformation of ghetto neighborhoods. More generally, we emphasize the way in which a number of social, political, and economic factors interact to produce high rates of deadly violence. Before presenting our argument, however, we critically assess two more popular explanations of lethal violence in America.

Popular Explanations of Violence

When politicians discuss the high U.S. murder rate, they often point an accusing finger at the criminal justice system. The courts and prisons let violent criminals off the hook too easily, they argue, sending the message that crime pays. This argument has been the main rationale for harsh new sentencing laws for adult and juvenile offenders, as well as for the increased use of the death penalty.

But this explanation ignores the fact that homicide rates are much lower in other western democracies that treat violent criminals, including murderers, less punitively than the United States. In the 1980s, before the introduction of harsh new sentencing laws in the United States, the murder rate in Canada was about one third of the U.S. rate; in England, it was about one seventh. If the politicians were right, we would expect to find that these two countries kept their murder rates under control by treating violent crime more harshly than the United States—but this was not the case.

A cross-national comparison of criminal punishment practices in the 1980s shows that the average U.S. prison term for homicide (50.5 months), a category that includes offenses ranging from first-degree murder to nonnegligent manslaughter, was roughly the same as the average terms served in both Canada (57 months) and England (42.5 months). For robbery, the average term served in the United States (20.9 months) was slightly shorter than the average term served in Canada (23.6 months) but considerably longer than the average term served in England (15.8 months). Overall, these comparisons indicate that U.S. sentences for violent crimes were similar to those in countries that had lower rates of homicide. The similarities end there, however. Less serious offenses—including property, drug, and public order offenses—were punished far more severely in the United States than in comparable countries (Lynch, 1995, p. 11). Moreover, the United States was (and remains) the only western democracy that imposed the death penalty on some of those convicted of murder.

If criminal justice leniency cannot explain the high U.S. homicide rate in the 1980s, it certainly cannot explain it in more recent years. For prisoners released in 1999, the average time served for homicide was 106 months—more than double the average time served in the 1980s (Maguire & Pastore, 2002, Table 6.40). As has been noted, sentences for nonviolent crimes have also become longer in recent years. In short, the United States is not more lenient—and is often more punitive—than comparable countries that have much lower levels of lethal violence.

Politicians and other opinion leaders are also quick to blame the mass media for high rates of lethal violence, apparently with good cause. By age 18, the average American adolescent has viewed about 200,000 acts of violence and 40,000 murders on television alone. The average body count in 1980s action films such as *Die Hard, Rambo III,* and *Total Recall* was just under 60 per movie (Courtright, 1996, pp. 249-250). More recent films, such as *Lethal Weapon 4, Scream 3,* and *I Know What You Did Last Summer,* depict comparable levels of mayhem. Quite plausibly, all this violent imagery encourages people to resort to violence in their own lives and desensitizes them to the real-life consequences of violence. Yet countries that have far lower rates of homicide than the United States, like Canada and Japan, have just as much (if not more) violence in their television programs and films (Zimring & Hawkins, 1997, p. 126). The argument that U.S. violence is caused by violent media imagery thus implies that life imitates art (we use the term loosely) only in the United States.

Images of violence in the mass media might, however, interact with factors peculiar to the United States to foster a relatively high U.S. homicide rate (Zimring & Hawkins, 1997; see also Reiner, 1997; Surette, 1998). In particular, more children in the United States grow up in a context characterized by poverty, neglect, and violence than do children in other industrialized democracies (Currie, 1998; Wilson, 1996). Such children might be especially vulnerable to images of violence in the mass media. Thus, although media violence is almost certainly not a direct cause of homicide, it might be one among many background factors. Unfortunately, there is little published research in the voluminous literature on mass media effects that tests this hypothesis convincingly (Zimring & Hawkins, 1997, pp. 124-137). In the sections that follow, we examine factors that we believe are more directly responsible for the high rate of lethal violence in the United States.

Guns

A National Rifle Association bumper sticker states, "Guns don't kill people, people kill people." Strictly speaking, the slogan is incontrovertible. But so, too, is the observation that people tend to kill people more frequently when guns are readily available. This is because gun assaults are far more likely to result in death than assaults with the next most deadly weapon, the knife (Zimring, 1968). And guns are the instrument of death in 7 out of 10 homicides in the United States, a figure that is unparalleled among industrial democracies (Zimring & Hawkins, 1997, p. 108).

The lethality of gun assaults helps to explain the high rate of homicide in the United States. In 1992, assaults in New York were 11 times more likely to result in death than were assaults in London. This difference is largely a consequence of the higher propensity of New Yorkers to attack one another with firearms: Whereas New York residents were as likely to attack one another with a gun as with a knife, Londoners were six times more likely to use a knife. If New Yorkers had assaulted one another with the same mix of weapons as Londoners, the number of deaths resulting from assault would have been about one third of the actual deaths from the assault figure of 2,152 (Zimring & Hawkins, 1997, p. 220).

The greater availability of guns in the United States also means that robberies are more likely to result in death. In 1992, the overall death rate for gun robberies in New York was 8.4 per 1,000, about 10 times greater than the death rate for nongun robberies. If the 91,000 New York City robberies in that year had resulted in death at the nongun death rate, 79 New Yorkers would have lost their lives in the course of a robbery. The actual number of deaths from robberies was 357 (Zimring & Hawkins, 1997, pp. 45-46).

It is possible that the extraordinary propensity of Americans to use guns in the commission of crimes and to settle disputes reflects a greater motivation to kill. This issue is far from settled, but researchers have accumulated a good deal of evidence suggesting that the ready availability of guns—rather than a greater determination to kill—accounts for the higher rate of homicide in the United States. For example, one study found that 70% of all homicide victims were killed by a single gunshot wound, and that attacks with guns and knives resulting in death were indistinguishable from attacks that did not cause death. On the basis of this evidence, the author of this study concluded that "most homicides were the result of ambiguously motivated assaults, so that the offender would risk his victim's death, but usually did not press on until death was assured" (Zimring & Hawkins, 1997, p. 114).

These findings are consistent with what convicted offenders say about their motives in discharging firearms. In interviews with 184 incarcerated people who fired a gun in the course of committing the offense for which they were serving time, only about one third claimed to have shot with the intent to kill. Larger percentages claimed to have fired to "scare the victim" or "to protect myself." Moreover, more than three quarters of these men claimed that they did not intend to actually use their firearm prior to the situation in which they ultimately took aim and fired (Wright & Rossi, 1994).

International comparisons also suggest that the greater availability of guns is a crucial cause of the U.S. homicide problem. Comparisons of Seattle and Vancouver, two cities on opposite sides of the U.S.-Canadian border, show that these cities have similar socioeconomic and demographic characteristics as well as comparable burglary and assault rates. Nevertheless, Seattle, with relatively lax gun control laws, has a homicide rate 60% higher than Vancouver's and a gun homicide rate 400% higher (Reiss & Roth, 1993, p. 268).

Gun availability is also implicated in the recent upsurge in juvenile homicide in the United States. Between 1984 and 1993, the homicide rate tripled for adolescents 13 through 17 years old and doubled for those 18 through 24. The rates have since come back down, but the sharp rise in youth violence in the late 1980s and early 1990s has something to teach us about the significance of guns. Throughout the entire period in question, the rate of nongun homicides committed by juveniles remained absolutely stable; only the rate of gun murders increased. The surge in juvenile homicide thus appears to be related to the spread of guns among youths (Blumstein & Cork, 1996).

Skeptics might object that something other than gun availability—such as the expanding role of youth in the drug market—is to blame. Later in this chapter, we will argue that drug dealing is, indeed, an important source of lethal violence, and that participation in the crack trade in the late 1980s and early 1990s did spur many youth to arm themselves. However, increased participation of youth in the drug trade does not account for all of the increase in gun-related homicide: The ratio of gun to nongun killings by juveniles rose in all six categories of the FBI's Supplementary Homicide Report, which include killings among family members and intimates, killings in the course of felonies, killings in the course of brawls and arguments, and gang-related killings. A surge in the practice of keeping and carrying guns seems to be a reasonable explanation of the spike in gun homicides among youths (Cook & Laub, 1998).

According to recent estimates, about 200 million guns, including 70 million handguns, are in circulation in the United States. Although the proportion of households possessing any type of firearm has declined from about 50% in the 1970s to 35%-40% in the 1990s, the percentage of households with a handgun increased during this period to about 25% (Wintemute, 2000). The United States now has more federally licensed gun dealers than gas stations (Wallman, 1997).

Perhaps most disturbing is the extent to which guns have proliferated among young people. In a survey of 96 randomly selected elementary, middle, and high schools,

> fifteen percent of students reported carrying a handgun in the past 30 days, and four percent reported taking a handgun to school during the year. Nine percent of the students reported shooting a gun at someone else, while eleven percent had been shot at during the past year. (Wilkinson & Fagan, 1996, p. 73)

The massacres of schoolchildren and their teachers by heavily armed classmates in Jonesboro, Arkansas; Littleton, Colorado; and elsewhere, recently explored in the popular film *Bowling for Columbine,* are an especially stark reminder of how serious the crisis has become. In the United States, guns are literally everywhere, and their contribution to the country's extraordinary rate of killing is evident.

Inequality and Homicide

Opponents of gun control often point out that widespread gun ownership is not associated with high rates of lethal violence in a few countries (such as Canada, Israel, and Switzerland) (Gurr, 1989). Human intentions do matter. People do, indeed, kill people. In the rest of this chapter, we consider the social, political, and economic factors that encourage Americans to use violence and risk death in the course of settling their disputes.

We begin with economic and racial inequality. A meta-analysis of the research on this subject reports that there is a "consensus that the incidence of homicide is higher in countries with greater income inequality" (Krahn, Hartnagel, & Gartrell, 1986, p. 269). In their analysis of 65 nations, these researchers found that the correlation between the homicide rate and various measures of economic inequality is especially strong in democracies and wealthier countries. A more recent study similarly found a strong relationship between economic discrimination and the homicide rate: Countries that practice "deliberate, invidious exclusion" on the basis of ascribed characteristics such as race have the highest rates of killing (Messner, 1989).

These cross-national comparisons suggest that the elevated rate of homicide in the United States is at least partially a consequence of the country's pronounced disparities in wealth and its history of racial discrimination. Exhibit 3.1 shows that the income gap between the rich and poor is much higher in the United States than in other western democracies. Furthermore, as Exhibits 3.2 and 3.3 show, economic inequality in the United States is structured along racial and ethnic lines and is especially devastating for children. Although often assumed to have been alleviated by racial reform, these inequalities actually deepened during the 1980s and early 1990s, with average African American and Hispanic family incomes dropping to 54% and 60%, respectively, of average white family income. In the late 1990s, these long-term trends finally reversed themselves, with minority households gaining a few percentage points against their white counterparts. In 2001, however, the income gaps remained huge.[1]

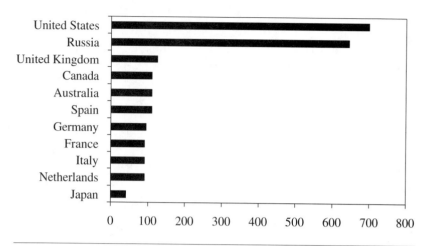

Exhibit 3.1   International Income Inequality

SOURCE: OECD (2000).

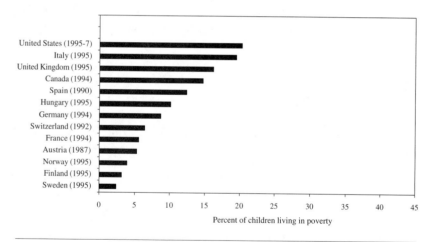

Exhibit 3.2   International Child Poverty

SOURCE: Vleminckx and Smeeding (2001).

A rich sociological tradition helps to explain the relationship between inequality and elevated levels of violence. Roughly 100 years ago, French sociologist Émile Durkheim argued that elevated levels of suicide and homicide reflect a societal breakdown in norms—"anomie," in the technical language of sociology—occasioned by a widening gap

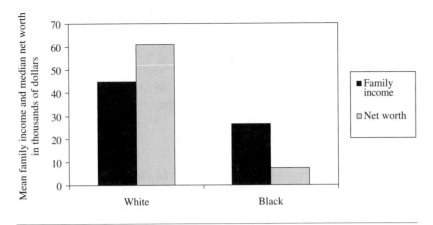

Exhibit 3.3   U.S. Economic Inequality by Race

SOURCE: U.S. Bureau of the Census (1998), Tables 51 and 55; Wolff (1998).

between people's dreams and aspirations, on one hand, and their actual life experiences, on the other. When such a breakdown prevails, people experience bouts of frustration, despair, and outright anger and become more prone to destruction of both self and other (Durkheim, 1951).

In the late 1930s, American sociologist Robert K. Merton employed the concept of anomie to explain the apparently high rate of crime in the United States relative to other, similar countries. Merton argued that a great deal of crime in the United States can be explained by a contradiction between the dominant cultural code, which prescribes material success above all else (the American Dream), and the economic organization of society, which denies to most people the routine means for achieving such success. To resolve this contradiction, Merton argued, many people turn to crime (as a way to achieve material success through alternative means) or addiction (as a way to escape the pressure to succeed) (Merton, 1938).

Anomie theory helps us to understand why the cross-national correlation between inequality and homicide is especially strong in democracies and wealthy countries. In democracies, the promise of equal access to "the good life" is most vigorously advanced, and thus, it is in democracies that arbitrary denial of opportunities is experienced as most intolerable. The fact that a great deal of frustration-induced violence gets acted out among family members, acquaintances, and neighbors rather than against the rich and powerful does not contradict this argument.

Rather, it suggests that people close at hand are simply convenient targets for pent-up anger (Messner, 1989, p. 598).[2]

But it is not just the anger and frustration born of high levels of inequality, or the strategic efforts of individuals to achieve material success against all odds, that help to explain the connection between inequality and violence. Countries with higher levels of social and economic inequality typically possess ecological and neighborhood conditions that directly contribute to high levels of violence.

The Ecology of Urban Violence

There is a tendency, when thinking about the causes of violence, to focus on the characteristics of individuals and groups, such as family history, level of education, and household income. These personal characteristics are less helpful in explaining serious violence than are the qualities of residential neighborhoods. Indeed, because lethal violence is overwhelmingly concentrated in poor urban communities, understanding these neighborhood characteristics is crucial. In the suburban areas where most white Americans live, rates of homicide are comparable to those in Finland. By contrast, half of all U.S. homicides occur in the 63 largest American cities—which house only 16% of the U.S. population (Sherman, 1997). Even within urban areas, the risk of homicide victimization is quite uneven: In areas of concentrated poverty, where racial minorities are more likely to live, rates of homicide are 20 times the national average (Sherman et al., 1997, p. v). An ecological or community-level approach is best able to explain the concentration of violence in poor urban communities.[3]

This type of explanation also has well-established roots in the sociological literature on crime and delinquency. More than five decades ago, in a landmark study, *Juvenile Delinquency and Urban Areas*, Clifford Shaw and Henry McKay reported that the distribution of delinquency across Chicago neighborhoods remained constant over many years despite population turnover. In other words, although the ethnic composition of these high-delinquency areas changed, the propensity of these neighborhoods to generate troublesome youths did not. To explain this pattern, these sociologists identified certain unchanging features of high-delinquency areas, especially their low economic status, ethnic heterogeneity, and high rates of residential mobility. These factors, they suggested, had the effect of undermining neighborhood social organization, especially the capacity of adults to exercise control over young people. In the absence of effective adult supervision and control, juvenile delinquency flourished (Shaw & McKay, 1942).[4]

Taking their lead from Shaw and McKay, contemporary researchers have demonstrated that the most violent urban neighborhoods are characterized by a cluster of "social dislocations." These dislocations include racial segregation, high rates of poverty, joblessness, family disruption, and residential instability (Land, McCall, & Cohen, 1990; Messner & Tardiff, 1986; Sampson, 1987, p. 366; Zimring & Hawkins, 1997). Elijah Anderson (1999) describes the residents of one such Philadelphia neighborhood in the 1990s:

> It is mostly a very poor neighborhood of women and small children, who make up extremely important kinship networks that work to sustain their members; at times, others are enlisted as fictive kin for needed help. These residents, if they are employed, work as dishwashers, mechanics, and domestics, as well as other menial jobs. . . . A large number of the women are on welfare. . . . When present at all, men appear most often in the roles of nephew, cousin, father, uncle, boyfriend, and son, but seldom husband. (pp. 27-28)

In such neighborhoods, poor, young, and overwhelmed single mothers are often unable to exercise control over children and adolescents, especially teenage peer groups in public spaces (Sampson, 1997).

Like Shaw and McKay, contemporary scholars have demonstrated that it is not the racial or ethnic composition of such places that explains their extraordinary rates of homicide. A comparison of two Manhattan neighborhoods in the mid-1980s illustrates this point well. The Bowery, with an only average-sized black population but a high concentration of poor people, had a homicide rate among the highest of the city's neighborhoods. By comparison, Stuyvesant Town-Cooper Village, with an average-sized black population but a relatively low poverty rate, had a homicide rate well below the average. Quantitative analysis of the relationship between neighborhood characteristics and homicide rates across Manhattan neighborhoods reinforces the obvious conclusion: It is the degree to which a neighborhood suffers from poverty-related social dislocations, not its racial composition, that helps to explain its homicide rate (Messner & Tardiff, 1986).

The Relevance of Race

This is not to say, however, that the problem of lethal violence in the United States is racially neutral. In the first place, residents of "high-poverty areas"—areas inhabited by high numbers of poor people—are overwhelmingly African American and/or Hispanic. In New York City, for example, 70% of the city's poor black and Hispanic residents live in high-poverty neighborhoods, but 70% of the city's poor whites live in nonpoverty neighborhoods (Sullivan, 1989).[5] Nationwide, nearly 7 out of 8 people living in a high-poverty urban area are members of a minority group. As one scholar, Loic Waquant, put it, "American urban poverty is pre-eminently a racial poverty . . . rooted in the ghetto as a specific social form and mechanism of racial domination" (Sampson, 1997, p. 68).

Second, to understand the expansion of ghetto poverty, we must examine the interplay between economic changes and racial discrimination. The most significant economic development in this context is the process called *deindustrialization.* This restructuring of the economy began in the 1970s and resulted in a massive loss of manufacturing jobs in central cities. In 1997, for example, New York City had approximately 925,000 manufacturing jobs, down from 1.5 million in 1978 (Perez-Pena, 1997, p. A14). The loss of manufacturing jobs in urban areas has not been fully offset by the expansion of the service sector, where wages for unskilled workers are markedly lower, and where jobs are more likely to be temporary and less likely to provide benefits such as health insurance.

The sharp increase in joblessness among African American males that resulted from this economic restructuring reduced the pool of "marriagable men," which in turn contributed to the proliferation of single-parent households and the intensification of inner-city poverty. Meanwhile, middle-class blacks seized the opportunities created by new laws banning discrimination in housing and fled the ghetto. In their wake, they left neighborhoods composed mainly of jobless men and poor, female-headed, single-parent families (Wilson, 1987). Research examining the relationships among homicide rates, levels of poverty, and family structure suggests that the increase in single-parent families in these poor communities has had significant consequences. In African American communities, for example, the percentage of families headed by a single parent is the strongest predictor of the homicide rate and is, in turn, strongly associated with the rate of joblessness among men (Sampson, 1987).[6]

Although deindustrialization was not motivated by racial considerations or intended to have racially disparate consequences, its effects have been particularly catastrophic for black urban communities because of the prior existence of racial segregation. Had poor blacks lived in racially

integrated neighborhoods throughout metropolitan areas, deindustrialization would have driven up rates of black poverty but would not have
produced isolated neighborhoods characterized by highly concentrated
poverty.[7]

Racial segregation is, of course, a product of racial discrimination.
In the South and elsewhere, local ordinances once prevented African
Americans from living in white neighborhoods. In the North, white
property owners attached "restrictive covenants" to their properties to
prevent transfer to blacks (and Jews). In the 1960s, under the rubric of
"urban renewal" (dubbed "Negro removal" by literary critic James
Baldwin), federal and municipal agencies destroyed about 20% of all
central-city housing occupied by blacks (Logan & Molotch, 1987,
p. 114). The federal government did eventually extend mortgage assistance—long the ticket to home ownership for whites—to African
Americans, but only to subsidize home ownership within all-black neighborhoods. New public housing was built but invariably located within
the confines of the ghetto (Wilson, 1996; see also Levine & Harmon,
1993).

Despite laws banning housing discrimination, the situation is not
much improved today. High levels of racial residential segregation cannot be explained by either the preferences of African Americans or their
socioeconomic situation. Rather, ongoing housing discrimination and
prejudice continue to keep many poor and working-class African
Americans in the ghetto (Massey, 1990, p. 354).

In sum, the relatively high rate of lethal violence in poor minority
neighborhoods is not a consequence of their racial composition. Instead,
it is related to the nature of the neighborhoods in which so many African
Americans and Latinos must struggle to make a life. Social inequality
and racial discrimination, both past and ongoing, have played a central
role in the formation of ghetto neighborhoods characterized by high
rates of poverty, joblessness, and single-parent families. In what follows,
we discuss two ways in which these social conditions give rise to high
levels of serious interpersonal violence.

The Drug Trade

One connection between the ecological conditions of poor communities and lethal violence is the drug trade. The concentration of street-
level drug dealing in ghetto neighborhoods is not new. Poor
neighborhoods inhabited by ethnic minorities have long acted as

"deviance service centers," providing illicit goods and services to surrounding communities (Hagan, 1994, p. 97). In the context of deindustrialization, however, the drug trade emerged as an especially important source of employment. With urban manufacturing jobs increasingly scarce, many people have found the drug market to be a more attractive alternative than low-paying, unstable, and often degrading work in the expanding service sector. On average, selling drugs pays somewhat better than the available service sector jobs. Moreover, the drug industry "offers hope, however illusory, of self-determination and economic independence, as contrasted with the petty humiliations and daily harassment faced in secondary service sector jobs" (Bourgeois, 1995, p. 141).

Unlike most legal work, however, drug dealing is highly dangerous. And it became dramatically more so in the 1980s and early 1990s with the advent of crack cocaine. The percentage of New York City homicides in which drugs played a significant role increased from 24% in 1984 to an astounding 53% in 1988 (when the popularity of crack cocaine peaked) (Goldstein, Brownstein, Ryan, & Belluci, 1989). Similarly, Washington, DC's homicide rate surged between 1986 and 1988 as the number of killings recorded as "drug related" climbed to 53% (Zimring & Hawkins, 1997, p. 248).[8] In the years since, the shrinking market for crack cocaine has been linked to a declining incidence of homicide (Johnson, Golub, & Dunlap, 2000).

These studies clearly show that drugs and violence are interrelated, but what is the nature of the relationship? Researchers have identified three types of drug-related homicide:

- "Psychopharmacological" killings are those caused by drug or alcohol intoxication, such as when a person gets high and acts out in a violent fashion.

- "Economic compulsive" killings are those committed in the course of property crimes, such as robberies, and motivated by the need for money to buy drugs.

- "Systemic" killings are the result of conducting business in an illegal market. Illegal markets are characterized by high profit margins and offer no recourse to the legal system to settle disputes.

Homicide records in New York City show that during the peak of the crack epidemic, only 15% of drug-related homicides seemed to have psychopharmacological causes, and just 4% fit the economic compulsive model. By contrast, nearly 80% of all drug-related homicides were systemic in nature. Moreover, these systemic killings constituted nearly 40% of all homicides during the sample period (Goldstein et al., 1989). Contrary to popular impressions, then, it is not the chemical effects of illicit drugs but the nature of the illegal drug trade that accounts for much drug-related violence.

Here are just three examples of the kinds of systemic conflicts generated by illegal drug markets:

[T]he victim in case #31 was a thirty-year-old male. He had been previously ousted from his drug sales location and had returned in an attempt to reassert his claim to the area. He was shot by a twenty-four-year-old male. Police report that this was not an isolated event, but part of a continuing turf war between two gangs. The perpetrator fled to Washington, DC, where he, in turn, was killed by associates of the victim.

In case #369 . . . the victim was a twenty-seven-year-old female crack user. The perpetrator was a twenty-two-year-old male who was both a crack user and a low-level crack dealer. He had lent her both money and crack, but she was not able to repay the debts. They engaged in an argument at a street crack sales location, which culminated in the woman being stabbed once in the chest.

In case #277, the victim was a thirty-two-year-old male. The perpetrator was a seventeen-year-old male. On a prior occasion, the victim had robbed the perpetrator of money and crack. The perpetrator subsequently shot the victim once in the abdomen in retaliation. (Goldstein et al., 1989, pp. 120-121)

All illegal drug markets tend to give rise to systemic violence, but the particular features of the crack trade and the socioeconomic context in which it emerged exacerbated this tendency. Crack was essentially a marketing innovation that made cocaine available in smaller and cheaper quantities to a broader segment of the public. The effects of crack cocaine are also extremely short lived. For both of these reasons, the crack market was, at its peak, characterized by a greater number of exchanges than is typically found in other drug markets. With an increase in the number of illicit exchanges comes an increase in the number of potential conflicts—and thus in the number of conflicts that can lead to murder. In addition, the fact that crack cocaine is relatively easy and cheap to make meant that people without much start-up capital could move into the trade, and the lack of legal alternatives enhanced their willingness to use and risk violence while doing so. The result was a high degree of instability in the market, a comparatively large number of exchanges, and intense competition over turf. For all these reasons, the crack trade in particular seems to have an especially strong link to lethal violence.

Ironically, the war on drugs has likely contributed to the problem of drug-related violence. Between 1980 and 2001, the number of people arrested on drug charges more than tripled to nearly 1.6 million (FBI, 2002, Table 29). During the same period, the number of people incarcerated on drug charges grew from roughly 40,000 to 450,000, or by more than 1,000% (King & Mauer, 2002a, p. 2). Arresting and jailing so many (alleged) drug dealers disrupts turf arrangements and triggers violent struggles to establish control over newly available territory. By destabilizing the drug trade, the police crackdown may have contributed to its violent character.

In addition, mass drug arrests have undermined the capacity of many minority men and women to obtain jobs and support families. Roughly 4 out of 5 people jailed for a drug offense are either black or Hispanic, and many of these are men from high-poverty, racially segregated neighborhoods. Jailed men do not marry and raise their children; neither do men who cannot get a good job because of a criminal record. In fact, studies have shown that those who have experienced incarceration are significantly less likely to obtain employment than are similarly situated defendants sentenced to alternatives (such as probation) (Freeman, 1991; Petersilia & Turner, 1986; Western & Beckett, 1999). By arresting and jailing such a large number of minorities, the war on drugs has become a significant source of joblessness and family disruption in poor neighborhoods, two social conditions that are strongly associated with high levels of homicide.

The Code of the Streets

Concentrated poverty generates cultural as well as economic adaptations, and these developments are also implicated in elevated rates of violence. Pervasive feelings of despair due to high rates of joblessness, widespread drug abuse, and severely limited educational and economic opportunities have led to the emergence of an oppositional "code of the streets" (Anderson, 1994, p. 82). In this section, we discuss the emergence of this code, paying particular attention to its implications for the problem of lethal violence. However, we wish to emphasize that the attitudes and practices described below are linked to cultural patterns that extend far beyond American inner cities. To borrow a distinction from sociologist William Julius Wilson, these cultural developments are "ghetto-related" but not "ghetto-specific" (Wilson, 1996). Those who articulate and live by the code are as American as apple pie.

At the heart of the code of the streets, according to sociologist Elijah Anderson, "is the issue of respect—loosely defined as being treated 'right,' or granted the deference one deserves" (Anderson, 1994, p. 82). Having respect means that one can avoid being bothered or menaced by others. This is especially important in violent areas, where vague slights can escalate into violent conflicts and where faith in the ability or willingness of the police to impose order is nonexistent. From a practical standpoint, "respect" is maintained through the projection of a menacing public presence: "One's bearing must send the unmistakable if sometimes subtle message to 'the next person' in public that one is capable of violence and mayhem when the situation requires it, that one can take care of oneself" (Anderson, 1994, p. 88). Anthropologist Philippe Bourgeois (1997) makes a similar point in his discussion of the "culture of terror" surrounding the drug trade:

> Behavior that appears irrationally violent and self-destructive to middle class (and working class) observers can be more accurately interpreted according to the logic of the underground economy as judicious public relations, advertising, rapport building, and long-term investment in one's "human capital." (p. 66)

Because of its utility in deterring aggression, young people living in poor urban areas often project a menacing posture whether they are genuinely committed to the code of the streets or not. But for the smaller number of young people who are heavily invested in street culture, respect is about more than warding off unwanted aggression. Hard won and easily lost, it is an absolute precondition for dignity and self-respect, especially for young men. "Manhood and self respect are flip sides of the same coin; physical and psychological well-being are inseparable and both require a sense of control, of being in charge" (Anderson, 1994, p. 89).

On the streets, respect is often pursued through character contests involving displays of masculine "nerve":

> Nerve is shown when one takes another person's possessions (the more valuable the better), "messes with" someone's woman, throws the first punch, "gets in someone's face," or pulls a trigger. Its proper display helps on the spot to check others who would violate one's person and also helps to build a reputation that works to prevent future challenges. But because such a show of nerve is a forceful expression of disrespect toward the person on the receiving end, the victim may be greatly offended and seek to retaliate with equal or greater force. A display of nerve, therefore, can easily provoke a life threatening response, and the background knowledge of that possibility has often been incorporated into the concept of nerve. (Anderson, 1994, p. 92)

The zero-sum nature of such character contests helps to explain why conflicts that seem petty to those on the outside can lead to violence and even murder.

> True nerve exposes a lack of fear of dying. Many feel that it is acceptable to risk dying over the principle of respect. In fact, among the hardcore street oriented, the clear risk of violent death may be preferable to being "dissed"[9] by another. (Anderson, 1994, p. 92)

This emphasis on getting respect is not unique to youth street cultures in the inner city. Neither is the notion that men must establish their masculinity by being tough in the face of challenges from other men. What is different is the context in which these displays of nerve and masculinity occur. Elsewhere in society, young men have multiple avenues for attaining status and demonstrating manhood. In increasingly poor and isolated urban neighborhoods, however, most of the conventional avenues for doing so are dead ends. This is even truer in prisons, where the code of the streets is found in its purest form. Ironically, the massive expansion of incarceration in the 1980s and 1990s has exposed ever-increasing numbers of people to this environment and has thus strengthened the hold that the code of the street has on some urban communities (Miller, 1996).

Conclusion

In this chapter, we have argued that the unusually high rate of homicide in the United States stems primarily from four interrelated factors: the ubiquity of guns, comparatively high levels of social and racial inequality and the concentrated urban poverty with which they are associated, the drug (and especially crack) trade, and a code of the streets that prizes respect and deference above all else. These deadly developments reinforce each other in complex ways. For example, the code of the streets has been strengthened by the spread of the drug trade and contributes to its lethal character. Both of these encourage the acquisition of firearms, even among those not directly involved in the drug trade. Inequality and racial discrimination facilitate violence by creating a sense of injustice and frustration and by contributing to the concentration of poverty in racially segregated neighborhoods. Concentrated poverty, in turn, encourages the code as well as the trade in drugs. No good purpose is achieved by trying to reduce this complexity to a simple mono-causal argument.

The U.S. homicide rate dropped between 1993 and 2000 by about one third. Politicians' claims notwithstanding, this welcome development does not necessarily mean that the "get tough on crime" policies are working effectively. As discussed previously, there is no clear or straightforward relationship between penal severity and the volume of crime in society (Zimring & Hawkins, 1995). This is true even in the context of recent U.S. history: In the first half of the 1980s, the homicide rate declined while the prison population expanded; in the second half of the 1980s, the homicide rate returned to its earlier level while the prison population continued its expansion (Tonry, 1995). Before abandoning these and other lessons of history, we ought to consider alternative explanations for the declining homicide rate.

The best alternative explanation concerns changes in the drug market. As we have seen, the spread of the drug trade stemming from the introduction of crack in the second half of the 1980s contributed to the rise in homicide in that period. In the 1990s, moreover, declines across metropolitan areas in the number of people arrested who tested positive for cocaine (a measure of the vitality of the crack trade) were closely associated with declines in homicide rates. In other words, the decline of the crack market appears to correspond to the decline in the incidence of lethal violence (Butterfield, 1997a, p. A10). We discuss this and additional explanations for the crime drop in Chapter 8.

Although the U.S. homicide rate is indeed high relative to other western democracies—and remains so even after the recent declines—this fact does not directly explain the country's imprisonment boom. However, it is possible that high levels of lethal violence lend credence to political claims regarding the severity of the U.S. crime problem and render some members of the American public more receptive to calls to crack down on criminal offenders. To better understand the context in which such popular perceptions and sentiments come into being, we turn to the areas of politics and culture. In the next chapter, we begin this inquiry by exploring the changing role of crime in political discourse.

4

The Politics of Crime

Over the past several decades, the U.S. government has enthusiastically declared and waged wars against crime and drugs. It is often assumed that these wars were a response to rising levels of crime and drug use. Like many popular theories, this assumption rests on a few kernels of truth: Crime—especially lethal violence—is a significant problem in the United States, the drug trade did expand in the 1970s and 1980s, and this trade frequently generates a good deal of violence. However, as we saw in Chapter 2, the best available evidence suggests that levels of crime did not increase significantly over the past 30 years and have actually dropped a good deal in the past decade—even as rates of incarceration have continued to climb. Similarly, levels of illegal drug use have declined sharply since their peak in the late 1970s. Even if the incidence of crime and drug use had been steadily increasing, this would not explain why crime and drugs came to play such a crucial role in national politics, why "getting tough" was seen as the best response to the crime and drug problems, or why political leaders of both parties came to accept this approach.

In this chapter, we focus squarely on this issue: Why have national-level politicians so vigorously waged a war on crime and drugs that has created the largest prison population in the world? We argue that in response to the social challenges of the 1960s, conservative political leaders—and, increasingly, those at the national level—began to highlight the problem of street crime in an attempt to steer state policy toward social control and away from social welfare.

That prominent national politicians began to construct these social problems in ways that imply the need for get-tough policies was not inevitable. Social problems like crime may be framed in a number of different ways, each of which has quite distinct policy implications. Crime, for example, may be depicted as evidence of the breakdown of law and order, of the demise of the traditional two-parent family, or of social and economic inequality. Thus, crime-related issues, like other social problems and issues, are socially and politically constructed: They acquire their meaning through struggles over their interpretation and representation. Social actors—sometimes called "claimsmakers" (Kitsuse & Spector, 1973)—compete for the public's attention and attempt to gain acceptance for the frames whose policy implications they prefer (Edelman, 1988; Gamson, 1992; Gamson & Lasch, 1983; Gamson & Modigliani, 1987; Gusfield, 1967; Hilgartner & Bosk, 1988).

The frames that come to dominate the political and cultural landscape are likely to have a significant impact on policy. For example, to the extent that crime is seen as a consequence of lenience within the criminal justice system, policies that get tough with criminal offenders seem most appropriate. Conversely, frames that depict crime as a consequence of poverty, unemployment, or inequality suggest the need for policies that address these social and economic conditions. Debates over penal policy are less influenced by social scientific research than by the way crime-related problems are framed in political discourse (Garland, 1990, p. 20).

In what follows, we show that conservative politicians have worked for decades to alter popular perceptions of crime, delinquency, addiction, and poverty, and to promote policies that involve "getting tough" and "cracking down." We also show that when advocating such policies, these political elites were not simply responding to popular beliefs and sentiments about crime and punishment, although they did help to shape the public's perceptions of the crime problem and preferences regarding what to do about it. Rather, their claims-making activities were part of a larger effort to realign the electorate in ways that favor the GOP and, even more significantly, to reorient state policy around social control rather than social welfare.

Over time, the responsiveness of electorally important segments of the public to the discourse of law and order did make it difficult for politicians to offer alternatives to the war on crime and drugs. By the late 1980s and into the 1990s, politicians of both parties were responding to popular desire for tough crime and drug policies. Today's tough-on-crime (and welfare) policies reflect the success of ongoing efforts to reframe the crime and drug problems as the consequence of excessive permissiveness.

Of course, the public is not always responsive to politicians' efforts to frame social problems in particular ways. In Chapter 6, we will explore popular views and sentiments in greater detail in order to illuminate why some members of the public did respond favorably to calls for law and order. We will also explore evidence that popular receptivity to the rhetoric of the war on crime has been more limited and superficial than is generally recognized, and pay particular attention to indications that public support for some aspects of it is eroding. For now, though, our emphasis is on the way in which politicians mobilized and framed the crime issue and the consequences of that mobilization for political culture and social policy.

Our analysis begins in the tumultuous decade of the 1960s, when southern officials first mobilized the discourse of law and order in their efforts to discredit the civil rights movement. As the decade progressed, conservative opponents of the welfare state also used this rhetoric to attack President Lyndon Johnson's Great Society programs and the structural explanations of poverty with which these programs were associated. Conservatives offered two theories of the newly politicized crime problem:

- An individualistic theory suggesting that both poverty and crime are freely chosen by dangerous and undeserving individuals who refuse to work for a living and are not penalized for doing so

- A cultural theory asserting that the "culture of welfare" is the primary cause of a variety of social ills, including poverty, crime, delinquency, and drug addiction

Although distinct in some ways, these individualistic and cultural theories both identify "permissiveness" as the underlying cause of crime and imply the need to strengthen the state's control apparatus. As a rallying cry for Republicans, the permissiveness frame helped forge the party's new (but unstable) political majority. In the 1980s and 1990s, the ascendance of this frame has also helped to legitimate the assault on the welfare state and the dramatic expansion of the penal system. In short, the construction of the crime issue as a consequence of excessive permissiveness has been extraordinarily useful to conservative opponents of civil rights and the welfare state.

The Origins of the Discourse of Law and Order

In the years following the U.S. Supreme Court's 1954 *Brown v. Board of Education* decision, civil rights activists across the South used direct action tactics and civil disobedience to force reluctant southern states to desegregate public facilities. In an effort to sway public opinion against the civil rights movement, southern governors and law enforcement officials characterized its tactics as "criminal" and indicative of the breakdown of "law and order."[1] Calling for a crackdown on the "hoodlums," "agitators," "street mobs," and "lawbreakers" who challenged segregation and African American disenfranchisement, these officials made rhetoric about crime a key component of political discourse on race relations.

As the debate over civil rights moved to Washington, depictions of civil rights protest as criminal rather than political in nature reached the national stage. For example, after President Kennedy unenthusiastically expressed his willingness to press for the passage of civil rights legislation in 1963, Republicans and southern Democrats assailed him for "rewarding lawbreakers" (Cronin, Cronin, & Milakovich, 1981). Later, Richard Nixon (1966) blamed civil rights leaders for the problems of crime and violence, arguing that

> the deterioration of respect for the rule of law can be traced directly to the spread of the corrosive doctrine that every citizen possesses an inherent right to decide for himself which laws to obey and when to disobey them. (p. 64)

Throughout this period, phrases like "crime in the streets" and "law and order" equated political dissent with crime and were used by conservatives in an attempt to heighten opposition to the civil rights movement. Conservatives also identified the civil rights movement—and, in particular, the philosophy of civil disobedience—as a leading cause of crime. Countering the trend toward lawlessness, they argued, would require holding criminals (including civil rights protesters) accountable for their actions through swift, certain, and severe punishment.

The rhetoric of "law and order" became more prominent in 1964, when Republican presidential candidate Barry Goldwater announced that "the abuse of law and order in this country is going to be an issue [in this election]—at least I'm going to make it one because I think the responsibility has to start some place" (Caplan, 1973, p. 585). Despite the fact that crime did not even appear on the list of issues identified by the public as the nation's most important, Goldwater, a prominent civil rights opponent, made "law and order" the centerpiece of his campaign and promised that his party would do more to protect it:

> Tonight there is violence in our streets, corruption in our highest offices, aimlessness among our youth, anxiety among our elderly. . . . Security from domestic violence, no less than from foreign aggression, is the most elementary form and fundamental purpose of any government, and a government that cannot fulfill this purpose is one that cannot command the loyalty of its citizens. History shows us that nothing prepares the way for tyranny more than the failure of public officials to keep the streets safe from bullies and marauders. We Republicans seek a government that attends to its fiscal climate, encouraging a free and a competitive economy and enforcing law and order. ("Goldwater's Acceptance Speech," 1964, p. A9)

There is no evidence that these early claims-making activities were a response to a demonstrable increase in public concern about crime. Opinion poll data show that other concerns—especially civil rights and the Vietnam War—were of far more concern to most Americans. On the other hand, it does appear that the tough anticrime rhetoric struck a chord among some voters; those opposed to social and racial reform were especially receptive to calls for law and order (Barkan & Cohn, 1994; Bennett & Tuchfarber, 1975; Cohn, Barkan, & Halteman, 1991; Corbett, 1981).

The responsiveness of these members of the electorate does not imply that they were manipulated or duped by political elites. Rather, the discourse of law and order provided a means by which a number of preexisting fears and concerns—about the pace and nature of social change, as well as the means used in an attempt to bring this change about—were tapped, organized, and given expression. As urban riots became a more frequent and highly publicized occurrence, the discourse of law and order provided a compelling means by which these concerns about social change, racial reform, and increasingly unruly forms of political protest could be expressed.

Ironically, it was the success of the civil rights movement in discrediting more explicit expressions of racist sentiment that led politicians to attempt to appeal to the public with rhetoric that tapped into white fears regarding racial reform in more subtle ways

(Omi, 1987; Omi & Winant, 1986). In subsequent years, conservative politicians also found the crime issue, with its racial subtext now firmly in place, useful in their attempt to redefine poverty as the consequence of individual failure and to recast welfare programs and their recipients in an unflattering light.

From the War on Poverty to the War on Crime

Throughout the 1960s, civil and welfare rights activists drew national attention to the issue of poverty. These activists not only highlighted the plight of the poor, but also argued that inequality of opportunity and racial discrimination ensured that poverty would remain widespread and concentrated in minority communities. To remedy this situation, they sought, among other things, to expand the Great Society welfare programs. These programs, they argued, were not only a humane and appropriate response to poverty, but also a means of addressing the crime problem. Politicians who also supported the Great Society programs echoed this view. Early in his administration, for example, President Johnson argued that programs that attacked social inequality were, in effect, anticrime programs:

> There is something mighty wrong when a candidate for the highest office bemoans violence in the streets but votes against the war on poverty, votes against the Civil Rights Act, and votes against major educational bills that come before him as a legislator. (Johnson, 1965, p. 1371)

By contrast, conservative opponents of the Great Society programs argued that poverty and crime were caused by a combination of bad people and excessive "permissiveness." Independent presidential candidate George Wallace ridiculed "soft social theories" of crime in especially memorable ways:

> If a criminal knocks you over the head on your way home from work, he will be out of jail before you're out of the hospital and the police-man who arrested him will be on trial. But some psychologist will say, well, he's not to blame, society is to blame. His father didn't take him to see the Pittsburgh Pirates when he was a little boy.[2]

According to this conservative argument, crime and related social problems originate in individual choice and greed rather than in social conditions; acting as though crime is affected by social conditions is not only wrong, but lets people off the hook when they make irresponsible choices.

For some opponents of the welfare state, discussions of street crime also illustrated the dysfunctionality of the poor that, they argued, was the true cause of their poverty. According to this culture-of-poverty thesis, poor people are poor because of their cultural values; programs such as Aid to Families with Dependent Children (AFDC) would only reward non-work-oriented lifestyles, thereby worsening the problems of poverty and crime. Furthermore, some suggested, the mere existence of welfare encouraged poor people to think that they are entitled to that which they have not earned. In this twist on the culture-of-poverty thesis, conservatives argued that the "culture of welfare" undermines the (already weak) self-discipline of the poor and promotes "parasitism"—both legal (welfare dependency) and illegal (crime) (Moynihan, 1973, p. 42).[3] As presidential candidate Barry Goldwater put it so succinctly,

> If it is entirely proper for the government to take away from some to give to others, then won't some be led to believe that they can rightfully take from anyone who has more than they? No wonder law and order has broken down, mob violence has engulfed great American cities, and our wives feel unsafe in the streets. (Matusow, 1984, p. 143)

In the mid-1960s, then, liberals and conservatives offered very different explanations of poverty and crime-related problems. According to liberals, social conditions—especially racial inequality and limited opportunities for youth—were the root causes of crime, poverty, and addiction. It is only by addressing these social conditions, they argued, that we may begin to ameliorate the problems they cause. By contrast, conservatives argued that social pressures such as racism, inadequate employment, lack of housing, low wages, and poor education do not cause crime. Instead, people are poor, criminal, or addicted to drugs because they made irresponsible or bad choices. Ironically, social programs aimed at helping the poor only encourage them to make these choices by fostering a culture of dependency and predation.

Highlighting the behavioral pathologies and, especially, the criminality of the poor was thus part of an attempt to transform their image from needy to undeserving. The changing racial composition of welfare recipients may also have facilitated this transformation of the public perception of the poor: Continued migration to northern cities from southern and rural areas meant that increasing numbers of those who received AFDC were African American women and their children. By emphasizing street crime and framing it as the consequence of bad people making bad choices, conservatives made it much less likely that members of the public would empathize with the plight of the poor and support measures to assist them. As historian Michael Katz (1989) suggested, when the poor appeared to be dangerous, they were perceived as the undeserving underclass.[4]

As early as 1965, the liberal emphasis on the root causes of crime began to weaken in the face of this conservative onslaught. Only 4 months after his election, for example, President Johnson declared in an unprecedented special message to Congress his new determination to fight crime: "I hope that 1965 will be regarded as the year when this country began in earnest a thorough and effective war against crime" (Johnson, 1966, p. 264). Toward that end, Johnson established the Law Enforcement Assistance Administration (LEAA), an agency with a mission to support local law enforcement. To coordinate law enforcement activities aimed at fighting drugs, Johnson also created the Bureau of Narcotics and Dangerous Drugs (now called the Drug Enforcement Agency). These initiatives represented a shift away from the view that the most important crime-fighting weapons were civil rights legislation, War on Poverty programs, and other policies aimed at promoting inclusion and social reform. Over time, the liberal commitment to assisting the poor also attenuated (Bayer, 1981).

The Republican Southern Strategy

The Republican commitment to waging war on crime intensified during and after 1968. During the campaign that year, Republican candidate Richard Nixon followed his conservative predecessors by rejecting social explanations of crime and arguing that the lenience of the criminal justice system was, in fact, to blame for crime and violence. Throughout his campaign, Nixon insisted that the "solution to the crime problem is not the quadrupling of funds for any governmental war on poverty but more convictions" (Marion, 1994, p. 70).

This rhetorical emphasis on crime was part of a political strategy, developed after the 1964 elections, aimed at weakening the electoral base of the Democratic Party: the New Deal coalition. This alliance of northern, urban ethnic groups and the white South had dominated electoral politics since 1932. But the fact that increasing numbers of African

Americans were migrating to the North and acquiring voting rights created quite a dilemma for Democratic officials interested in attracting African American voters while simultaneously maintaining white southern allegiance to the party. In 1948, Democratic President Harry Truman responded to the growing number of African American voters by pressing for a relatively strong civil rights platform, and the first serious signs of strain in the Democratic partnership appeared. In protest, white southerners organized a states' rights party, and in the subsequent election, four Deep South states (Louisiana, South Carolina, Alabama, and Mississippi) delivered their electoral votes to this insurgent political force. Democrats moved quickly to pull in disaffected white southerners only to have the Republican share of the African American vote increase from 21% in 1952 to 39% in 1956 (Phillips, 1969).

By drawing public attention to the plight of African Americans in the South, civil rights activists forced the Democratic Party to choose between its southern white and northern African American constituencies. Nightly newscasts during the period featured peaceful civil rights protesters being hauled off, rounded up, and otherwise brutalized by southern law enforcement agents. Not surprisingly, support for the civil rights cause grew among nonsouthern whites. This development, along with the increasing numbers of African American voters, eventually led the Democratic Party to cast its lot with African Americans and their northern allies.

Although this decision secured for the Democrats the loyalty of most African American voters, it alienated some of those traditionally loyal to the Democratic Party, particularly white southerners. "Millions of voters, pried loose from their habitual loyalty to the Democratic Party, were now a volatile force, surging through the electoral system without the channeling restraints of Party attachment" (Edsall & Edsall, 1991, p. 41). These voters were "available for courting," and the Republicans moved swiftly to seize the opportunity.

Initially, the GOP targeted white southerners—voters who had formerly composed the Democrats' "solid South"—as potential "swing voters." This strategy certainly paid off: The formerly Democratic South is now overwhelmingly Republican, a trend that the resurgence of evangelicalism, concentrated in the so-called Bible Belt, has helped to solidify.

Over time, Republican analysts began to suggest that northern white suburbanites; ethnic Catholics in the Northeast and Midwest; and white, blue-collar workers might also be receptive to their socially conservative and racially coded rhetoric. Some conservative political strategists frankly admitted that appealing to racial fears and antagonisms was central to this strategy. For example, political analyst and consultant Kevin Phillips argued that a Republican victory and long-term realignment was possible primarily on the basis of racial issues, and therefore suggested the use of coded anti-black campaign rhetoric (Phillips, 1969, p. 39). Similarly, John Ehrlichmann, Special Counsel to the President, described the Nixon administration's campaign strategy of 1968 in this way: "We'll go after the racists. That subliminal appeal to the anti-African-American voter was always present in Nixon's statements and speeches" (Ehrlichmann, 1970, p. 233).

New sets of Republican constituencies were thus courted through the use of racially charged code words—phrases and symbols that "refer indirectly to racial themes but do not directly challenge popular democratic or egalitarian ideals" (Omi & Winant, 1986, p. 120). The discourse of "law and order" is an excellent example of such coded language, and allowed for the indirect expression of racially charged fears and antagonisms.[5] In the context of increasingly unruly street protests, urban riots, and media reports that the crime rate was rising, the capacity of conservatives to mobilize, shape, and express these racial fears and tensions became a particularly important political resource.

As the traditional working-class coalition that buttressed the Democratic Party was ruptured along racial lines, race eclipsed class as the organizing principle of American politics. By 1972, attitudes on racial issues, rather than socioeconomic status, were the primary determinant of voters' political self-identification (Edsall & Edsall, 1991, p. 150). The "southern strategy," as this tactic came to be known, eventually enabled the Republican Party to create a new division between some (mostly white) working- and middle-class voters and the traditional Republican elite, on one hand, and "liberal elites" and the (disproportionately African American and Latino) poor on the other.

The initial success of the "southern strategy" helps to explain why the liberal commitment to tackling the root causes of crime weakened over the course of the 1960s. At first glance, the Democratic embracement of law and order is puzzling: Throughout this period, much of the public retained the view that crime has environmental and social causes and remained committed to addressing these. But leaders in the Democratic Party were especially worried about the views and sentiments of a particular segment of the voting public: swing voters. Like their Republican counterparts, Democratic strategists had noted that economically liberal but socially conservative white voters were shifting their loyalties to the Republicans—and were strongly attracted to the Republican campaign for law and order. The liberal backpedaling on crime appears to have been part of an attempt to woo these voters back to the Democratic Party.

The long-term result of the GOP's southern strategy has been not so much a partisan realignment that works consistently in its favor, but rather the destabilization of the electoral system. The number of swing voters (as well as nonvoters) has grown, and voters increasingly cast their ballot for the candidate (rather than the party) they prefer. Analysis of these swing voters—variously referred to as the forgotten workers; Reagan Democrats; waitress moms; lunch-pail dads; soccer moms; and, most recently, office park dads—has become something of an industry among pollsters and political analysts.

The increased importance of these swing voters, along with Republican and Democratic reluctance to target and mobilize alienated (and disproportionately young, poor, and nonwhite) nonvoters and the winner-take-all electoral college system, encourage candidates from both parties to avoid taking anything that might be perceived as a controversial stand. Of course, the perceived need to court swing voters sometimes conflicts with the parties' need to maintain the allegiance of their more loyal base. But in the case of crime, the apparent popularity of the get-tough approach, especially among swing voters, meant that challenges to the war on crime have been few and far between.

The shift in liberal political discourse also occurred in the context of growing criticism, from scholars and activists across the political spectrum, of rehabilitation (Bayer, 1981). Not surprisingly, conservatives opposed rehabilitation on the grounds that punishment must be harsh and painful if it is to deter crime. But many liberals also became critical of policies associated with rehabilitation during this period, arguing that open-ended ("indeterminate") sentences designed to facilitate the correction of offenders created the potential for the intrusive, discriminatory, and arbitrary exercise of power. Under the weight of these twin (if quite distinctive) critiques, the rehabilitative project was called into question. The declining legitimacy of rehabilitation as a penal philosophy undoubtedly made it more difficult for liberal politicians to offer a clear alternative to the conservative calls to crack down on criminals, and may also have facilitated the Democratic leap onto the law-and-order bandwagon.

Nixon's Federalist Dilemma

After assuming office, the Nixon administration was forced to contend with the fact that the federal government has little authority to deal directly with street crime outside of Washington, DC. Administration insiders concluded that the only thing they could do was "exercise vigorous symbolic leadership." Toward that end, they waged war on crime by adopting "tough-sounding rhetoric" and pressing for largely ineffectual but highly symbolic legislation (Epstein, 1977, p. 69). Not fooled, journalists began to report that, despite Nixon's tough talk, the crime rate was still rising.

Nixon administration officials attempted to resolve this dilemma in several ways. First, Nixon requested—and received—a massive increase in LEAA funds to support local law enforcement (Baum, 1996, p. 41; Epstein, 1977, p. 69). Second, new statistical artifacts were created in the hope that these would permit a more flattering assessment of Nixon's capacities as a crime fighter (Milakovich & Weis, 1975).[6] Most important, however, was the administration's identification of narcotics control—for which the federal government has significant responsibility—as a crucial anticrime weapon (Epstein, 1977).[7]

To explain and legitimate this new focus on drugs, administration officials argued that drug addicts commit the majority of street crimes to pay for their habits.[8] In fact, the evidence marshaled to support this claim was quite problematic. For example, in a well-publicized speech in 1971, Nixon claimed that drug addicts steal more than $2 billion worth of property per year. According to the FBI, however, the total value of all property stolen in the United States that year was $1.3 billion (Baum, 1996). Despite these kinds of problems, fighting drugs became a crucial weapon in the war on crime.[9]

The Assault on Defendants' Rights

The Nixon administration's claim that crime is a consequence of "permissiveness" also had important implications for criminal and constitutional law. Under the leadership of Justice Earl Warren, the U.S. Supreme Court had strengthened the protections offered to criminal defendants throughout the 1960s. For example, in *Mapp v. Ohio* (1961), the court ruled that state police officers, like federal law enforcement agents, were, under most circumstances, obliged to obtain a search warrant before conducting a search or seizing evidence.[10] In *Gideon v.*

Wainwright (1963), the Court ruled that people accused of a crime were guaranteed the right to counsel. In *Escobedo v. Illinois* (1964), coerced confessions were deemed inadmissible. And in *Miranda v. Arizona* (1966), the Court ordered that suspects must be informed of their legal rights upon arrest and that any illegally obtained evidence would be inadmissible in the courts. Finally, under the Warren Court, defendants were permitted to argue that they had been entrapped when the idea of the crime in question originated with the police or when police conduct "fell below standards for the proper use of governmental power" (Davey, 1995, p. 106).

Many of these legal rights and protections were undermined or abandoned altogether during the Nixon era. Some of the legislation sponsored by the Nixon administration directly challenged these legal protections (Bertram, Blachman, Sharpe, & Andreas, 1996). By appointing several conservatives (including Warren Burger and William Rehnquist) to the Supreme Court, Nixon ensured that defendants' rights were further weakened. For example, in 1973, the Burger Court undermined the Warren Court's interpretation of the Fourth Amendment's prohibition against unwarranted searches and seizures by ruling that if an arrest is lawful, "a search incident to the arrest requires no additional justification" (Davey, 1995, p. 124). All of these efforts to undermine criminal defendants' rights were rooted in the notion that the excessive lenience of the criminal justice system was an important cause of crime. Although these changes in criminal and constitutional law did diminish defendants' rights, but researchers have concluded that they did not have a demonstrable effect on the rates of arrest, conviction, or incarceration (Davey, 1995, p. 107).

The Reagan Years

Despite the centrality of the law and order discourse to the GOP's electoral strategy, the salience of the crime and drug issues declined dramatically following President Nixon's departure from office in 1974. Neither President Ford nor President Carter mentioned crime-related issues in their State of the Union addresses or took much legislative action on those issues.[11] As a result of this inattention, both the crime and drug issues largely disappeared from national political discourse in the latter part of the 1970s.

During and after the 1980 election campaign, however, the crime issue once again assumed a central place on the national political agenda.

Candidate and President Ronald Reagan, following the trail first blazed by his conservative predecessors, lavished attention on the problem of "crime in the streets" and promised to enhance the federal government's role in combating it. Once in office, Reagan instructed the new U.S. Attorney General, William French Smith, to establish a task force to recommend "ways in which the federal government can do more to combat violent crime" (U.S. Department of Justice, 1981, p. v) and began to pressure federal law enforcement agencies to shift their focus from white-collar offenses to street crime. By October 1981, less than 1 year into the new administration, the Justice Department announced its intention to cut in half the number of specialists assigned to identify and prosecute white-collar criminals. The Reagan administration's crackdown on crime also explicitly excluded domestic violence on the grounds that it was "not the kind of street violence about which it was most concerned" (Davis, 1983, p. 127).

In subsequent years, President Reagan frequently returned to the topic of crime, striking all of the now-familiar conservative themes. Time and again, for example, he rejected the notion that crime and related social ills have socioeconomic causes:

> Here in the richest nation in the world, where more crime is committed than in any other nation, we are told that the answer to this problem is to reduce our poverty. This isn't the answer. . . . Government's function is to protect society from the criminal, not the other way around. (Reagan, 1984b, p. 252)

Reagan also echoed his conservative predecessors on the putative relationship between crime and welfare. The naive view that "blocked opportunities" cause crime, Reagan suggested, led liberals to believe that the "war on poverty" would solve the problem. In fact, it is the government's attempt to ameliorate poverty—not poverty itself—that causes crime:

> By nearly every measure, the position of poor Americans worsened under the leadership of our opponents. Teenage drug use, out-of-wedlock births, and crime increased dramatically. Urban neighborhoods and schools deteriorated. Those whom the government intended to help discovered a cycle of dependency that could not be broken. Government became a drug, providing temporary relief, but addiction as well. (Reagan, 1984a, p. 1013)

Thus, like Nixon and others before him, Reagan argued that welfare programs such as AFDC not only "keep the poor poor" but also accounted, along with lenient crime policies, for the rising crime rate. In fact, studies investigating the relationship of welfare and crime have found that greater welfare spending is associated with lower—not higher—levels of crime.[12]

Under Reagan, it became even more clear that conservatives sought not only electoral success, but a fundamental reconceptualization of the purpose and function of government. Administration officials argued quite explicitly that their liberal predecessors had distorted the government's functions. The state would be on more legitimate constitutional grounds and would more effectively help the poor, they suggested, by scaling back public assistance programs and expanding the criminal justice system and law enforcement:

> [T]his is precisely what we're trying to do to the bloated Federal Government today: remove it from interfering in areas where it doesn't belong, but at the same time strengthen its ability to perform its constitutional and legitimate functions. . . . In the area of public order and law enforcement, for example, we're reversing a dangerous trend of the last decade. While crime was steadily increasing, the Federal commitment in terms of personnel was steadily shrinking. (Reagan, 1989, p. 238)

Reagan thus articulated the central premise of the conservative project of state reconstruction: Public assistance for the poor is an illegitimate state function; policing and social control constitute its real "constitutional" obligation (Reagan, 1984c, p. 672). The conservative mobilization of crime-related issues was thus a key component of the effort to legitimate the shift from the "welfare state" to the "security state." This reinterpretation of governmental responsibilities has affected not only federal priorities, but state-level spending as well (see Exhibit 4.1).

Once again, conservative claims-making on the crime issue was not a response to a clear shift in public attitudes or beliefs. Prior to the Reagan administration's renewal of the war on crime, the view that crime had its origins in welfare dependence and humankind's propensity for evil was not widely supported. In fact, most Americans continued to attribute crime to socioeconomic conditions throughout the late 1970s and into the early 1980s. In 1981, for example, a national poll found that most Americans believed that unemployment was the main cause of

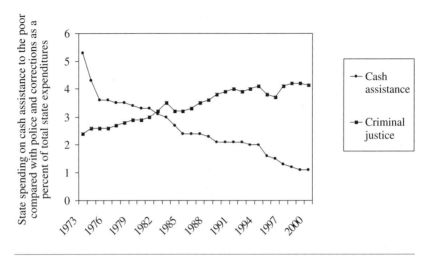

Exhibit 4.1   State Welfare and Criminal Justice Spending

SOURCE: U.S. Department of Commerce (1974-2001).

Note: Cash assistance figures for 1997-2000 calculated from U.S. Department of Commerce (1998-2001).

crime. Similarly, a 1982 ABC News Poll found that 58% of Americans saw unemployment and poverty as the most important causes of crime; only 12% identified "lenient courts" as the main source of this problem (Flanagan, 1987). As the decade progressed, however, public opinion did shift in more punitive directions.

From the War on Crime to the War on Drugs

When it came time to translate its rhetoric into policy initiatives, the Reagan administration faced the same dilemma as the Nixon administration had before it: In the United States, fighting conventional street crime is primarily the responsibility of state and local government. Once again, the identification of drugs as a crucial cause of crime partially resolved this dilemma. In 1981, FBI Director William Webster announced, "The drug problem has become so widespread that the FBI must assume a larger role in attacking the problem" ("FBI Director Weighs War," 1981, p. A27).

As a result of the Reagan administration's renewed interest in battling drugs, federal law enforcement agencies were able to stave off the

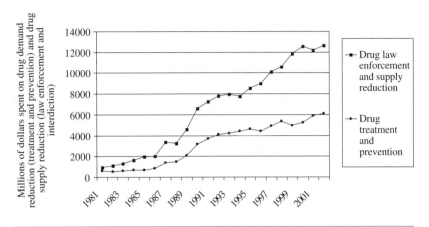

Exhibit 4.2   National Drug Demand and Supply Reduction Spending

SOURCE: ONDCP (1992), pp. 216-219; ONDCP (1998), Table 5; ONDCP (1999), Table 5; ONDCP (2002), Table 4.

General Accounting Office's proposed, across-the-board budget cuts. By contrast, funding for agencies with responsibility for drug treatment, prevention, and education was sharply curtailed. By 1985, 78% of the funds allocated to the drug problem went to law enforcement; only 22% went to drug treatment and prevention (Executive Office of the President, 1990). The only agencies that fared worse than those with drug treatment and prevention responsibilities in the 1982 budget were child nutrition (down 34%), urban development action grants (down 35%), and school milk programs (down 78%) (Baum, 1996, p. 145). As illustrated in Exhibit 4.2, the Reagan administration's early emphasis on the need for a tough approach to drugs gave law enforcement agencies a distinct advantage in the bureaucratic scramble for antidrug funds.

In sum, the Reagan administration's emphasis on the need for a tough approach to crime facilitated the emergence of the war on drugs and shaped the nature of that campaign. The administration's analysis of the causes of the drug problem was remarkably similar to its assessment of the crime problem: Drug use and abuse were a consequence of bad people rather than dangerous social conditions. "Narco-traffickers" and "drug pushers," they argued, were especially evil individuals motivated solely by greed. Drug users were also individually culpable:

If this problem is to be solved, drug users can no longer excuse themselves by blaming society. As individuals, they're responsible. The rest of us must be clear that . . . we will no longer tolerate the illegal use of drugs by anyone. (Bush, 1990, p. 624)

This belief in the importance of individual accountability also guided the recommendations made by the Department of Education under the leadership of (future drug czar) William Bennett. Students caught with drugs, Bennett argued, should be kicked out of school. Counseling these kids not only smacked of moral relativism but implied that drug abuse has root causes that are worth exploring (Baum, 1996, p. 221).

Although public opinion has not been irrelevant to the development of federal drug policy, the get-tough approach to drugs, like the war on crime before it, was not primarily a response to changes in public attitudes. As of 1981, only 3% of the American public believed that cutting the drug supply was the most important thing that could be done to reduce crime; 22% felt that reducing unemployment would be most effective. Furthermore, the percentage of poll respondents identifying drug abuse as the nation's most important problem had dropped from 20% in 1973 to 2% in 1974 and hovered between 0% and 2% until 1982. Thus, public opinion polls do not indicate that there was an upsurge in concern about drugs prior to Reagan's declaration of war, nor is there evidence of widespread support for the idea that fighting crime and drugs through tough law enforcement was the best solution to these problems (Gallup, 1990; see also Roberts, 1992).

The Escalation of the War on Drugs

Political and media attention to "the drug issue" intensified significantly in the summer of 1986. In part, this surge in attention to the drug issue was a response to the cocaine-related deaths of athletes Len Bias and Don Rogers and the increasing visibility of the crack cocaine market. The claims-making activities of federal officials also played a key role.[13]

In October 1985, the DEA sent Robert Stutman to serve as the director of its New York City office. Stutman made a concerted effort to draw journalists' attention to the spread of crack. "The agents would hear me give hundreds of presentations to the media as I attempted to call attention to the drug scourge," he wrote later (Stutman, 1992, p. 148). He explains his strategy as follows:

In order to convince Washington, I needed to make it [drugs] a national issue and quickly. I began a lobbying effort and I used the media. The media were only too willing to cooperate, because as far as the New York media [were] concerned, crack was the hottest combat reporting story to come along since the end of the Vietnam war. (p. 217)

This campaign appears to have been quite effective. The number of drug-related stories appearing in the *New York Times* increased from 43 in the latter half of 1985 to 220 in the second half of 1986 (Danielman & Reese, 1989). Other media outlets soon followed suit.

In an attempt to ensure that their party was perceived as taking action on the drug issue, Democrats in the House began putting together legislation calling for increased antidrug spending. In September 1986, the House passed legislation that allocated $2 billion to the antidrug crusade for 1987, required the participation of the military in narcotics control efforts, imposed severe penalties for possession of small amounts of crack cocaine, and allowed the death penalty for some drug-related crimes and the admission of some illegally obtained evidence in drug trials. Later that month, the Senate proposed even tougher antidrug legislation, and in October, President Reagan signed the Anti-Drug Abuse Act of 1986 into law. In addition to the House proposals described above, this legislation prescribed harsh mandatory minimum sentences for some drug offenses (Windelsham, 1998, p. 26).

Between 1986 and 1990, a period that bridged the administrations of Ronald Reagan and George Bush, drug use was one of the nation's most publicized issues. The 1988 Anti-Drug Abuse Act added more mandatory minimum sentencing statutes, including a 5-year minimum sentence for first-time offenders convicted of possessing five or more grams of crack cocaine (Windelsham, 1998, p. 26). Now, heightened public concern about drugs reached its zenith immediately following President Bush's national address in 1989, in which he focused exclusively on the drug crisis. As Exhibit 4.3 indicates, federal funds allocated to the battle against drugs grew rapidly. In fact, federal antidrug spending was greater under President Bush than under all presidents since Richard Nixon—combined.

The crime issue also enjoyed a high profile in the 1988 presidential campaign, in part as a result of George Bush, Sr.'s successful manipulation of what came to be known as the "Willie Horton" incident. Horton, a convicted murderer who had served most of his prison sentence, absconded from a Massachusetts furlough program while Michael

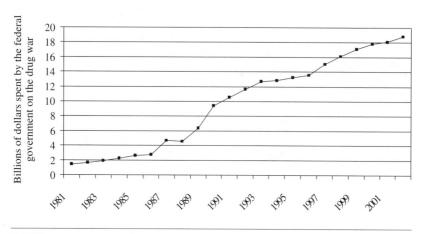

Exhibit 4.3   National Drug Control Spending

SOURCE: ONDCP (1992), p. 219; ONDCP (1999), Table 5; ONDCP (2002), Table 4.

Dukakis, Bush's Democratic rival, was governor. While on the loose, Horton kidnapped a couple in Maryland and raped the woman. During the 1988 campaign, Bush and his supporters used the incident in stump speeches and television commercials to mobilize outrage about crime and blame it on "liberal Democrats" like Dukakis. As one of Bush's political operatives explained, the incident was "a wonderful mix of liberalism and a big black rapist" (Karst, 1993, pp. 73-74).

The Triumph of Law and Order

The outbreak of the Persian Gulf War in early 1991 eclipsed domestic issues, and President Bush largely ignored crime and drugs during the 1992 campaign season. This shift probably reflects the inefficacy of the war on drugs (as indicated by increases in drug-related emergency room visits and in the overall supply of cocaine and heroin within the United States), as well as candidate Clinton's relative invulnerability on these issues.

Like many "new" Democrats, 1992 presidential hopeful Bill Clinton was determined not to suffer the fate of the previous Democratic presidential candidate, Michael Dukakis, who was portrayed by the Bush administration as hopelessly "soft on crime." As both governor and presidential candidate, Clinton expressed strong support for expanded police efforts, more aggressive border interdiction programs, and tougher penalties for drug offenders. The 1992 Democratic platform also embraced the idea that levels of crime and drug use are a direct function of crime control efforts: "The simplest and most direct way to restore order in our cities is to put more police on the streets" (Michelowski, 1993, p. 6).

Despite his record as governor and his relatively tough talk during the election campaign, some speculated that on ascension to office, Bill Clinton would create space for alternatives to the get-tough approach. His record and campaign rhetoric were somewhat ambiguous in this regard. On one hand, Clinton emphasized the need for greater law enforcement efforts and boot camps for juvenile offenders, and he touted his record on capital punishment. (Perhaps to make the point, Clinton returned to Arkansas in the midst of the 1992 campaign to oversee the execution of a convicted killer with an IQ in the 70s.)

On the other hand, both before and after the election, Clinton occasionally evinced glimmers of a more sociological analysis of the crime problem. For example, in a speech to the Democratic Leadership Council shortly after the Los Angeles riots, Clinton characterized looters as people whose "lives and bond to the larger community had been shredded by the hard knife of experience." He also criticized the Reagan-Bush administrations for blaming crime problems on "them"—poor, nonwhite Americans. A year after the election, Clinton still, at least occasionally, expressed these views:

> We have to rebuild families and communities in this country. We've got to take more responsibility for these little kids before they grow up and start shooting each other. I know the budget is tight, but I'm telling you, we have to deal with family, community and education, and find jobs for members of society's underclass to bring structure to their lives. ("Clinton Nurtures High Hopes," 1993, p. 2794)

In short, Clinton and his deputies sometimes espoused the notion that crime and drug abuse are related to social conditions, giving some observers hope that the new administration would advocate alternative approaches to these problems.

This potential was not realized. In August 1993, Republicans announced an anticrime legislative package calling for increased federal aid for local law enforcement, enhanced federal support for prison construction for states willing to adopt "truth-in-sentencing" provisions, more mandatory minimum penalties, and new restrictions on the federal appeals process for death row inmates. One week later, Clinton and several key congressional Democrats proposed their own anticrime legislation, calling for much the same. The only meaningful differences between the two parties' proposals were their positions on gun control, crime prevention programs, and the requirement that federal aid to local law enforcement be used to bolster community policing efforts (all of which the Democrats favored and the Republicans opposed) (Idelson, 1993; Windelsham, 1998, p. 31). Although these differences are not insignificant,[14] both parties overwhelmingly emphasized the need to spend more on police and prisons. Only the Congressional Black Caucus developed anticrime proposals oriented toward a radically different goal: to "prevent crime [by making social investments, particularly in urban areas] and reform the criminal justice system to make it more fair" (Windelsham, 1998, p. 50).[15]

The publicity associated with these legislative proposals appears to have had an impact on public concern about crime. The percentage of those polled who felt that crime was the nation's most important problem increased from 9% in June 1993 (when Republican legislators announced their new campaign) to 22% in October and to 32% by January 1994 (Public Opinion Survey, 1994).[16] Attention to the crime issue increased still further when President Clinton used his 1994 State of the Union address to urge more congressional action, including the adoption of a federal equivalent of California's three-strikes law (which made life imprisonment mandatory for three-time convicts). Later that year, a national poll found that 72% of the voters endorsed these three-strikes provisions; 28% opposed them (Windelsham, 1998, p. 68). Most Democrats—pleased with new poll results indicating that Republicans no longer enjoyed an advantage on the crime issue[17]—continued to support the expansion of the criminal justice system while offering only tepid criticism of some mandatory sentencing provisions and mild support for some preventive measures (Idelson, 1994).[18]

The final version of the Violent Crime Control and Law Enforcement Act of 1994 authorized $6.9 billion for crime prevention efforts, $13.8 billion for law enforcement, and $9.8 billion for state prison construction. The cost of the bill, originally estimated at $5.9 billion, was now estimated to be $30.2 billion (Idelson, 1995). The legislation was sent to President Clinton in August 1994 and was hailed as a victory for the Democrats, who "were able to wrest the crime issue from the Republicans and make it their own" (Masci, 1994, p. 271).

With Republicans demanding still-tougher solutions to the crime problem, House and Senate campaigns in the fall of 1994 focused more on crime than on any other issue. In Florida, gubernatorial candidate (and brother of the current president) Jeb Bush called for corporal punishment of the sort practiced in Singapore. On the television program *Meet the Press*, Texas Senator Phil Graham promised a "real crime bill" that "grabs violent criminals by the throat, puts them in prison, and that stops building prisons like Holiday Inns." In North Carolina, congressional candidate Fredrick Kenneth Heineman urged that provisions of the North American Free Trade Agreement be used to export U.S. criminals to Mexico, "where they can be warehoused more cheaply" (Sasson, 1995b, p. 165).

Under the leadership of then-House Minority leader Newt Gingrich, the Republican Party enthusiastically announced its "Contract With America"—including new anticrime proposals. This legislative package proposed further strengthening truth-in-sentencing, mandatory minimum sentencing, and death penalty provisions and weakening restrictions on the admission of illegally obtained evidence. In addition, the Republicans proposed eliminating funding for all preventive measures. Privately, Republicans justified this move by expressing doubt regarding the efficacy of crime prevention programs and by pointing out that their main beneficiaries were the urban poor—a group famous for its loyalty to the Democratic Party (Windelsham, 1998).

The goals advanced in the Contract With America were subsequently embodied in a series of bills passed easily in the House in February 1995. Although President Clinton and the Democrats did manage to retain separate funds for community policing efforts and the ban on assault weapons, the 1996 legislation largely embodied the get-tough approach to crime and decimated federal support for crime prevention programs. Asked to explain President Clinton's failure to provide any real alternative to these proposals, one administration official said, "You can't appear soft on crime when crime hysteria is sweeping the country. Maybe the national temper will change, and maybe, if it does, we'll do it right later" (Kramer, 1994, p. 29). Since that time, few congressional representatives have been willing to deviate from the bipartisan consensus in favor of "getting tough."

During this period, both the federal government and many states passed punitive laws that not only subjected offenders—especially drug offenders—to long sentences, but also imposed sanctions that begin when the sentence runs out. One federal law denied convicts the right to live in—or even to visit relatives in—public housing. Another denied any person convicted of a drug felony of the right to welfare benefits, including food stamps, for the rest of his or her life. And many states adopted laws that denied felons the right to vote, sometimes for life. (As of 2002, an estimated 3.9 million Americans, including 13% of African American men, are disenfranchised as a result of such laws, a development that shaped the outcome of the presidential elections of 2000.) Some jobs— such as plumbing, real estate, and barbering—were also deemed off-limits by some states for offenders following their release. Although the intent of these laws was to deter offenders and protect the public, many experts are concerned that their main effect has been to make it more difficult for released prisoners to establish a conventional life (Butterfield, 2002a).

Expanding the War on Crime

Early in the 21st century, the war on crime is expanding in new ways. Just 6 weeks after the September 11, 2001 attacks on the Pentagon and World Trade Center, Congress passed one of the broadest anticrime bills in American history. The USA Patriot Act (short for Uniting and Strengthening America by Providing Appropriate Tools Required to Intercept and Obstruct Terrorism) was passed on October 26, 2001, at the height of the anthrax scare, a time when many legislators did not even have access to their offices. Not too surprisingly, the statute was adopted without much debate, despite the fact that the 342-page document amended a wide array of federal statutes covering everything from immigration law to privacy for library and bookstore patrons. Some of the more controversial provisions of the Patriot Act:

• Broaden the definition of terrorism to include any act not committed for personal gain in which a weapon or dangerous device is used. Under this definition, those involved in a barroom brawl may be guilty of terrorism (Cole, 2002).

• Define the provision of aid to any group deemed terrorist by the U.S. government as terrorist activity. Under this definition, provision of schoolbooks to many South African antiapartheid groups in the 1980s would have constituted "terrorist activity," as many such groups— including the Party of Nelson Mandela, the African National Congress— were deemed terrorist by U.S. authorities (Solomon, 2002).

- Enable the U.S. Attorney General to detain noncitizens (and in some instances, U.S. citizens who are also citizens of other countries) indefinitely by stating that there are "reasonable grounds to believe that they are engaged in terrorist activity." These grounds cannot be contested by those detained, and detainees do not have the right to legal counsel or even family visitation. As of October 2002, between 1,500 and 2,000 people have been detained in the search for terrorists. None of the detainees has been charged in connection with the attacks of September 11, 2001, although many have been deported for minor violations of immigration regulations (Cole, 2002).

- Allow the government to conduct "roving" (moving) wiretaps and searches without establishing probable cause of a crime. Among other things, this means that library officials and booksellers are obligated to hand over patron records to law enforcement officials without "probable cause" that the suspect is engaged in terrorist activity. Librarians and booksellers are also prohibited from informing their patrons that they are being investigated (Cole, 2002).

Of course, many other provisions of the USA Patriot Act have stirred up controversy. Belated concern about aspects of the bill led various congressional committees to hold hearings on aspects of the bill *after* its adoption. Government surveillance of U.S. residents who gather at religious services or political events has been particularly alarming to some (Minow, 2002). But so far, neither Democrats nor Republicans in Congress have been willing to challenge the bill in any sustained manner. The fear of being labeled "soft on terror" now stifles debate in much the same way that the fear of being seen as "soft on crime" has for decades.

Even as the country recovered from the attacks of September 11, 2001, a new crime-related scandal burst onto the front pages, this time featuring allegations of misconduct in the boardrooms of some of the nation's most prominent Fortune 500 firms. In these cases, high-ranking executives were accused of knowingly "cooking the books" in order to overstate the profitability of their companies. Knowing the real deal, these insiders then sold their stock at high prices, leaving employees to incur the hit when stock values subsequently plummeted. Some employees lost not only their jobs, but also, in some cases, their entire retirement savings. As revelations of this and other kinds of corporate fraud rocked the country, Congress passed legislation that increased the penalty for some kinds of corporate fraud from 5 to 25 years. As in previous years, fear of opposing what seemed to be a tide of public outrage led many representatives to vote for a bill about which they had many reservations. As one senator said, "Nobody wants to get out ahead of that get-tough train" (Johnson, 2002, p. 454).

The seeming severity of the increased penalties for some forms of criminal fraud has left some wondering if tough criminal sanctions will be any more successful in deterring corporate crime than they have been in deterring street crime (Johnson, 2002). Whatever the answer may be, fears that corporate executives are being highly—and overly—criminalized seem misplaced. Much corporate misconduct is not prohibited by criminal law, and the prison and jail populations remain overwhelmingly poor and disproportionately nonwhite—and will continue to be for the foreseeable future. Furthermore, the financial price tag of corporate crime far exceeds that of street crime. According to a recent FBI estimate, the combined cost of burglary and robbery is $4 billion a year. By contrast, the annual cost of white-collar fraud is thought to be around $200 billion (Simpson, 2002). Estimates of the cost of white-collar crime would undoubtedly be much higher if more corporate misconduct was defined as a crime in the first place. As one scholar recently put it, "The biggest scandal of all is how much bad [corporate] behavior is perfectly legal" (Johnson, 2002, p. 458).

In short, both the scope of the war on crime and the federal government's role in it have expanded significantly as a result of the increased federal involvement in the war on crime, as well as congressional action against terrorism and corporate crime. At the same time, some state governments are quietly attempting to undo some of the more draconian and extreme aspects of the get-tough approach to crime and drugs.

During the legislative season of 2001, for example, state governments across the country adopted legislation that either slowed or reversed tough sentencing policies in an effort to reduce levels of incarceration. These efforts took different forms: Five states expanded drug treatment programs that provide judges with alternative sentencing options, four states revised mandatory sentencing laws, and seven states passed legislation designed to ease prison overcrowding (Sentencing Project, n.d.). Declining levels of crime, concern about the massive numbers of released felons reentering the work force with little education and few skills, and decreasing tax revenues and worsening budget crises all seem to have fueled support for these measures (King & Mauer, 2002b; see also Butterfield, 2001; Kasindorf, 2002).

In the fall of 2002, faced with very serious budget deficits, many states began to take more drastic measures to reduce prison populations and cut correctional costs. In Oklahoma, for example, Republican Governor Frank Keating asked the Pardon and Parole Board to find a way to release 1,000 nonviolent inmates. Looking for ways to make an even more significant impact on the state budget, several other states are considering overhauling draconian drug laws passed in previous decades (King & Mauer, 2002b; see also Butterfield, 2001; Kasindorf, 2002). By contrast, national political leaders, including congressional representatives, remain committed to the war on crime and have refused to modify the harsh sentencing provisions of the Anti-Drug Abuse Act of 1986 or repeal tough mandatory minimums for other offenses. Consequently, the federal prison population continues to grow quite rapidly while the number of state prisoners is stabilizing. In the year 2000, the state prison population increased by 0.3%, whereas the federal prison population grew by 8% (Sentencing Project, n.d.-f).

Conclusion

Beginning in the 1960s, conservative politicians at the national level began to focus an unusual degree of attention on the problem of street crime. That they did so is somewhat surprising: Not only is the capacity of federal government officials to respond to this type of crime fairly limited, but there was no indication that public concern about crime had increased or that the public believed that getting tough was the best way to address this problem. Similarly, in the 1980s, conservatives called for the wars on crime and drugs *before* the public demonstrated any increased desire for such measures. These politicians made law and order a centerpiece of their political platforms, promoted the view that these social ills stem from permissiveness in the forms of criminal justice leniency and welfare dependency, and argued for tough criminal justice and welfare policies in order to address the problem.

If not a response to clear public demands to "get tough" on crime, how can the rise of the crime issue to the center of the political stage be explained? The conservative initiative on these issues was part of a larger effort to forge a new Republican electoral majority following the collapse of the New Deal coalition. Doing so involved reaching out to formerly Democratic, white voters who had been alienated by the (belated and reluctant) Democratic embrace of the civil rights cause. Rhetoric about the collapse of law and order, crime in the streets, and the need for strength in the face of chaos proved to be a successful means of doing so.

Conservative initiative on the crime issue has also been aimed at shifting the government's role and responsibilities from the provision of social welfare toward the protection of personal security. The get-tough policies that have resulted from this campaign are not supported by the findings of most sociological research, which suggest that severity of punishment does not have a significant deterrent effect and that welfare spending reduces rather than increases crime. Nevertheless, these policies have been largely supported by both Republican and Democratic politicians for complex political reasons, and, to a significant extent, by members of the public. In the following chapters, we turn our attention to the mass media and their role in fueling support for the war on crime and drugs.

5

Crime in the Media

Americans have a love-hate relationship with crime. On one hand, we abhor it, decry its apparent increase, and worry about the safety of our loved ones and ourselves. At the same time, we are fascinated with crime—we cannot get enough of it. Indeed, crime-related news stories are among the most widely read, and many of the most popular entertainment shows also focus on crime and violence. Of course, it is difficult to determine whether our enthusiasm for crime stories is a consequence of their ubiquity or whether crime stories are ubiquitous because we so relish them. In either case, crime is one of the most consistent topics covered by the news media, and both news and entertainment programs that focus on crime are widely viewed by the public. In fact, many researchers have found that the mass media are the main source of the public's information about crime.

In this chapter, our focus is on both news and entertainment media (although we hasten to point out that the line between these genres is often—and increasingly—blurry). Our theoretical interest is in the way media contributed to public concern about crime and generated support for law and order messages over the past 30 years. Given this focus, much of the material we discuss covers the 1970s, 1980s, and 1990s. This historical material is a vital part of our story—one we bring up to the present day. We begin with crime in the news.

Crime in the News

Over the past three decades, the news media kept a steady spotlight on the issue of crime. Between 1990 and 1999, the major networks (ABC,

NBC, and CBS) devoted more coverage to crime than any other topic on their nightly national newscasts (Dorfman & Schiraldi, 2001, p. 9; "Living in Fear," 1998). On local television news, stories about violent crime consumed 30% of all news time, displacing coverage of other pressing issues. In comparison to crime, topics like government (11%), health (7%), education (4%), and poverty (2%) receive far less attention (Klite, Bardwell, & Salzman, 1995).

At particular times and in particular places, coverage of crime and drugs has surged beyond this already high plateau. In some cases, like Denver (in 1992) and Boston (in 1997), the triggering events for these upsurges in media attention to crime included murders of "ideal victims"—individuals deemed by society to be either especially vulnerable or especially blameless. In Boston, the 1997 rape and murder of 10-year-old Jeffrey Curley was linked to a number of other grisly murders and reported intensively by the local press. News coverage of "the killing season" (as one local newspaper dubbed it) was so intense that the state legislature debated and came within one vote of adopting a death penalty statute, despite the fact that the state's overall murder rate had been declining for several years.[1]

Nationwide, surges in media coverage of crime and drugs have typically been triggered by increased attention to crime-related issues by public officials and politicians. In 1986, for example, in the wake of the cocaine-related deaths of athletes Len Bias and Don Rogers, federal drug enforcement and treatment agencies worked doggedly to promote journalistic attention to drugs. The National Institute of Drug Awareness (NIDA) launched its most ambitious outreach program, "Cocaine, the Big Lie," featuring 13 public service announcements that aired between 1,500 and 2,500 times per month on 75 local television networks (Forman & Lachter, 1989, chap. 3). Meanwhile, the Drug Enforcement Agency (DEA) and other government officials issued hundreds of press releases and gave innumerable interviews. Because the news media tend to identify government officials as authoritative sources, drug coverage increased dramatically on the major television networks and news weeklies, with literally hundreds of items on the topic appearing in the summer and fall of that year (Reinarman, 1995).

The pattern repeated itself in the first half of the 1990s, but this time, the focus was on violent crime. The rate of violent crime in the United States began its decade-long decline in 1992. Nevertheless, between 1993 and 1994, as the White House and Congress struggled over a new national initiative on violent crime, television and newspaper coverage of the issue

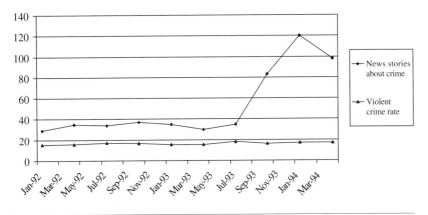

Exhibit 5.1   Television and Newspaper Coverage of Crime

SOURCE: Chiricos, T., Eschholz, S., & Gertz, M. (1997).

Note: Media coverage includes television and newspaper stories about violence. The violent crime rate is measured in terms of the number of violent crimes known to the police per 10,000 population.

increased by more than 400% (see Exhibit 5.1) (Chiricos, Eschholz, & Gertz, 1997). Between 1990 and 1998—a period in which the homicide rate declined by 33%—network news coverage of homicide increased by 473% (Dorfman & Schiraldi, 2001, p. 10).

Crimes, Criminals, and Victims in the News

One of the most noteworthy characteristics of contemporary crime news has been its tendency to focus on the rarest types of crime, such as murder and robbery. According to one study, although they comprise less than two tenths of 1% of all arrests, murders account for between 27% and 29% of all crimes reported on the evening news (Dorfman & Schiraldi, 2001, p. 9). A meta-analysis of 36 content analyses of crime news underscores this finding, concluding that eight stories about violent crime appeared for every two stories about property crime. By contrast, official statistics show that more than nine property crimes occur for every one violent crime. Other kinds of illegalities, such as corporate and state crime, tend to be either reported as "business news" or ignored in favor of violent "street crime" (Marsh, 1991, p. 73). This focus on the comparatively rare violent cases is more pronounced in the electronic media (radio and television) and in local and tabloid newspapers than in "high-brow" publications such as the *New York Times* (Beckett, 1996; Skidmore, 1995).

The news media have also been more likely to report instances of violent crime committed by strangers than those committed by acquaintances or intimates (especially domestic violence) (Reiner, 1997). As a result, criminal offenders have typically been portrayed as predatory outsiders rather than as friends and family members. Over the past century, these predatory criminals have been depicted as ever more barbaric and irrational, and their crimes are presented as more and more violent and unpredictable (Surette, 1994, pp. 134-135; see also Barak, 1994). Sexual violence, for example, has been covered extensively by the news media, but the cases deemed newsworthy have been almost exclusively those involving predatory strangers as suspects (especially cases involving multiple victims). These stories reinforce the notion that sex crimes are committed only by "sex fiends"—crazy and irrational individuals—and both reflect and perpetuate the myth that sexual violence is not committed by known and trusted individuals (Soothhill & Walby, 1991). In fact, the majority of rapes are committed by people known to the victims (Beirne & Messerschmidt, 1991).

Network news stories in which African Americans are accused of crimes have been more likely to involve violence or drugs than news stories featuring white defendants (Entman, 1994). This fact alone is difficult to interpret: African Americans have also been arrested for violent and drug-related crime at a higher rate than whites. However, blacks charged with violent offenses are often depicted differently from whites charged with violent offenses. Studies of local and national news have found that African Americans arrested for violent crimes were more likely to be depicted in the physical custody of police (e.g., spread-eagled against the side of a police cruiser) and to be dressed sloppily. Blacks were less likely than whites to be identified by name in still photographs or to be represented through sound bites from defense attorneys. Together, these differences had the effect of making African Americans accused of violent crimes appear more menacing than whites accused of violent crimes.[2]

News media depictions of crime victims have also been misleading. In the news, when crime victims are depicted, they are typically white, female, and affluent (Chermak, 1995; Elias, 1993; Reiner, 1997, p. 201). One content analysis of national and local television newscasts, for example, found that when the race and gender of crime victims could be identified, white females were the most common category of victims (see

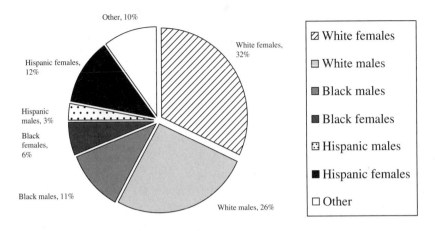

Exhibit 5.2   Crime Victims in the News

SOURCE: Chiricos, T., Eschholz, S., & Gertz, M. (1997).

Note: Figures are based on a 9-week analysis of news in Tallahassee, Florida, in 1995.

Exhibit 5.2) (Chiricos et al., 1997, p. 354). In fact, young men of color—especially those living in poor and urban areas—experience the highest rates of victimization, and white females report the lowest. This pattern is illustrated by comparison of the coverage of a pair of recent New York City homicides. The murder of Marvin Watson, a 22-year-old electrician, elicited no media coverage. The killing a few weeks later of Amy Watkins, a 26-year-old graduate student studying to become a social worker, was covered extensively by local and national media; reporters camped out at the crime scene, and tabloids ran the story on their covers. Both Watson and Watkins were new to the city, and both were "innocent victims." The only apparent difference between the two is that she was a middle-class white woman and he a working-class black man (Yardley, 1999, p. A1).

Framing Crime News

In general, crime-related news stories provide detailed accounts of individual criminal events. Comparatively little attention is paid to broader trends in crime, and few stories attempt to put the crime problem in a larger perspective (Reiner, 1997). As one researcher explained, crime news tends to be framed "episodically" rather than "thematically" (Iyengar, 1991). Coverage of child sexual abuse, for example, has typically ignored issues of gender and power in the family, and instead highlighted the pathology of individual perpetrators or the failures of social workers in particular cases (Nava, 1988; Reiner, 1997, p. 202). Similarly, coverage of urban riots has tended to depict such political disorder as instances of criminality and to ignore the larger structural and political forces involved (Iyengar, 1991; Nava, 1988).

Crime stories are somewhat more likely to be framed thematically (in terms of causes and possible remedies) in news weeklies and the commentary sections of newspapers (Barlow, 1998; Elias, 1993; Sasson, 1995b). In these venues, crime is sometimes depicted as a consequence of poverty, family breakdown, or violence in the mass media. In the 1980s and 90s, however, the most common frame treated crime as a consequence of the failures of the criminal justice system: Criminals escape punishment because of legal technicalities, liberal judges, and permissive laws. According to this perspective, the best way to lower the rate of crime is to impose more certain and more severe punishment and to incapacitate offenders for longer periods of time.[3]

There is evidence that the dominance of this way of framing crime-related issues has much to do with the media's tendency to define government and law enforcement officials as "authoritative" and "objective" sources. One analysis of news media representations of the drug issue, for example, found that stories featuring state officials as news sources were far more likely to depict the drug problem in ways that imply the need to get tough on drugs and drug users, and that the predominance of these sources accounts for the overwhelming depiction of drug use as a law-and-order issue during this period. By contrast, stories in which state actors did not appear as sources were much more heterogeneous in their meanings and policy implications (Beckett, 1995).

One fascinating study suggests that the tendency among reporters to frame crime-related stories in terms of criminal justice leniency may also be related to issues of race and class. In the early 1980s, the typical cocaine-related network news story focused on white recreational users who snorted the drug in its powder form. These stories frequently relied on news sources associated with the drug treatment industry and emphasized the possibility of rehabilitation (the "recovery" frame). By late 1985, however, this frame was supplanted by a new one depicting cities in a state of siege (the "siege" frame). Increasingly, cocaine-related news stories featured poor and nonwhite users and dealers of crack cocaine. At the same time, law enforcement officials demanding tougher responses to the drug problem took the place of the medical and treatment experts previously identified as drug authorities. As the 1980s progressed, journalists increasingly used an overtly "campaigning" voice to demonstrate their clear disapproval of the drug scene and those who populated it. And as a result of their reliance on law enforcement sources, camera crews began using handheld cameras to cover crack house raids from the vantage point of the police (Reeves & Campbell, 1994).

More recently, chinks have appeared in the edifice of law-and-order framing of the drug problem. The appearance of more critical frames was triggered by the recommendation of the Sentencing Commission that those provisions of the Anti-Drug Abuse Act that mandate 5-year minimum terms in federal prison for even small-scale crack offenders be substantially modified. In the debate that ensued, more critical perspectives on the drug problem received a significant amount of exposure in the news media, and previously ignored issues—including the social and economic conditions that shape the problem of drug use and distribution, the racially biased consequences of current sentencing statutes, and the overrepresentation of black youth in the criminal justice system— were identified in the mass media as important components of the drug problem. Some stories went so far as to suggest that many aspects of what is now considered the "drug problem" are actually drug *policy* problems. Ironically, the weakening of the dominant framing of the drug problem as a problem caused by excessive criminal justice lenience also confirms the impact of official news sources on news content: It was the collapse of consensus among state officials, along with effective grassroots organization, that facilitated the change in the nature of drug coverage.

Understanding Crime News

How do we understand the media's growing preoccupation with violent crimes committed by predatory strangers? How do we make sense of the media's tendency to frame crime in terms of failures of the justice system? Three main factors help to account for these tendencies:

News values. Journalists define *news* as that which is out of the ordinary (Ericson, Baranek, & Chan, 1991; Hall, Critcher, Jefferson, Clarke, & Roberts, 1978).[4] By definition, criminal events involve the violation of official rules and therefore satisfy this criterion. Stories about crime provide society with a fascinating and never-ending series of conflicts between good and evil. This conflict is captured most dramatically in stories about violent, predatory crimes committed against people believed to be vulnerable and blameless, and this helps to explain the overrepresentation of white, female victims in the news (Best, 1999).

Organizational needs. Given that the mass media are for-profit enterprises with an interest in increasing market share and advertising revenue, the apparent popularity of crime stories certainly helps to explain why the news media focus on crime. The CBS special *48 Hours on Crack Street,* for example, was the highest rated of any similar program in 5 years.

Reliance on official sources. The tendency of journalists to rely on law enforcement agents, politicians, and government officials for information also influences the volume and content of crime news (Beckett, 1995, 1997; Chermak, 1994; Elias, 1993; Fishman, 1978). This practice is by no means unusual: In general, journalists prefer politicians and government bureaucrats as news sources (Fishman, 1978; Sherizen, 1978). Officials are often seen as authoritative and thus lend legitimacy to the often ambiguous journalistic enterprise (Gans, 1979; Morgan, 1986; Nimmo, 1964; Sigal, 1973; Whitney, Fritzer, Jones, Mazzarella, & Rakow, 1989). Officials are also able to supply journalists with a steady diet of appropriately formatted and timely information—a necessity in the deadline-driven world of modern journalism (Becker, 1967; Gans, 1979; Hall et al., 1978; Herman & Chomsky, 1988; Schudson, 1978; Tuchman, 1978; Whitney et al., 1989).

Increasingly, criminal justice officials attempt to shape the way in which their performance is depicted in the news (Kasinsky, 1994; Schlesinger & Tumber, 1994). For example, police organizations work hard to ensure that instances of excessive use of force are either discredited or framed within the "one bad apple" theory, which holds that such problems are not institutionally based but are the consequence of a few "rotten" individuals (Reiner, 1997). It is true, of course, that not all such efforts are successful.

Consider, for example, news coverage of the 1991 beating of motorist Rodney King by officers of the Los Angeles Police Department (LAPD). News accounts of the Rodney King affair did not represent it as an isolated event, but framed the LAPD's excessive use of force as a widespread phenomenon resulting from strained police-community relations. Two factors help to explain the reluctance of the media to adopt the

LAPD's perspective in their coverage of the King beating. First, the dramatic nature of the videotaped beating made it more difficult for LAPD officials to define the meaning of the event for the public or journalists. Second, the availability of "respectable" independent sources and the presence of conflict between elites on the subject of police brutality in general, and the King beating in particular, meant that no one source was able to establish a dominant interpretation of these events (Lawrence, 1996).

In the routine course of events, however, official sources are often successful in their efforts to shape the news (Herman & Chomsky, 1988; Schlesinger, 1990; Schlesinger, Tumber, & Murdock, 1991). As was discussed previously, public officials played a key role in drawing attention to drugs in the 1980s and 1990s, and stories that relied on such official sources were much less likely to offer criticisms of the government's antidrug strategy (Beckett, 1995, 1997). Furthermore, although conflict between political elites increases the likelihood that media coverage will present alternative perspectives, the usual reluctance of media personnel to rely on nonofficial sources (such as crime victims, grassroots or public interest organizations, or criminal suspects) means that the range of perspectives depicted in the news typically remains fairly narrow (Herman & Chomsky, 1988). In short, although nonelite sources sometimes are able to establish themselves as authoritative news sources, the news media tend to reproduce the perspectives of the law enforcement officials and politicians who serve as their main news sources.

Crime as Entertainment

Much to the chagrin of social critics and reformers, fictional stories about crime and law enforcement have long been staples of American popular culture. In the first half of the 20th century, critics worried that popular gangster films glorified criminals and encouraged disrespect for the law. In recent decades, many have argued that media images of murder and mayhem desensitize people to the real-life consequences of violence and may even encourage copycat crime. Today, a new set of concerns has emerged alongside these venerable criticisms: Some observers now worry that the "surplus visibility" of violence and crime in popular entertainment has become a key source of popular fear and anxiety about crime (Donovan, 1998). According to these critics, media depictions of violence are problematic not because they cause crime, but because they generate fear and reinforce popular support for harsher punishment.

As a result of these concerns, images of crime and violence in the entertainment media have become one of the most heavily studied topics in the social sciences. Many of these studies compare representations of crime and violence in popular entertainment with crime data. For example, one group of researchers has charted the crime rate for the world of prime-time television since the mid-1950s. In the first decade of their study, the real-world rate was 2 violent crimes per 1,000 Americans. On prime-time television, however, characters were committing violent crimes at a rate of 40 per 1,000 characters. In the second decade of the study, the real-world rate of violent crime increased, but on television, it shot up even faster. In the third decade of the study, the rate of violent crime decreased somewhat on television and increased in the real world. Nevertheless, the gap between the two remained enormous (Lichter, Lichter, & Rothman, 1994, p. 276).[5]

The difference between crime rates on television and in the real world is most striking with respect to murder. Over the past four decades, the rate at which Americans have killed one another has varied between 5 and 10 murders annually per 100,000 population. On prime-time television, the average homicide rate has varied between 7 and 10 for every *100* characters—about 1,000 times the real-life rate (Lichter et al., 1994, p. 275). These figures translate into an average of a dozen televised murders for every prime-time viewing slot, every day of the year (Lichter et al., 1994, p. 299).

In the 2000s, television's most violent shows have been aired on subscription cable. Shows like HBO's *The Sopranos*, about a New Jersey organized crime family, and *Oz*, about the fictitious Ozwold maximum security prison, featured scenes of graphic violence that are more typical of R-rated movies than television. The opening episode of *Oz*, for example, depicted a stabbing, a prison rape, beatings of inmates by guards, the torture of an inmate by a prison gang, the suffocation of an AIDS patient, and the immolation of an inmate strapped to a gurney. Interspersed throughout were flashbacks of the prisoners' former crimes, including still more murders.

Depictions of crime and violence have also been abundant in film. In fact, in 2000, both prime-time television shows and the 50 top-grossing movies each averaged an identical 15 episodes of violence per hour (Lichter, Lichter, Amundson, & Butterworth, 2002). One recent study found that the share of movies with crime as a dominant theme has remained more or less stable at around 20% since 1945. The volume of violence within these films, however, has increased substantially. Until the mid-1960s, movies rarely depicted crimes other than the ones that animated their central narratives. The murder that sparked the who-dunit, in other words, was the only murder in the film. In recent years, films have increasingly depicted a host of ancillary and incidental crimes, to the point where characters like Dirty Harry cannot go for a hamburger without coming across a bank robbery in progress. In the world of feature films, violence is no longer unusual. It is, rather, a pervasive feature of everyday life (Reiner, 1997).

The surge in celluloid violence has not been restricted to crime films. One new study examined the five top-grossing films for the years 1964, 1974, 1984, and 1994. The study's sample includes conventional crime films such as *Beverly Hills Cop*, but also box office hits with no apparent relationship to crime, like *The Lion King* and *Forrest Gump*. The authors found that the total number of acts of violence in these films increased substantially during the first three sample periods before leveling off in the fourth. More striking, though, is the surge in the share of violent acts depicted in a graphic (detailed and realistic) fashion. Whereas the most successful films of 1964 depicted 2 violent acts, and the films of 1974 depicted 12 such violent acts, the popular films of the 1990s featured 64 violent acts (Shipley & Cavender, 2001).

The general picture that emerges from this body of research is that the world of popular entertainment is far more violent than the real world, and that it has grown more so in recent history. Does this make-believe violence intensify fear and concern about crime in everyday life? Have fictional representations of crime contributed to Americans' punitive mood and hence their demands for a tougher and more expansive criminal justice system? Comparisons between the fictional and the real are an interesting first step but do not answer these questions. Tallying instances of fictional violence tells us nothing about the meanings these images have for the public. Dramas about crime and law enforcement may foster fear of a chaotic and risky world, but the opposite is also possible: Perhaps such shows reassure people who are already anxious that heroic law enforcers are making the world a safer place. Similarly, whether or not fictional representations of crime encourage popular punitiveness probably depends on the way criminals, law enforcers, and the American justice system are presented and perceived by the audience.

To begin assessing the significance of images of crime and violence in popular entertainment, we ask three sets of questions: First, what stories are told about crime and violence in popular entertainment? What do these stories imply about the nature of lawbreakers, police, and the criminal justice system? Second, how do fictional representations of crime and law enforcement relate to claims-making about these matters in the political sphere? Finally, how do audiences respond to media representations of violence, crime, and law enforcement? What are the effects of these representations on the feelings, perceptions, and attitudes of the general public? In the sections that follow, we examine depictions of crime and law enforcement on television police dramas, in films and made-for-TV movies, and in reality-based cop shows. In the final part of the chapter, we consider the effects of these popular entertainments on the perceptions and views of the public.

The Police Drama

Over the past 40 years, between 20% and 40% of prime-time television programs have focused on law enforcement, making the crime drama the single most popular form of television entertainment (Surette, 1998, p. 36). By the late 1980s—the last time anyone counted—more than 500 different television serials had dealt with crime and law enforcement (Stark, 1987, p. 244). In a given week of prime-time viewing, the typical audience member will watch 30 police officers, 7 lawyers, and 3 judges but only 1 scientist or engineer and only a small number of blue-collar workers (Carlson, 1985, p. 29).

In recent years, as a consequence of the proliferation of cable television stations, the police drama—or something very much like it—has become more ubiquitous still. Today, niche stations each broadcast their own version of the cop show. The Animal Channel, for example, offers a show that "chronicles the drama of New York City law enforcement officers seeking to protect pets." The Outdoor Channel airs *Texas Trophy Hunters,* a show depicting sting operations targeted at unlicensed deer hunters by fish and game agents. And the Travel Channel offers *It Happened Here: Crime Scene,* a show that takes viewers on tours of sites of historical crimes (Koch, 2002).

The early police dramas of the 1950s and 1960s—*Dragnet, Naked City, The Untouchables,* and *Hawaii Five-O,* to name a few—established the basic parameters of the cop show genre. Like the westerns that they imitated, these shows constructed a two-dimensional moral order. The criminals were unambiguously awful characters. Motivated by either unadulterated greed or mental disturbance, they preyed on innocent citizens: "They threatened helpless widows, accosted women and children, and kicked puppies and kittens" (Lichter et al., 1994, p. 303).

By contrast, the police were exceptionally good, if not quite heroic or larger than life. Epitomized by *Dragnet*'s Joe Friday, they were detached professionals simply trying to do their job (Lichter et al., 1994, p. 303). Friday's signature sign-on—"This is the City of Los Angeles. I work here. I carry a badge."—epitomized the law officer's commitment to duty and to the letter of the law. In short, this was "a world where clean cut paragons of decency uphold social mores against deviants and evil-doers, where moral and legal standards never diverge, where disorder and ambiguity are dispatched with equal disdain" (Lichter et al., 1994, p. 302).

Variations on the genre have proliferated over the years:

- *Cop as Action Hero Shows*. Shows like *77 Sunset Strip* (1950s), *Starsky and Hutch* (1970s), and *Martial Law* (1990s) featured hip crime-fighting duos: "They make their own rules, they drive a distinctive car, they shoot guns, they save each other's lives, they chase bad guys very fast in their distinctive car, they get hurt, they don't die, they always get their man" (Stark, 1987, p. 252).

- *Cop as Social Worker Shows*. Shows like *The Mod Squad* (1960s) and *The Rookies* (1970s) softened Joe Friday's image for a more socially conscious audience.

- *Private Eye as Cop Shows*. Shows like *Charlie's Angels* (1970s), *Cannon* (1970s), and *Magnum P.I.* (1980s) expanded the ranks of crime fighters to include private detectives.

- *Civilian-Sleuth Shows*. These shows opened up the crime-fighting profession to an insurance investigator (*Longstreet*, 1970s); a talented medical examiner (*Quincy*, 1980s); an author of crime fiction (*Murder She Wrote*, 1990s); and, most recently, laboratory scientists (*CSI*, 2000s).

- *Cop Shows as Sitcoms*. Shows like *Barney Miller* (1980s) and *Night Court* (1990s) offered rare satirical alternatives to the regular fare.

- *Cop Shows as Soap Operas*. The most recent additions to the mix are shows like *Hill Street Blues* (1980s), *Cagney and Lacey* (1980s), and *N.Y.P.D. Blue* (1990s), which explore the personal lives and relation-ships of their characters while tracking multiple story lines across weekly episodes.

The crime shows have, on occasion, reflected changes in the broader political climate. In the early 1970s, for example, network executives tried to capture the rebellious spirit of the times by airing shows about crusading, activist attorneys (*The Young Lawyers, Storefront Lawyers*). Ten years later, they responded to Ronald Reagan's tough-on-crime platform by ordering a new batch of cop shows, including *Hill Street Blues* (Gitlin, 1983, p. 274). A few years after that, television producers dramatized the Reagan administration's war on drugs in a new *Cop as action hero* show, *Miami Vice:* "The national taste had no problem seeing Colombian drug dealers shot on a weekly basis," commented the show's producer, Dick Wolf (Lichter et al., 1994, p. 31). (The networks had already helped set the stage for the drug war by nearly doubling the number of prime-time depictions of drug crimes between 1975 and 1985; Lichter et al., 1994, p. 287.) Finally, in the 1990s, network executives rushed to fill the void left by the conclusion of the O.J. Simpson murder trial by airing a prime-time look-alike, *Murder One.*

Looking beyond these short-term efforts to tap into the prevailing mood, two developments in the cop show genre are especially striking. The first is a common narrative in which the police take extralegal action to counterbalance what are portrayed as undue constraints on their crime-fighting duties. The second is the introduction of characters—on both sides of law enforcement—who are morally complex, exhibiting both flaws and heroic qualities.

Vigilante Police. Since the 1970s, the theme of bureaucratic and legal constraints on law enforcers—and the concomitant necessity of extralegal police action—have become increasingly prominent. In shows such as *Kojak, Adam-12,* and *Streets of San Francisco,* laws and bureaucratic rules aimed at protecting the civil liberties of suspects were depicted as impediments to police investigations. Faced with the possibility of seeing their honest arrests rejected because of these legal "technicalities," characters such as Telly Savalas's *Kojak* ("Who loves you, baby?") were obsessed with "the way criminals were 'getting off' because the police were not allowed to do their job properly." A smart legal aid lawyer, this detective would say, wants only to "get criminals back on the street" (Stark, 1987, p. 262). Dedicated to "getting their man" in the face of these constraints, these law enforcers routinely strong-armed witnesses, conducted illegal searches, coerced confessions, and engaged in other illegal behaviors—all in the pursuit of justice.

Indeed, one analysis of 15 police dramas aired in a single week in the 1970s identified 21 constitutional violations by the police and 15 instances of police brutality (Carlson, 1985, p. 43). Another analysis from the same period found that "illegal searches were portrayed as essential, always turning up a vital missing piece of evidence. Witnesses brutalized by police often provided the crucial lead that resulted in the capture of vicious criminals" (Haney & Manzolati, 1983, p. 128). In more than 70% of the cases where the police mentioned the Constitution, the courts, or judges, the reference was negative or critical. These studies concluded that the message on television crime shows is that "the law and the Constitution stand in the way of effective solutions to our crime problem" (Haney & Manzolati, 1983, p. 128).

This emphasis on legal constraint and the need for extralegal action by law enforcers persisted in the 1980s and 1990s. On *Hill Street Blues,* for example, Captain Furillo has "had it up to here with looters, rapists, con-artists, lawyers, and liberal politicians" and asks sarcastically, "Now, whose civil rights have we violated today, Counselor?" (Stark, 1987, p. 276). During the show's second season, public defender Joyce Davenport considers quitting her job after the monster who killed her colleague is released on a technicality. By the end of the season, Davenport is packing a gun (Gitlin, 1983, p. 317). In the same vein, story lines for the current hit program *Law and Order* typically revolve around open-and-shut cases that get complicated when liberal judges order suppression of key pieces of evidence, effectively sending the prosecutors and detectives back to square one.

Given the apparent difficulty of making arrests stick in court, it is no wonder that television cops do whatever they can to elicit confessions. In *N.Y.P.D. Blue,* for example, Detective Sipowitz, a recovering alcoholic, routinely slaps suspects around during interrogations. On FX Network's new show *The Shield,* Detective Vic Mackey is both a "hero and a villain" who "gets the job done, often with his fists." In the words of the show's creator, "He lives by a code that justifies what he does. He feels he has the freedom to go after bad people in any way, in order to make our lives safer" (Weintraub, 2002, p. B1).

In all of these shows, what makes the suppression of key evidence seem especially outrageous—and the frequent police trespasses on suspects' rights tolerable—is the fact that in almost every case, viewers know for certain who the bad guys really are. The notion that restraints on police conduct exist because the police often do not know who is guilty is difficult to recover from these entertainment narratives (Crew, 1990).

One reason the theme of legal constraint and police vigilantism has become a key characteristic of police dramas is that it features the timeless conflict between the individual and the organization, allowing for the narration of a kind of rugged American individualism. The maverick who answers to his (and sometimes her) own conscience, works according to his or her own rules, and triumphs where rule-bound organizations have failed is the very stuff of American heroism—and it makes for great television (Sparks, 1992b; see also Crew, 1990).

But in cop shows and films, this theme has clear political implications. In particular, it resonates with conservative political attacks on Supreme Court decisions that, according to critics, "handcuff" the police. These police dramas, in other words, provide an abundance of images that seem to confirm that "the system is set up to protect the rights of criminals and not victims," "the police are handcuffed by the courts," "prisons have revolving doors," and "criminals get off on technicalities." In reality, few felony arrests are rejected by either prosecutors or judges as a result of procedural errors.[6] Nevertheless, as we will see in Chapter 6, these staple slogans of conservative political rhetoric on crime have been accepted by many members of the general public.

Moral Complexity. The second long-term thematic development in cop shows emerged in the early 1980s. Whereas the police dramas of the 1950s, 1960s, and 1970s depicted a simple struggle of good versus evil, more recent police dramas tend to present characters and situations that are more morally complex. These changes began with *Hill Street Blues* and *Cagney & Lacey* in the 1980s, and they flowered in the 1990s with *Homicide: Life on the Streets* and *N.Y.P.D. Blue*. Police in these new dramas are depicted more realistically, as complex individuals with personal strengths—which still typically include integrity and commitment to protecting the public—but also with very real personal flaws. In several of the new police dramas, leading characters are portrayed as (surprisingly likable) recovering alcoholics, beneath-the-surface racists, or unregenerate sexists. At the margins of these dramas, moreover, are various "bad cops" enmeshed in criminal conspiracies whose investigation by the Internal Affairs Division constitutes an increasingly common subplot.

An episode of *Homicide* illustrates this more complex construction of cops. In the weeks leading up to the episode, Detective Kellerman has been in a downward spiral after covering up the circumstances of his killing of the notorious drug dealer Luther Mahoney. Under investigation by Internal Affairs and taunted by Luther's sister (who threatens that she has a videotape of the killing), he has begun drinking heavily. Then, in the episode in question, after staggering drunk out of a bar, he picks a fight with a couple of men who are simply hanging out on the corner. He beats one of the two mercilessly, stopping only when interrupted by a police cruiser that happens on the scene. Questioned by the uniformed officers, he explains—struggling not to slur his speech—that the man on the ground is a "collar" who should be taken to jail. He then leaves the scene. Eventually, in a later episode, Kellerman is forced to retire.

Kellerman is not, however, simply a bad cop. When he shot Luther Mahoney and set in motion the events that led to his downfall, his motivations were noble. Mahoney was an especially evil character who had managed time and again to avoid prosecution and threatened to do so again. Moreover, the shooting itself was an ambiguous affair: Kellerman burst onto the scene just as Mahoney was about to kill Kellerman's partner, Detective Lewis. Ordered by Kellerman to drop his gun, Mahoney instead dangled it aimlessly by his index finger. It was only after several attempts to get Mahoney to drop the gun that Kellerman opened fire. In some respects, therefore, even this representation of trigger-happy policing could be interpreted as a familiar tale of justified police vigilantism in the face of evil criminals and a legal system that will not lock them up.

Greater moral complexity sometimes extends to portrayals of criminals. Most shows still feature odious and evil professional criminals, motivated by greed and rationally calculating their crimes (Reiner, 1997, p. 208; see also Lichter et al., 1994, pp. 290-300; Surette, 1998, pp. 39-40). Increasingly, however, cop shows also situate street crime in the context of the harsh conditions of ghetto life:

> In shows like *Cagney & Lacey* and *Hill Street Blues* police officers had to face the fact that not all criminals were bad people, and that all bad people were not necessarily criminals. Driven by passion or desperation, criminals lacked the premeditated, evil nature seen so often in earlier shows. In other cases very abusive or opportunistic people who deserved arrest were beyond the reach of the law. (Lichter et al., 1994, p. 312)

This more nuanced portrayal of police and criminals reflects, in part, television and film's stylistic turn toward "gritty realism," which has had a variety of implications for police dramas. Since *Hill Street Blues,* for example, shows have been more willing to depict members of minority groups as criminal offenders. Network executives still prefer the politically safe practice of featuring white street criminals, but the new police dramas increasingly reflect the reality that those arrested for drug and violent crimes are disproportionately people of color. These shows are also more realistic in terms of how they represent violence and its consequences, a fact that has earned them a stamp of approval from at least one group of researchers monitoring media violence (see University of California, Los Angeles, 1999).[7]

But the moral complexity of these newer police dramas is about more than mere style; it also reflects political concern about contemporary law enforcement, social inequality, and race relations. In other words, real-world voices of opposition are occasionally given expression in these programs. Therefore, in general, we agree with the media scholar John Fiske that these newer police dramas, like most television programs, are "producerly texts": They do not strong-arm their viewers into a single moral conclusion or perspective on reality, but are open to multiple interpretations (Fiske, 1987). Although the core of their narratives remains squarely within the cop show genre—valorous law enforcers standing between innocent civilians and the world of violent criminals—the newer cop shows sometimes convey a range of additional images that might be interpreted in a variety of ways.

The Crime Film

In several respects, the evolution of crime films has mirrored the television police drama. Between the end of World War II and the mid-1960s, movies with law enforcement themes uniformly depicted the police as helpful and virtuous and criminals as bad guys responsible for their own troubles. The movies of this period invariably concluded with the villains brought to justice and peace restored (Powers, Rothman, & Rothman, 1996).

There was nothing accidental about the ubiquity of this simplistic good-versus-evil morality play. To preempt government censorship, the five giant studios that dominated film production during this period promulgated a Production Code that banned more controversial story lines. For example, the Production Code stipulated that

> law, natural or human, shall not be ridiculed, nor shall sympathy be created for its violation. [Crimes] shall never be presented in such a way as to throw sympathy with the crime as against law and justice or to inspire others with a desire for imitation. (Powers et al., 1996, p. 106)

In the 1970s, as the big studios' control over the film industry diminished, representations of crime and justice became more ambivalent. Cops were increasingly depicted as either corrupt or as the first to initiate violence. For example, in the film *Serpico* (1974), police officers kill one of their own to cover up widespread corruption. Before 1965, only 1 in 6 celluloid cops committed a crime and only 1 in 10 resorted to violence; thereafter, approximately half of all cops were depicted as criminal or violent (Powers et al., 1996, p. 108).

During the same period, criminals were, for the first time, occasionally represented as victims of circumstances beyond their personal control (Powers et al., 1996, p. 112), even as their violent deeds became more sadistic and gratuitous (Allen, Livingstone, & Reiner, 1998). Criminals were also scripted as protagonists with greater frequency (Allen et al., 1998; see also Rafter, 2000). These developments did not destroy the conventional crime film model. In the 2000s, most big-screen police officers are depicted as heroic and most criminals as evil. But like the television police drama, the crime film became more ambivalent after 1970, with cops increasingly depicted as playing by the same rules as criminals (Allen et al., 1998, p. 111).

Images of crime victims also have changed over the past four decades. One content analysis of roughly 150 big box office crime movies released after 1945 found that just 1 in 4 of the earlier movies showed crime victims as traumatized. After 1980, however, roughly three quarters of the films depicted victims as suffering extreme trauma. "By positioning the audience as sympathetic to the victims," the authors of this study speculate, "later films may in fact make the audience more inclined to abhor violence and crime in general" (Allen et al., 1998, p. 67).

Like the police drama, the theme of vigilante justice is increasingly central to the crime film. Before the mid-1960s, roughly 1 in 10 celluloid cops resorted to vigilante tactics; thereafter, the number rose to roughly 8 in 10. In the earlier period, movies were as likely as not to conclude with the major villain brought to justice. Today, this is almost never the case. Instead, criminals are typically dispatched in a hail of bullets (Allen et al., 1998, p. 68).

Narratives of the maverick cop have been especially prevalent in cop-as-action-hero movies like *Dirty Harry* (1972), *The Enforcer* (1977), and *Death Wish II* (1982), as well as in comedies like *Beverly Hills Cop* (1985). In these movies, conventional police officers are portrayed as too constrained—either by their superiors or by the law—to function as effective crime fighters. Instead, superhuman cops must break department regulations and disregard the civil liberties of virtually everyone to "get the job done." For example, in *Lethal Weapon IV* (1998), the crime-fighting duo of Martin Riggs (Mel Gibson) and Roger Murtaugh (Danny Glover) are promoted to the rank of captain to get them off the streets where their crime-fighting antics are proving too costly for the City of Los Angeles. Nevertheless, in a rapid-fire sequence of car chases, gun battles, and martial arts maneuvers, the maverick L.A.P.D. cops hunt down and kill the movie's Chinese slave-trader villains. Looking back on the past three decades of crime movies, one research team concludes, "Hollywood's representation of police work looks more like organized vigilantism than the measured use of force in bringing criminals to justice" (Allen et al., 1998, p. 102).

Now and again, crime films and made-for-TV movies have proven especially effective in drawing public attention to particular crimes and criminal justice issues. For example, the so-called slasher films popular in the 1980s and 1990s—including *Scream* (1996), *Silence of the Lambs* (1991), and the *Friday the Thirteenth* series (1980s)—focused attention on the problem of serial murder (see Jenkins, 1994). Similarly, made-for-TV movies like *The Burning Bed* (1985) drew a great deal of attention to domestic violence (see Rapping, 1994). Made-for-TV movies have also helped to disseminate and popularize the core claims of the victim's rights movement—claims that will be discussed in Chapter 7.

The Reality-Based Cop Show

As discussed above, the news media provided intense coverage of the war on drugs in the 1980s, including dramatic footage of border seizures and police raids on crack houses. The news footage for these stories was frequently shot live and from the vantage point of the police, typically by reporters tagging along on police raids. It was in this context that the new reality-based police shows were introduced to the American public.[8]

A curious hybrid of news and entertainment, these shows consist of either actual video footage of police pursuing and apprehending suspects or dramatic recreations of crimes and arrests. In those shows that rely on footage of actual events, police officers often serve as program "hosts," providing narrative and commentary. Insofar as they claim to be strictly factual, these shows are distinct from the police dramas discussed in the previous section. But these programs are not exactly news: The episodes are not dated and are often shown in reruns. The most popular such show has been Fox TV's *COPS*, which depicts raw footage from a variety of U.S. cities. Other such programs include *Real Stories of the Highway Patrol, Bounty Hunters, L.A.P.D. Life on the Beat, Top Cops,* and *America's Most Wanted*.

One might assume, based on the proliferation of these shows, that they command a large audience. Actually, the evidence suggests otherwise. In one sample week in the mid-1990s, the Nielsen Company reported that reality-based police shows attracted viewers from about 9% of all households with television sets. The comparable figure for the average network prime-time show during that week was 12%; the most popular shows (*Seinfeld, Home Improvement, 60 Minutes*) drew between 17.5% and 22%. In terms of audience share—a measure of a show's audience size relative to other shows in the same time slot—the reality shows typically drew about 15%, a weak showing compared to the 22% to 39% commanded by the most popular shows. "In short," one observer has noted, "no matter how you measure it, reality crime programs are not wildly popular. They have an audience, but, by industry standards, it is neither large nor particularly lucrative" (Fishman, 1998, p. 39). Although audiences for the reality-based shows may be small by industry standards, they are still quite significant. A rating of 9%, after all, translated in the mid-1990s to nearly 9 million households, comparable to the audience for the networks' evening newscasts (Fishman, 1998).

An additional consideration helps to explain why reality-based cop shows have become a staple of prime-time television. Television networks profit by either expanding their audiences or, as in the case of the reality-based police shows, reducing their production costs. Because these shows rely on footage of real-life cops, the producers have no writers, set designers, or make-up artists to pay. Best of all, these shows have no expensive stars. Production of a single episode of a hit comedy can cost millions of dollars. By contrast, it costs only $250,000 to produce six half-hour segments—a full week's worth of programming—of *Real Stories of the Highway Patrol*. In an era of declining overall audience size for all network television, the cost savings afforded by these shows likely explains why they have proliferated so rapidly (Fishman, 1998).

For viewers who do tune into these cheaply produced pseudo-documentaries, what is the attraction? One keen interpreter of the reality-based shows argues that they offer viewers the twin pleasures of voyeurism and identification with authority:

> Voyeurism is taking pleasure from viewing the private or forbidden. The viewer overrules the wishes of others that the object of viewing remain secreted. Viewing may thus be experienced as an act of domination. The voyeurism of *Cops* is intertwined with its authoritarian pleasures. The seductions or pleasures of one type of power—voyeuristically intruding into the private or forbidden—are meshed with the seductions of another type of power: identifying with the sanctioned authority of the police. (Doyle, 1998, p. 53)[9]

The reality-based programs may also attract viewers by appealing to their sense of civic duty. *America's Most Wanted*, for example, urges audience members to help fight crime by calling a tips hotline with information on the whereabouts of criminals depicted in the weekly program. In the mid-1990s, this show received 3,000 telephone calls per weekly episode (Donovan, 1998).

Reality-based cop shows differ from the new television police dramas in several ways. First, even in the newer dramas, criminals are largely depicted as white and as either professional crooks or corrupt businessmen. In contrast, in the reality-based shows, the objects of police attention are typically poor and members of minority groups (Lichter et al., 1994, p. 294). In fact, one content analysis (Kooistra, Mahoney, & Westervelt, 1998) found that the show *COPS* overrepresents blacks as offenders, especially when it comes to violent crime: "In all, 26 of the 34 violent crimes (76%) and seven of nine property offenses (78%) were allegedly committed by nonwhites" (p. 141). Whereas blacks tended to be associated with violent crimes, whites were typically depicted as engaging in less serious crimes, such as prostitution and leaving the scene of an accident.

Second, in the carefully constructed reality-based programs, the moral ambiguity of *N.Y.P.D. Blue* and *Homicide* is nowhere to be found. The cops are portrayed as honest, hard-working, and deeply committed to protecting the public. Whenever the story line permits, they are treated as heroes. The suspects, on the other hand, are frequently "described in terms that connote physical ugliness. They are depicted as dangerous, depraved, unremorseful people" (Cavender, 1998, p. 79). Journalist Debra Seagal, who at one time logged raw footage for the show *American Detective*, explains how the editing process works:

By the time our 9 million viewers flip on their tubes, we've reduced fifty or sixty hours of mundane and compromising video into short, action-packed segments of tantalizing, crack filled, dope-dealing, junkie-busting cop culture. How easily we downplay the pathos of the suspect; how cleverly we breeze past the complexities that cast doubt on the very system that has produced the criminal activity in the first place. How effortlessly we smooth out the indiscretions of the lumpen detectives and casually make them appear as pistol-flailing heroes rushing across the screen. (Seagal, 1993, p. 54)

The good-versus-evil story line is constructed from the raw footage by way of exclusion. Images of police brutality, abuse of power, and corruption are edited out. Images of suspects that might elicit sympathy— or of suspects or witnesses responding with hostility to the presence of the television camera—are similarly excised. And in the most straight-forward exclusion of all, camera crews are rarely assigned to tag along with police in neighborhoods where middle-class deviance might be uncovered.

Seagal describes some of the material that winds up on the cutting-room floor. In one strip of raw footage, two Latino suspects are seen emerging from a car after a high-speed chase with their hands in the air. "Get on the ground, cocksucker!" a police officer screams. "I'll blow your motherfucking head off." Viewers of *American Detective* will never hear this; nor will they see the violence that ensues as officers kick the suspects in the stomach, face, and head:

Our main cameraman focuses on the detectives ambling around their fallen prey like hunters after a wild-game safari; a lot of vainglorious, congratulatory back-slapping ensues. Our secondary cameraman holds a long, extreme close-up of a suspect while his mouth bleeds into the dirt. I feel like I'm dying, he wheezes, and turns his head away from the camera. One [*American Detective*] producer shook his head at the vio-lence. "Too bad," he said. "Too bad we can't use that footage." This was clearly a case of too much reality for reality-based TV. (Seagal, 1993, p. 55)

Finally, in the reality-based cop shows, in contradistinction to the best of the police dramas, only one perspective on reality is presented— that of the show's narrating host. Several of the reality-based shows, including *COPS* and *L.A.P.D. Life on the Beat,* have police officers as guest hosts. Others, such as *America's Most Wanted* and *Unsolved*

Mysteries, have permanent celebrity hosts. In either case, it is the host's interpretation—and almost never that of witnesses, victims, or suspects—that imbues the images on the screen with meaning.

Consider a typical vignette from the show *COPS:* The cameras roll as a Latina woman is arrested for selling cocaine to an informant working for the police. When told that she is "going away" for at least 3 years, the woman breaks down sobbing. The host police officer sums up the segment with this observation: "What made her do it? I don't know, the devil made her do it." Audience members, of course, are never made privy to the woman's own explanation for why she "did it" (Stojanovich, 1997).

In these shows, moreover, the host's perspective rarely strays far from the "permissiveness" theme that dominates political discourse on crime (see Chapter 4). A victim's rights activist and host of the show *America's Most Wanted* conveys the central message in these words, broadcast as a teaser for the program:

> You know what I'm sick of? Criminals who serve only a fraction of their sentences. Sexual predators who are released to live next door to you and your children and you don't even know it. Drug dealers who think they run these streets. This is a society where criminals have all the rights and victims don't have any. Well, it's going to change. You're going to make that happen. The new "America's Most Wanted." America fights back. Premieres next Saturday after "Cops" on non-stop Fox. (Doyle, 1998, p. 53)

The moral simplicity and narrative closure of the reality-based shows have led some observers to declare that they are, in fact, less real than the best of their fictional counterparts (Donovan, 1998; Seagal, 1993). Be this as it may, both fictional and reality-based cop shows depict a world that is filled with predatory violence—a world in which well-intentioned police officers are doing their best to protect the public in spite of laws and judges that favor the rights of criminals over the lives of honest citizens. These themes are given the hard sell in the reality-based cop shows and in the more archaic police dramas. In the new "gritty realism" dramas, these themes are soft peddled—and sometimes even contradicted—but are generally present for those who are inclined to seize on them. What is the impact of this familiar narrative on its audience? In general, how have media images of crime and law enforcement affected the feelings and beliefs of the American public? These are the questions explored in the next section.

Media Imagery and Public Opinion

Newspapers, television, and film, like parents and schools, influence people's ways of thinking, feeling, and being in the world. Whatever effects the media have on beliefs are likely to accumulate over long stretches of time and interact with other social forces (Jeffres & Perloff, 1997, pp. 86-97). This fact makes assessing the effects of media exposure exceedingly difficult. How can we disentangle the impact of the mass media from the influences of other institutions in society?

One approach, most closely associated with George Gerbner and his colleagues at the University of Pennsylvania's Annenberg School for Communication, draws on survey data to compare the attitudes and feelings of heavy and light television viewers. In a series of annual content analyses of prime-time television, Gerbner and his colleagues contrasted the "mean and scary" world of television with the real world as portrayed by official statistics. They simultaneously administered surveys of the general public regarding television viewing habits and perceptions of social reality. To highlight their interest in the cumulative effects of television viewing, they called this methodology "cultivation analysis."

In general, Gerbner and his colleagues found that heavy television viewers are more likely to see the world as a mean and scary place than are light television viewers. Heavy viewers, for example, are more likely to overestimate the number of people who commit serious crimes, as well as the percentage of people involved in violence. Similarly, heavy television viewers are more likely to distrust others, fear walking alone at night in their own neighborhood, and report that crime is a "very serious personal problem" (Morgan & Signorielli, 1990). In short, as one member of the research team stated, "television's mean and dangerous world tends to cultivate a sense of relative danger, mistrust, insecurity, vulnerability, dependence, and—despite its supposedly 'entertaining' nature—alienation and gloom" (Signorielli, 1990, p. 88).

Researchers testing cultivation theory have qualified these findings in a number of ways. One researcher found that the media had a more pronounced impact on people who regard television dramas as "realistic" (Potter, 1986). Other researchers report that heavy viewing contributes to fear of the world "out there" but not of the immediate neighborhood (Coleman, 1993; Heath & Gilbert, 1996; Heath & Petraitis, 1987). Gerbner's own research team has suggested that the media's contribution to fear may consist largely of "mainstreaming"— the tendency to heighten fear among heavy television viewers who belong to demographic groups that typically express moderate levels of fear. For example, heavy television viewing tends to increase fear among respondents with medium to high incomes but not among respondents with low incomes (Gerbner, Gross, Morgan, & Signorielli, 1980).

Most cultivation analysis examines the effects of television as a whole. Some analysts, however, have focused on shows with law enforcement themes. One such researcher found adolescent heavy viewers of fictional crime dramas to be more fearful of victimization and view the police more positively than light viewers. Adolescent heavy viewers were also found to be less supportive of civil liberties (Carlson, 1985).[10] In another study, regular viewers of reality-based crime shows provided higher-than-average estimates of crime prevalence, and, in contradistinction to heavy viewers of fictional police dramas, higher-than-average estimates of crime prevalence among African Americans (Oliver & Armstrong, 1998).

Cultivation research has been criticized on a number of grounds. In some studies, the statistical relationship between heavy viewing and fear of crime is either relatively weak or disappears after the introduction of statistical controls for age, education, and income (Heath & Gilbert, 1996; Reiner, 1997). Cultivation researchers respond that because even light viewers watch a substantial amount of television, modest differences between light and heavy viewers may indicate a substantial cultivation effect for all television viewers.[11]

Cultivation research has also been criticized for assuming that television viewing causes fear. It is possible that fearful people are drawn to television's depictions of crime and violence, and that television exposure does not have the causal effects Gerbner and his colleagues claim (see especially Sparks, 1992b; Zillmann & Wakshlag, 1985). The basic allure of crime dramas, these skeptics contend, is that they promise to reassure the already anxious; their popularity is a measure, not a cause, of popular anxiety about crime. An alternative but similar argument holds that feelings of vindictiveness toward criminals draw certain people to television's images of aggressive law enforcement.

The difficulty of isolating the causal impact of exposure to the media has encouraged some researchers to turn to experimental techniques. Such research typically involves exposing experimental and control groups to systematically altered media content (a process known as "priming"), and then following-up with survey questions on crime-related attitudes and feelings. Such studies find that people exposed to media depictions of violent crimes are subsequently more likely than viewers in control groups to perceive other crimes as more serious and to support punitive anti-crime measures. They also find that respondents who learn about a criminal case from the news media are far more likely to believe that the sentence delivered was too lenient than those who read the actual court documents (63% vs. 19%) (Roberts & Doob, 1990; Roberts & Edwards, 1992).

Experimental studies by Shanto Iyengar and colleagues have also examined the impact of news frames and racialized images of criminal offenders. In one study, the television crime story to which research subjects were exposed varied along two dimensions. Some stories framed crime "episodically"—they depicted a single instance of violent crime. In others, violent crime was framed "thematically"—that is, discussed as a social problem and situated in its larger social context. Researchers also varied the racial identity of those visually depicted as "the criminal." Not surprisingly, those who viewed stories that framed violent crime in "episodic" terms were more likely to attribute crime to individual rather than social causes. But the more dramatic finding in this study was the significance of race: Stories that featured violent black criminals were more than twice as likely as stories depicting violent white criminals to elicit individualistic (rather than social) attributions of responsibility for the problem of crime (Iyengar, 1995, p. 196).

In a follow-up study, Iyengar (with Franklin Gilliam) exposed groups of research subjects to three digitally altered variations of a crime news story. In the first variation, the 5-minute story included a 5-second mug shot of a black offender. In the second scenario, the story was the same, but the mug shot was digitally altered to depict a white offender. In the third, the mug shot was excluded, and no clues were provided with respect to the racial identity of the offender. The results indicated that the brief exposure to the mug shot of a black offender not only increased the tendency of white viewers to attribute crime to individual failings as opposed to social problems, it also increased the share that were willing to support punitive anticrime policies such as "three strikes and you're out" and the death penalty. Just as remarkable, 60% of viewers who saw the story with no image of a perpetrator falsely recalled seeing one, and 70% of these believed the perpetrator to be an African American. The researchers attribute this surprising finding to the familiarity of viewers with a standard violent crime news "script" that features African American offenders: "Lacking concrete evidence about the perpetrators, viewers infer what must have happened" (Gilliam & Iyengar, 2000, p. 564).

In sum, recent experimental research confirms that news reports of violent crime do tend to increase punitive attitudes among viewers, and that this effect is especially pronounced among white viewers of news items describing crimes committed by African Americans.

Conclusion

Over the past three decades, crime has consistently been a dominant feature of both news and entertainment media. In the first part of this chapter, we argued that the rapid growth in crime-related news reflects news values; media outlets' pursuit of market share; and the media's tendency to rely on state officials, many of whom have sought, for political reasons, to call attention to the crime and drug problems. We also showed that most crime news focused on violent assaults by predatory strangers and tended to frame these happenings as isolated events rather than as part of a broader social problem. In those cases in which crime was treated more thematically, the alleged lenience of the criminal justice system was emphasized.

In the second part of the chapter, we showed that the fictional "reel" world of film and television has long been far more violent than the real world and has become even more violent in the past 30 years. Moreover, the police are increasingly depicted as stymied in their pursuit of criminals by liberal-minded due-process restrictions. Although the moral categories of the police drama are, in some cases, less clearly drawn today than in the past, new reality-based television cop shows resemble the crime dramas of the 1950s in their unambiguous "us versus them" depictions. Therefore, in general, most contemporary crime narratives still resonate with key elements of the conservative discourse on crime.

In particular, entertainment crime narratives encourage three ideologically loaded notions:

- Offenders are professional criminals—clever, clear-headed, and motivated by unadulterated greed. (This conception contrasts sharply with the notion that the behavior of many criminals is shaped by the "code of the streets" discussed in Chapter 3.)

- The interests of public safety and justice are ill served by liberal judges and lawyers who are—sometimes to the point of absurdity—preoccupied with the rights of defendants.

- Hard-working, dedicated cops are out there every day doing their best in the face of these difficult challenges.

Empirical assessments of the general impact on popular perceptions of mass-mediated depictions of crime, violence, and law enforcement are methodologically difficult. Cultivation studies have found that heavy television viewers tend to be more fearful and mistrusting, to view the police more positively, and to express greater hostility toward civil liberties. But because crime-related programs may, in fact, attract the already fearful (for reassurance) and the vindictive (for vicarious vindication), these studies are unable to disentangle cause and effect. However, experimental studies consistently support the conclusions of cultivation researchers by showing that news media depictions of violent criminal acts (which are quite characteristic of crime news) encourage punitive attitudes, especially when the offenders depicted are African American.

In the next chapter, we continue our discussion of popular opinion. Why are people so worried about crime, and why do they seem to favor punitive approaches to the problem?

6

Crime and Public Opinion

One version of the conventional wisdom on the expansion of the penal system goes like this: Whatever crime rates may be doing, the American public has become more fearful of crime and increasingly punitive in its policy preferences. Although these sentiments are not necessarily a response to trends in criminal activity, they are widespread and are the driving force behind the war on crime and drugs. This view is conveyed in the following excerpt from a 1994 *Time* magazine article titled "Lock 'Em Up!":

> With outraged Americans saying that crime is their No. 1 concern, politicians are again talking tough. But are they making sense?
>
> "WHAT ARE WE GOING TO DO ABOUT these kids (monsters) who kill with guns??? Line them up against the wall and get a firing squad and pull, pull, pull. I am volunteering to pull, pull, pull."
>
> That's not a rap lyric. It's from an anonymous letter to a judge in Dade County, Florida—part of the shared unconscious talking. And suddenly we're all ears. In one of the most startling spikes in the history of polling, large numbers of Americans are abruptly calling crime their greatest concern. Confronted by clear evidence of a big issue, politicians everywhere, including the one in the White House, are reaching for their loudest guns: prisons, boot camps, mandatory sentences. Months before the start of baseball season, the air is full of shouts of "Three strikes and you're out." (Lacayo, 1994, p. 50)[1]

In this chapter, we review evidence that casts serious doubt on the claim that the war on crime is primarily a response to the spread and dominance of such sentiments. We show that over the past three decades, fear of crime has been surprisingly stable, and that, with some notable exceptions, it is not nearly as widespread as media accounts suggest. We also show that crime-related issues rise to the top of the popular agenda in response to political and media activity around crime—not the other way around. By focusing on violent crime perpetrated by racial minorities, and by perpetuating inaccurate perceptions of the criminal justice system, politicians and the news media have amplified and intensified popular fear and punitiveness.

Despite this pattern, the public has not become uniformly or even primarily punitive. Evidence from surveys and ethnographic research indicates that *both* tough-on-crime rhetoric and alternatives to it have resonated with much of the public, even at the peak of the wars on crime and drugs. In recent years, support for these wars has diminished, and support for alternatives to it has grown. Thus, although some members of the public have supported the punitive anticrime and anti-drug policies of recent decades, and this support was intensified by political and media representations of crime, it nevertheless remained far more qualified and conflicted than is commonly recognized. This is particularly true for African Americans, who suffer the highest rates of criminal victimization and are most often the target of criminal justice institutions.

Fear of Crime

In survey research, the standard measure of fear of crime is the question, "Is there any area right around here—that is, within a mile—where you would be afraid to walk alone at night?" If rising fear of crime explains the political response to crime, we would expect to see the level of reported fear of "walking alone at night" increase over time. As Exhibit 6.1 shows, however, slightly more than a third of the population consistently reports fearfulness.

This exhibit shows that the percentage of Americans who are afraid to walk near their homes at night has remained remarkably stable over time and has declined some in recent years. It is not clear, however, how much these survey results really tell us. As several researchers have recently pointed out, the "walking alone at night" question does not tap feelings of fear and dread that respondents may experience in the course of other routine activities (Ferraro, 1995; Ferraro & LaGrange, 1987; Haghighi & Sorensen, 1996). Rather, the question asks respondents to imagine how they would feel were they to engage in the kind of activity

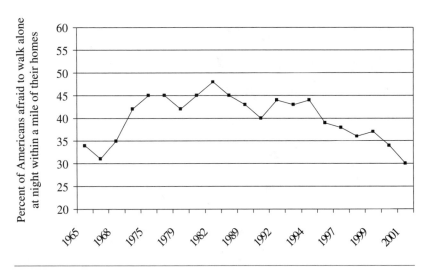

Exhibit 6.1   Fear of Walking Alone at Night

SOURCE: Maguire and Pastore (1998), Table 2.35; Maguire and Pastore (2002), Table 2.4; Warr (1995).

that some people—especially women and the elderly—are likely to avoid (Ferraro, 1995; Liska, Sanchirico, & Reed, 1988, p. 827; Skogan & Maxfield, 1981). Therefore, questions that tap more directly into feelings of fear that people experience in their actual, everyday lives are more useful and have been incorporated into more recent studies.

In one national survey, for example, respondents were asked how frequently they worry about various types of crime. Of the survey findings, two are especially noteworthy.

First, respondents appear relatively well informed about the chances of experiencing various kinds of crime. For example, respondents perceive the likelihood of experiencing a burglary or auto theft as much greater than the likelihood of being murdered (see Exhibit 6.2). Second, with a few important exceptions (discussed later), most people do not feel themselves to be personally in great danger of serious victimization. Less than a fifth of Americans, for example, worry "somewhat frequently" or "very frequently" about getting murdered, and less than a third worry about getting mugged (see Exhibit 6.2).

In addition, national pollsters began to ask whether people felt afraid in their homes at night, something that most people cannot avoid.

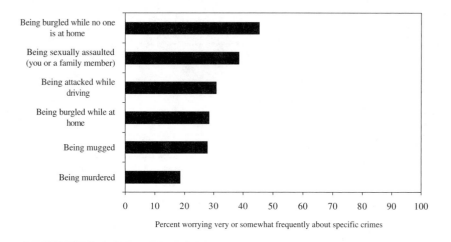

Exhibit 6.2   Worry About Specific Crimes

SOURCE: Flanagan and Longmire (1996), p. 25.

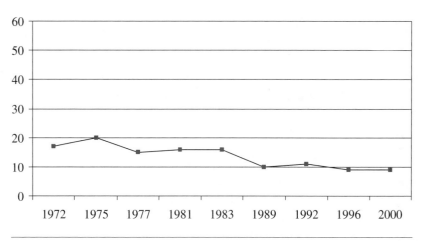

Exhibit 6.3   Percentage of Americans Who Feel Unsafe in Their Homes at Night

SOURCE: Maguire and Pastore (n.d.), Table 2.40.

The results indicate that most Americans have felt and continue to feel safe in their homes after dark (see Exhibit 6.3).

There are a few important exceptions to the conclusion that levels of fear are relatively low. The elderly are more likely to fear being a victim of crime than their reported rates of victimization would lead one to expect, probably because older people feel less able to defend themselves if attacked. Women of all races report comparatively high levels of fear, especially with respect to sexual assault. In fact, women's fear of sexual assault—a crime women worry about more frequently than murder—significantly diminishes their sense of security and increases the extent to which they feel vulnerable to all types of victimization. Like older people, women may also feel unable to protect themselves if attacked; they are also aware that they are at far greater risk of being sexually assaulted than are men (Ferraro, 1995, pp. 88, 100; see also Gordon & Riger, 1989; Stanko, 1985, 1990). Finally, minority men and women report higher levels of fear of violent crime than do whites. This pattern is largely explicable in terms of rates of criminal victimization: In the United States, minorities are more likely to be the victim of a crime, and are more fearful as a result (Ferraro, 1995, p. 64).

This does not suggest, however, that people's feelings about crime are based solely on the level and distribution of criminal victimization in their demographic group.[2] A number of studies indicate that a variety of environmental stimuli are also associated with fear of crime. These triggers include "incivilities" such as aggressive panhandling, distrust of the police, and media imagery of the sort discussed in Chapter 5 (Box, Hale, & Andrews, 1988; Ferraro, 1995; Lewis & Salem, 1986). In arriving at assessments of personal risk, people draw on the various resources available in their immediate environment, including, but not limited to, environmental cues, information gleaned from the mass media, and personal experiences with crime.

In sum, although fear of crime is not uncommon, attributing the punitive drift in criminal justice to widespread and increasing fear of crime is not supported by the available survey data. Whether researchers ask the hypothetical "walking alone at night" question or tap directly into everyday fears of crime, Americans report a relatively stable level of fear, and one that is generally lower than some media accounts and scholars imply.

Crime as a Social Problem

Although most Americans may not be terribly worried about the potential for personal victimization, they may still be highly concerned about crime as a social problem for the nation as a whole. Information about such concern (as opposed to fear) is typically culled from surveys that ask respondents to name "the most important problem facing the country." Of course, people might feel that crime is an important problem, but not the *most* important problem; to the extent that this is the case, this measure underestimates public concern about crime.

As Exhibit 6.4 shows, the percentage of respondents identifying crime or drugs as the nation's most important problem is far more volatile than fear of crime. Prior to the 1980s, issues pertaining to the economy (such as unemployment and government spending) and international relations topped the list of national concerns, although the percentage of people identifying crime, riots, and lawlessness as the nation's most important problems did rise to approximately 30% in 1968, a year known for antiwar demonstrations around the globe as well as President Nixon's campaign for "law and order." In 1988 and 1989, drugs surged to the top of the list of "America's most serious" problems. In subsequent years, public concern about drugs declined, but it was soon replaced by rising concern about crime.[3] By the year 2000, only tiny percentages of Americans identified either crime or drugs as the most pressing national problem.

In sum, these data show that Americans consider crime and drugs to be serious social problems—at least some of the time. But we should not jump to the conclusion that this concern is the driving force behind the politicization of the crime and drug issues in the 1960s, 1980s, and 1990s. Indeed, there is evidence that levels of public concern are highly responsive to levels of political initiative on the crime and drug issues. When politicians pay a great deal of attention to the crime problem, and their claims-making activities are reported in the media, the percentage of Americans who identify crime as the most important problem increases. When politicians stop emphasizing crime and drugs, public concern about crime and drugs (at least as captured by the "most important problem" question) declines. Thus, when it comes to concern about crime and drugs, it appears that the public is following the leadership of politicians and the media, not the other way around.[4]

The surge in popular concern about drug abuse in 1989 provides an especially vivid illustration of this process. "This is the first time since taking the oath of office that I felt an issue was so important, so threatening, that it warranted talking directly with you, the American people," President Bush, Sr. declared on September 5, 1989, in his first nationally televised address after taking office. "All of us agree that the gravest domestic threat facing our nation today is drugs" (Bertram et al., 1996, pp. 113-114). The president described a series of new antidrug initiatives, including creation of the office of "drug czar," and stepped up

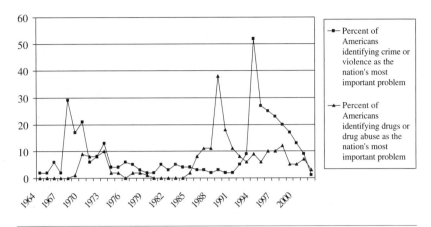

Exhibit 6.4   Concern About Crime and Drug Problems

SOURCE: Gallup (1990); Maguire and Pastore (1997), Table 2.1; Maguire and Pastore (n.d.), Table 2.1.

Note: When more than one Gallup Poll was administered in a given year, we report the results of the last survey taken in that year.

military involvement in drug interdiction. To dramatize the seriousness of the problem, he waved before the cameras a clear plastic bag of cocaine and stated ominously that it had been purchased "in the shadow of the White House" (Bertram et al., 1996, pp. 113-114). (In fact, the cocaine had been purchased near the White House, but the person who sold it was lured there from elsewhere in the city to help make the president's appeal more dramatic.)

The groundwork for the president's message had already been established by the national press. Acting on an earlier White House announcement that Bush would deliver a major address on drugs in September, the three major networks increased coverage of the issue. In the 2½ weeks prior to the speech, ABC, NBC, and CBS aired an average of nearly three stories each night on the issue, up from an average of fewer than one story per night in the weeks prior to the announcement of the president's plan. In the week following the address, coverage increased to an average of nearly four stories per night (Bertram et al., 1996, p. 115).

The public apparently received the message loud and clear. The share of respondents naming drugs as the "most important problem" surged in the aftermath of the president's speech from an already high mark of 27% in May to an astonishing 64% in September. By November, the numbers dropped back to 38%.

Several years later, the topic changed from drugs to crime, but the pattern remained more or less the same. In August 1993, the Republicans in Congress—eager to reclaim the crime issue so effectively neutralized by Clinton in the 1992 presidential election—announced a major new package of anticrime legislation. Clinton and the Democrats responded with their own rival package, effectively setting the stage for a contest over which political party was tougher on crime. As both houses of Congress debated omnibus crime bills, local congressional races featured an unprecedented torrent of tough-on-crime posturing.

In December 1993, the Senate passed a version of the crime bill providing for massive federal support to states for hiring police and building prisons. A few weeks later, 37% of Americans, an unprecedented proportion, named crime the most important problem facing the country. In the ensuing months, political and media attention to the issue of crime intensified still further. President Clinton announced his support for a federal "three strikes and you're out" law in his State of the Union address, the House of Representatives adopted its own version of the crime bill, and the national media covered the issue in a series of magazine cover stories and network news special reports. In addition, the national press provided saturation coverage of a number of sensational crimes and trials, including the abduction and murder of 12-year-old Polly Klaas, the massacre on the Long Island Commuter Train, and the trial of the Menendez brothers for the murder of their parents (Alderman, 1994).[5] In August, the month President Clinton—amid maximum fanfare—signed the crime bill into law, public concern about crime reached its apex when 52% of those polled identified crime as the nation's most important problem.

In sum, popular concern about crime and drugs as social problems historically has been lower than concern about such issues as the economy and war and peace. But public concern about crime and drugs, as measured by the "most important problem" question, has also proven quite volatile and highly influenced by politicians and the mass media. This should hardly come as surprising news; in general, when people are asked about the country's (as compared with their own) problems, they reflect not only on their personal experiences, but also on what they have seen and heard in the mass media and from their political leaders. This is not to say that politicians can mobilize popular concern about any issue, or that public concern about crime is not genuine. The public worries about crime and drugs, but this worry is not the driving force behind the massive political and media attention to these issues. On the relatively rare occasions when the public has put crime or drugs at the top of its list of concerns, it has done so in the context of massive political initiative and media coverage.

Popular Punitiveness

What about Americans' preferences regarding crime control policy? Is it true that the public is highly punitive and growing more so? There are a few kernels of truth to this bit of conventional wisdom. The most reliable trend data on public opinion about crime control consists of questions regarding the death penalty and the harshness of the courts. Between the mid-1960s and early 1970s, fewer than half of the respondents in national surveys expressed support for the death penalty for people convicted of murder. By 1976, the share of the public supporting the death penalty had climbed to 66%; by 1988, it had reached nearly 80%. Support for capital punishment remained at this high level for several years, but has declined somewhat recently (see Exhibit 6.5).

National surveys also indicate a sharp increase, albeit concentrated in the late 1960s and early 1970s, in the percentage of Americans critical of their local courts. In 1965, 48.9% of respondents expressed the view that the courts in their area "do not deal harshly enough" with criminals. By 1969, that percentage had increased to nearly 75%, and between 1976 and 1995, approximately 80% of respondents expressed this view. In 1994, the same year 52% of Americans identified crime as the nation's most important problem, a record 85% also reported that the courts were not harsh enough (Maguire & Pastore, 1997, Table 2.5; Stinchcombe et al., 1980, p. 31). Since then, however, the percentage of Americans complaining about the lenience of the courts has declined, dropping to 68% in 2000 (Maguire & Pastore, n.d., Table 2.54).

Because these trend data consist of responses to just two questions, they might be considered a precarious basis for drawing conclusions about the mood of the public regarding criminals. A number of national surveys conducted in the early and mid-1990s, however, also found growing and widespread support for most get-tough policies and initiatives. In particular, large majorities of respondents favored imposing mandatory sentences (including three-strikes laws) (Maguire & Pastore, 1996, Table 2.35); restricting bail and parole for violent offenders (Maguire & Pastore, 1995, Table 2.39); treating juvenile violent offenders

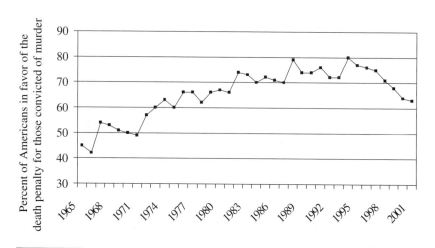

Exhibit 6.5   Support for the Death Penalty

SOURCE: Maguire and Pastore (1997), Table 2.55; Maguire and Pastore (2001), Table 2.61; Warr (1995). Estimate for 2001 taken from "Stop the Killing Machine" (2001).

Note: When more than one Gallup Poll was administered in a given year, we report the results of the last survey taken in that year.

as adults (Maguire & Pastore, 1997, Table 2.59); and building new prisons (Maguire & Pastore, 1995, Table 2.48). Moreover, most Americans complained during this period that prison conditions were too comfortable (Roberts & Stalans, 1997, p. 48), and, according to some surveys, that the government should focus on "punishing" rather than "rehabilitating" violent offenders (Gerber & Engelhardt-Greer, 1996; Maguire & Pastore, 1995, Table 2.46; Maguire & Pastore, 1997, Table 2.56). Although these attitudes are found in all demographic groups, they are more widespread among men, whites, those who live in the South and West, and self-identified conservatives (Bowers, 1993; Ellsworth & Gross, 1994; Gaubatz, 1995; Gerber & Engelhardt-Greer, 1996; McCorkle, 1993; Roberts, 1992).

Qualitative research conducted during this period also found relatively widespread support for the notion that the criminal justice system is too lenient with offenders. For example, in focus group discussions conducted in Boston in the early 1990s, a number of participants argued vigorously that the crime problem is, in large measure, attributable to permissive judges.[6] In the following discussion, for example, participants argue that the hands of the police are "tied" by judges who naively insist that "there's a little bit of good in everybody."

Facilitator:	O.K. Next question. "Do you think the crime problem is getting worse or better, and why?"
Edward:	I think it's getting worse to some extent, because the hands of the police and the judicial system—not so much the judicial system—the hands of the police and the prison system are somewhat tied, so that the punishment is almost a joke.
Sally:	Doesn't fit the crime.
Edward:	And if you're a hardcore criminal, you don't really get punished.
Rhoda:	When a police officer makes an arrest, before he finishes his paperwork, the damn criminal is back on the street.
Unknown Voice:	Right. I know.
Rhoda:	The courts have no room for them. There's no follow-up.
Christine:	It's easy to be a criminal.
Rhoda:	Jails. The courts don't follow through. They're let out in the street, and then the cop doesn't even finish his paperwork and the guy's back out in the street. Ninety percent of the cops don't even want to go to court anymore. It's not worth the effort.
Edward:	It's discouraging.
Rhoda:	It is. They're discouraged. I mean when we were assaulted, Christine and I, the cop literally said, do you want to push this? Yeah, I want him off the street! Of course I want to push it!
Edward:	And the judicial system is very set up to protect the rights—But you're far more protected if you're a criminal than if you're a victim, which is very frustrating.
Unknown Voice:	Mmhm.
Martha:	You're telling the truth. The police make the arrests, but nothing happens. If you're a policeman and you arrested a hardened criminal, and you're sitting in court and all of a sudden this sweetheart of a judge— "There's a little bit of good in everybody." If he

knew how little there was in some of them, he wouldn't sleep nights! So the little so-and-so gets— goes free. And he goes out and he does it again. He says, what do I have to worry about? I can commit this crime many times. And they do. They do. They keep repeating their crime, because they have no fear. (Sasson, 1995b, pp. 39-40)

Discussion participants also criticized allegedly cushy prison conditions. In the following extract, they describe prisons as "country clubs" that provide amenities unaffordable to law-abiding citizens. Harsher prison conditions, they argue, are both well deserved ("if they're going to act like animals, they should be treated like animals") and more likely to discourage crime:

Deborah:	There's no rehabilitation services available, or no deterrent services either. Because we were talking earlier about quadruple bunking them for example. You know, make prison a really—
Lloyd:	Not a kiddy club.
Deborah:	Yeah. A real terrible place to be—
Karl:	Take away the TV.
Lloyd:	The gyms, the swimming pools—
Georgia:	Let them know that they're there for a reason.
Lloyd:	[Take away] the cable TVs.
Deborah:	[Over clamor] If they're going to act like animals, they should be treated like animals.
Lloyd:	People here in the winter have it so bad that they'd rather go into jail because it's so good there. Three squares. A place to work out. A place to watch TV. A place to go swimming, or whatever. And read and get a little bit of knowledge and stuff, and then it's warm. And then they come out in the summertime.
Georgia:	And if they're there long enough, they can come out with a Ph.D.
Unknown voice:	Mmhm.
	[A few minutes later, in response to a trigger statement:]
Lloyd:	I feel strongly on that one. That one is something that has to be addressed. That's why we're trying to make

	more prisons and stuff like that. But they need to make them less plush, right, and more of them.
Unknown voice:	Mmhm.
Chuck:	Make it what it is—it's a jail. [Over clamor] It's a prison.
Unknown Voice:	Quadruple bunk 'em.
Chuck:	It's not a country club. It's not a camp. It's not a summer camp, you know. It's not body-building camp. You know, most of these guys go in the joint, they come out, they look like Arnold Schwarzenegger.
Unknown Voice:	Sure you're right. Sure you're right.
Unknown Voice:	Pumping iron every day.
Unknown Voice:	Eating good.
Chuck:	If you don't want to work, you don't have to work.
Karl:	You know how much it costs a year to keep one in prison?
Deborah:	Something outrageous.
Karl:	$46,000.
Deborah:	More than they pay me.
Lloyd:	Is it?
Karl:	To keep *one*. $46,000 for *one*.
Deborah:	Wow. (Sasson, 1995b, pp. 44-45)

In only 1 of 20 focus group discussions did a participant challenge this characterization of prison conditions. Notably, this dissenter had worked as a top administrator in the Massachusetts prison system.

In sum, both quantitative and qualitative research finds evidence of growing support for the get-tough policies of the war on crime and drugs throughout the 1980s and into the 1990s. However, the results of more recent surveys indicate that support for these policies is beginning to erode. As was mentioned earlier, both support for capital punishment and the perception that the courts are not harsh enough have declined over the past few years. Similarly, the percentage of poll respondents favoring three strikes and other mandatory sentencing laws declined from 55% in 1995 to 38% in 2000 (Bank, 2002), and in 2001, the percentage favoring the legalization of marijuana reached a record high of 34% (Maguire & Pastore, n.d., Table 2.0011). That same year, more than 52% felt that drug use should be treated like a disease; only 35% favored continuing to treat it primarily as a crime (Maguire & Pastore, n.d., Table 2.50).

In the next section, we further explore the sources of the spread of the get-tough mood in the 1980s and early to mid-1990s. We also analyze the coexistence of popular punitiveness with ongoing—and increasing— public support for alternative approaches to the crime problem.

Understanding Popular Punitiveness

As discussed in detail in Chapters 2 and 3, the United States does not have unusually high levels of crime, but it does endure an unusually high rate of lethal violence. Some have suggested that the frequency of homicide creates a more generalized fear of crime and thus fuels support for tough criminal justice policies. This argument is supported by evidence that fear of crime was relatively high during the 1980s, when homicide rates were also relatively high, and by evidence that both homicide rates and fear of crime have declined over the past decade.

But other bits of evidence are inconsistent with this argument. First, levels of fear have been fairly stable compared to the homicide rate. Second, fear of crime does not necessarily lead to punitiveness, and those who are not personally fearful are often among the most punitive (Stinchcombe et al., 1980). Finally, killers make up only a tiny percentage of officially sanctioned criminals. It appears, then, that high rates of homicide play a small and indirect role in the generation of popular support for get-tough crime policies. What other factors help us to explain why Americans *sometimes* express harsh views regarding criminal offenders in general? Why did these sentiments become so widespread in our recent past? We begin our analysis with a discussion of certain dimensions of American culture that encourage support for harsher forms of punishment, and then consider the ways in which media imagery and race relations contribute to public punitiveness. We conclude with some speculations about why public support for the wars on crime and drugs appears to be eroding.

Individualism and Self-Reliance

Analysts of American political culture have long noted the extraordinary salience of two closely related values:[7]

Self-reliance stresses the responsibility of each individual for herself or himself: People should stand on their own two feet! If in the gutter, they should pull themselves up by their own bootstraps! Self-reliance celebrates the self-made person who perseveres in the face of obstacles and achieves material success through hard work. *Individualism* highlights the importance of individuality, autonomy, and free choice. Each person ought to be regarded first and foremost as a unique individual, and only after that as a member of an ethnic group or larger collectivity. Individualism celebrates personal choices—doing your own thing—in matters of politics and lifestyles. Individuality, autonomy, and freedom to choose are valued in their own right and inso-far as they permit individuals to discover and develop their "true" selves.

For many Americans, these core values are important wellsprings of optimism. The belief that individual effort alone shapes the quality of one's life means that ordinary people can surmount personal hardships—including handicaps associated with social class, race, and gender—and make something extraordinary of themselves. The flip side of adherence to the values of self-reliance and individualism is the view that crime, like all forms of action, is strictly a matter of individual choice and motiva-tion. Were crime viewed as a choice made in the context of socially struc-tured beliefs, constraints, and opportunities—as sociological theories tend to suggest—then crime control strategies emphasizing prevention and rehabilitation would seem to be the most logical. But insofar as crime is viewed as a personal choice, pure and simple, crime control strategies oriented toward deterrence and punishment make the most sense. It is in this way that the values of self-reliance and individualism in American political culture provide fertile soil for punitive rhetoric and beliefs.

Media Imagery

If core aspects of American political culture create the potential for punitiveness, then the crime-related images and messages that saturate the mass media play a vital role in actualizing this tendency. One way the media accomplish this triggering function is by misleading and misin-forming the public about crime and the criminal justice system. These erroneous beliefs tend to fuel support for punitive anticrime measures.

Study after study has shown that Americans tend to overestimate the national crime rate, especially levels of violent victimization, as well as rates of recidivism (Roberts & Stalans, 1997, pp. 207-209; see also Diamond & Stalans, 1989, pp. 87-88). Crime-related news stories and police dramas—especially those of the reality genre—focus on vio-lent crimes committed by strangers and fuel the public's tendency to overestimate the seriousness of the typical criminal offense (Roberts & Stalans, 1997, pp. 207-209; see also Diamond & Stalans, 1989, pp. 87-88). Such stories also intensify viewers' felt need for enhanced punishment and intensify racial animosity among whites. A recent study, for example, found that exposure to a news story about crime featuring a violent, nonwhite offender (as many do) increases support for punitive anticrime measures and heightens negative attitudes about African Americans among whites (Gilliam & Iyengar, 2000). Such stories not only reinforce the erroneous perception that most crime is violent, they also portray crime as perpetrated by dangerous "others." In turn, people who regard criminals as dangerous, malevolent (and nonwhite) outsiders are likely to support harsher crime control measures (see Roberts, 1992, pp. 109-121; Roberts & Stalans, 1997, p. 33; Zimring & Hawkins, 1997, pp. 12-13).[8]

Following the lead of political leaders who routinely complain about "soft-on-crime judges," the mass media also mislead the public about criminal justice practices. Routine news stories about criminal trials, for example, rarely provide adequate information to allow members of the public to grasp the reasons behind sentencing decisions (Roberts & Stalans, 1997, p. 216). Thematic news stories about the criminal justice system, as discussed in Chapter 5, typically highlight only the institution's most egregious failures, such as the early release of offenders who go on to commit new violent crimes.[9] Entertainment crime programs return time and again to narratives of police vigilantism necessitated by judges and criminal justice bureaucrats more concerned with protecting the rights of criminals than with ensuring the public's safety.

In these various ways, the mass media depict the criminal justice system as inefficient, ineffectual, and toothless. These images clearly affect public perceptions of the criminal courts. In one series of studies, for example, researchers found that 63% of the research subjects who read news media accounts of criminal cases felt that the sentences were too lenient, whereas only 19% of those who read the summary of the actual court documents felt that way (Roberts & Doob, 1990). In this way, media reportage contributes to the perception that the courts routinely let hardened and violent criminals off the hook.

Apparently as a result of the images presented in the media and elsewhere, most people significantly underestimate the severity of punishments actually meted out by the justice system (Bowers, 1993; Roberts & Stalans, 1997, p. 44). One study found that Florida residents expected inmates to serve an average of 40% of their original sentence; in fact, the law requires that they serve 85% of that sentence (Sentencing

Project, n.d.-b). In Oregon, a survey found that many citizens believed that violent offenders were being released early from prison due to overcrowding; in fact, neither violent nor nonviolent offenders were being released for this reason (Sentencing Project, n.d.-b).

Ironically, the public's sentencing preferences appear to be *less* punitive than those administered by the criminal justice system. In one study, researchers compared sentences prescribed by the Federal Sentencing Guidelines to sentences preferred by members of the public for selected crime vignettes. (Each crime vignette described a criminal event and provided brief background information on the defendant to be sentenced.) In most cases, the public's sentencing preferences closely matched those prescribed by the federal guidelines. However, in almost every case in which there was a disparity between the two, the federal guidelines were harsher.[10]

For example, the federal guidelines' sentence for the "trafficking in crack cocaine" vignette (22 years in prison) was more than twice as long as the median respondent sentence for the same crime vignette (10 years). Federal guidelines' sentences were about twice as severe as those preferred by the public for kidnapping in which a victim is unhurt (11.3 years vs. 6 years), carjacking in which the victim is unhurt (11.3 years vs. 5 years), and bank robbery in which a weapon is fired at the ceiling (11.3 years vs. 5 years). In sum, when it comes to the concrete task of sentencing criminal defendants, the public does not appear to be harsher than the courts (Rossi & Berk, 1997).

Evidence of the mass media's influence on popular conceptions of the criminal justice system can also be found in the everyday discourse of regular people. Consider, for example, the extracts from focus group discussions quoted earlier. In the first extract, participants claim that "the hands of the police are . . . tied," the punishment "doesn't fit the crime," and "you're far more protected if you're a criminal than if you're a victim." These slogans were not conceived from scratch, but were borrowed from the mass media and reflect the tendency of the public to underestimate actual sentences. Similarly, these discussion participants routinely advanced claims about the criminal justice system that originate in the broader public discourse—for example, claiming in the second extract that prisoners enjoy cable television, swimming pools, and the opportunity to work toward a PhD. They also refer to the cost to taxpayers of keeping an offender behind bars for a year. These slogans and "facts" about the justice system are part of a larger public discourse whose principal venue is the mass media.[11]

Modern Racism

There is evidence that punitiveness is also, at least among some, a manifestation of hostility toward African Americans and Latinos and ongoing opposition to policies that are aimed at actualizing racial equality. This was especially true in the earlier years of the war on crime. In the early 1970s, in the midst of President Nixon's war on crime, researchers found that those expressing the highest degree of concern about crime also tended to be opposed to racial reform. For example, one study reported that 42% of those who strongly disapproved of racial and social reform efforts identified crime as the nation's most important problem, compared with only 13% of those who strongly approved of reform efforts (Furstenberg, 1971). Others also found that racial attitudes were an important predictor of support for law-and-order rhetoric. For example, one researcher found that "those who support a hard line on law and order issues tend to be more racist and sexist, tend not to support equal rights for unpopular minorities . . . and they have a more negative view of welfare recipients" (Corbett, 1981, p. 337; see also Bennett & Tuchfarber, 1975). Opposition to busing was also strongly associated with white support for punitive anticrime policies (Stinchcombe et al., 1980).

Although this association between opposition to programs and policies aimed at bringing about racial equality and support for tough anticrime policies has abated somewhat, it has not disappeared. Survey research continues to show that people who report higher levels of racial prejudice also tend to have more punitive attitudes on the topic of crime control. In one national survey, for example, both antipathy toward African Americans and racial stereotyping were found to be statistically significant predictors of support for the death penalty, even after controlling for a battery of alternative predictors (Barkan & Cohn, 1994; see also Cohn et al., 1991). Similarly, in the study comparing popular sentencing preferences to the federal guidelines, respondents' attitudes toward civil rights were found to be a key predictor of punitiveness. Specifically, respondents who believed minorities have "too few" civil rights (about a quarter of the sample expressed this view) assigned an average sentence of 2 years. By contrast, the average sentence assigned by respondents who believed minorities have "too many" civil rights (also about a quarter of the total sample) was 3.8 years. The difference was even more stark with respect to the specific crime of drug trafficking: The average sentence assigned for this crime by civil rights supporters was 3.4 years; by civil rights opponents, 8.8 years (Rossi & Berk, 1997).[12]

It is important to note that survey respondents who express racial prejudice through criminal justice punitiveness have had a great deal of encouragement. Conservative law-and-order discourse—with its rhetorical origins in the struggle waged by southern politicians against civil rights activists—has frequently been mobilized to make veiled (and hence deniable) references to threats posed by minorities (see Chapter 4). In more recent years, this discourse has been joined by race-coded claims about the burdens imposed on taxpayers by welfare cheats, freeloaders, drug users, and so on, especially in the context of the debate over welfare reform (Edsall & Edsall, 1991; Gerber & Engelhardt-Greer, 1996, p. 71). Finally, television crime news and the new reality crime programs associate blackness and brownness with crime, and they do so in emotionally charged ways that encourage punitiveness among the viewing public.

The picture of an angry and vengeful public tainted by racism and clamoring for more prisons and more executions is, however, quite partial. As we shall see, the evidence suggests that even as support for tough anti-crime policies was growing, most Americans also supported alternatives to the get-tough policies emanating from the state and federal governments. It appears, then, that popular sentiments are far more complex—even contradictory—than is often appreciated.

Alternatives to Punitiveness

As Exhibit 6.6 shows, most Americans preferred that money be spent on crime prevention programs rather than on law enforcement and prison construction, even when popular punitiveness was at its peak (Maguire & Pastore, 1996, Table 2.37; Roberts & Stalans, 1997, p. 123).[13] In 1989, when levels of support for capital punishment were quite high and the vast majority of Americans believed the courts were too lenient, 61% of those polled preferred that money be spent on solving "social and economic problems" that underlie crime; only 32% favored spending more on law enforcement (Maguire & Pastore, n.d., Table 2.46). In 1994, when three-strikes laws appeared to be quite popular, 53% of those polled favored spending on prevention and rehabilitation, whereas 43% favored beefing up enforcement and punishment (Maguire & Pastore, n.d., Table 2.37). This preference for prevention has become even more pronounced in recent years: In 2000, fully 68%

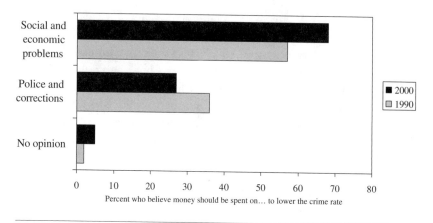

Percent who believe money should be spent on... to lower the crime rate

Exhibit 6.6   Support for Various Anticrime Strategies

SOURCE: Maguire and Pastore (2001), Table 2.46.

favored attacking social problems in order to reduce crime, whereas only 27% wished to enhance law enforcement (Maguire & Pastore, n.d., Table 2.46).

Popular support for crime prevention is rooted in the widespread notion that crime is a result not only of criminal justice leniency, but also of environmental factors, such as family and community breakdown, poverty, drug addiction, and guns. In fact, Americans are more inclined to identify these environmental factors than criminal justice leniency as a cause of crime (Flanagan, 1987, pp. 231-243; Maguire & Pastore, 1996, Tables 2.22 and 2.23). Ethnographic research also finds that many people attribute crime to a breakdown in the moral order, especially in the traditional authority structures of family and community (Crime and Justice Foundation, 1991; Doble, Immerwahr, & Richardson, 1991; Doble & Klein, 1989, p. 38; Sasson, 1995b).[14] "Basically the reason [we have so much crime]," explained one participant in the Boston focus group discussions, "is because society's whole moral structure and moral fiber has broken down, where people don't feel like they have to live by the rules" (Sasson, 1995b, p. 66). These discussions focused heavily on the failures of parents to supervise, discipline, and accept responsibility for their children. For example:

Gloria: I feel as though [crime is] happening because of the homes that some of these young people may come out of. Lack of super-vision, lack of parents—parents being parents.

Ben: No guidance. ["Right!"—a voice interjects.] A few years back on TV, you remember, "It's 11:00 o'clock, do you know where your children are?" And the answer to that today is "Yeah, they're outside on the street somewhere."

Gloria: No commitment in the home, no commitment in schools. Parents do not go to parent/teacher meetings. They don't go to the schools until the student has a real serious problem.

Ben: And then they get angry with the teacher.

Gloria: Yes. Or angry with the principal, or angry with the guidance counselor, or angry with the bus drivers. It's everybody else's fault.

Ben: There is no respect. (Sasson, 1995b, p. 66)

Discussion participants also attributed crime to the disintegration of the close-knit communities of their childhoods. These communities, they suggested, provided both mutual support as well as discipline. As one discussion participant vividly recalled:

I'll chime in. I grew up in a neighborhood—what I'll call a real neighborhood. And I grew up very poor. But one thing about growing up as poor as I did is that we had a sense of community. And we really had to work as a community, because individually the people of the community could not have survived by themselves. The only way that we could survive is that we had to pull together as a community. An example of that is that we were constantly without food. I did not eat every day. What we do sometimes is we would go around to the various neighbors, I need a cup of flour, I need a cup of milk. Go tell Ms. Sue to send me some baking powder and salt. And we would borrow amongst ourselves in order to make that bread. Children just got together and played. This is one thing that—children today, I come in the neighborhood and say "where are the children?" [In my] day you see like tons of children. We just played together as big groups of children when I was growing up. And there was spanking rights throughout the neighborhood and this type of thing. And I long for that. (Sasson, 1995b, p. 73)

This "social breakdown" perspective is often the basis for the public's abiding support for crime prevention initiatives. To the extent that people believe that faltering families and communities are the wellsprings of crime, they support efforts to shore up these institutions and provide alternative means of encouraging young people to stay on the straight and narrow. The relationship between this emphasis on social breakdown as a cause of crime and support for crime prevention initiatives was sometimes made quite explicit in the discussions:

> When you talk about education and family values and all that sort of thing, it's giving people options—it's—there are some very [good] programs in terms of when you challenge the kids and when you get them involved in art programs and sports programs and you basically get them using their time in more of a constructive fashion, [then] they don't have as much time to basically sit around and feel bored and look for trouble to get into. I think we've all been there as kids ourselves. . . . I think that would help, definitely, in terms of reducing the crime. And also, it's not only going to do it because you're keeping the kids busy, but it's also because you're teaching them good value systems at the same time. (Sasson, 1995b, p. 75)

Although often described as a liberal alternative to the get-tough approach, the social breakdown perspective is potentially compatible with key elements in conservative political discourse. In particular, concern about family breakdown, the decline of traditional authority structures, and limits on parents' right to inflict corporal punishment resonate with conservative calls for traditional family values, attacks on the welfare state, and attempts to impose order through get-tough criminal justice initiatives. On the other hand, support for community-based prevention programs fits nicely with the liberal emphasis on strengthening the social fabric in order to reduce crime.

In addition to crime prevention, most Americans continue to support rehabilitation (Gerber & Engelhardt-Greer, 1996; McCorkle, 1993; Roberts & Stalans, 1997, p. 200). In fact, in one national survey taken at the height of the crime war, a plurality of respondents indicated that the most important goal of prison, for those already behind bars, is "rehabilitation" rather than "punishment" or "crime prevention/deterrence."[15] In a separate study on public attitudes toward rehabilitation, criminologist Frances Cullen and his associates conclude,

> [C]itizens do not feel that time in prison should be wasted; prisons should not be warehouses or places that inflict pain without clear purpose. Instead, most citizens take a more pragmatic stance: Inmates should be given the education, training, employment experiences, and, perhaps, counseling that will enable them to become productive citizens. (Cullen, Skovron, Scott, & Burton, 1990, p. 256)

The recent passage of ballot initiatives calling for treatment rather than jail for nonviolent drug users, as well as surveys in which 75% of those polled prefer mandatory drug treatment over jail time for drug users, indicate widespread support for drug treatment (Bank, 2002).

Finally, a growing body of evidence indicates that most Americans respond favorably when asked about specific alternatives to both incarceration and capital punishment. In focus group interviews, for example, researchers have found that most participants support intermediate sanctions—such as community service, boot camp, and restitution to crime victims—as alternatives to incarceration, especially for nonviolent offenders. "As long as the crime did not involve violence," one group of researchers reports, "only small numbers favored incarceration after learning about alternatives, even with offenders who had multiple convictions" (Doble & Klein, 1989, p. 38; see also Crime and Justice Foundation, 1991; Doble et al., 1991; Sentencing Project, n.d.-b). Support for alternatives even extends to the death penalty. In one national survey—as well as statewide surveys in Florida, California, Georgia, and New York—a majority of respondents choose a sentence of life in prison without the possibility of parole rather than the death penalty for first-degree murderers when restitution to the victim's family is ordered as part of the package.[16]

These findings suggest a need to qualify the image of a highly punitive public. The widespread perception that the criminal justice system is too lenient is based on the impression that the punishments handed out are much less severe than they actually are, rather than a legal system that is out of touch with the public. Even when most Americans responded favorably to get-tough proposals such as three-strikes laws, the majority of Americans continued to prefer crime prevention programs when given a choice between the two. What most people seem to be demanding of the criminal justice system is protection from violent offenders and punishments that effectively communicate societal disapproval of crime.[17] Most Americans express support for alternatives to incarceration and execution that are consistent with these goals.

Minority Dissent

African Americans experience disproportionately high rates of serious criminal victimization and express higher-than-average levels of fear. As a result, it is hardly surprising that attitudes among African Americans toward individuals charged with criminal offenses, although still less severe than those of whites (see Maguire & Pastore, 1997, Table 2.69),[18] have hardened somewhat in recent decades. The share of African Americans expressing support for the death penalty for people convicted of murder, for example, increased from 44% in 1976 to 54% in 1996 (Secret & Johnson, 1989).

At the same time, African Americans, especially young men, have been the targets of aggressive law enforcement initiatives and, as a consequence, have been disproportionately affected by the wars on crime and drugs (Chambliss, 1994; Davis, 1992; Donziger, 1996; Miller, 1996; Tonry, 1995). This fact, along with highly publicized cases of police brutality, harassment of African American suspects, and widespread racial profiling by police departments across the country, explains African Americans' growing alienation from the institutions of criminal justice.

This alienation was widely recognized for the first time during the 1995 murder trial of black football superstar O.J. Simpson. Although most white Americans believed Simpson to be guilty, most African Americans believed it was plausible that he was framed by racist cops (Whitaker, 1995, p. 24). Undoubtedly, African Americans' views on the case were influenced by the Fuhrman tapes—audiotapes in which the lead police investigator in the Simpson case says, "Anything out of a nigger's mouth . . . is a f—ing lie" and that "If you did the things that they teach you in the academy, you'd never get a f—ing thing done" (text omitted in original). In the words of one journalist writing at the time of the trial, "Those tapes confirmed what many African Americans had always known or suspected—that many white cops hate black people, and see nothing wrong with violating civil rights or tampering with evidence to put away anyone they're convinced deserves it" (Whitaker, 1995, p. 24).

When asked in a 2002 national survey whether the police treat people fairly, 61% of white Americans answered in the affirmative, but only 43% of African Americans and 41% of Latinos did (Maguire & Pastore, n.d., Table 2.29). Similarly, only 16% of whites but 42% of African Americans and 39% of Latinos are afraid that the police will stop and arrest them for no reason (Maguire & Pastore, n.d., Table 2.30). These sentiments extend to the criminal justice system as a whole: When asked, "Who do you think is treated more harshly in this country's criminal justice system?" 74% of African Americans (compared to 35% of whites) indicated that blacks are treated more harshly. Interestingly,

African American perceptions of injustice are not limited to the issue of race. In the 1995 National Criminal Justice Opinion Survey, African Americans were substantially more likely than whites to perceive judicial bias in the "treatment of rich and poor" as well as in the "treatment of minorities" (Myers, 1996, p. 52; for similar findings, see Hagan & Albonetti, 1982, pp. 329-355; Wortley, Macmillan, & Hagan, 1997).

Ethnographic researchers have reported that conspiracy theories about crime and drugs are widespread in African American communities (see Sasson, 1995a; Turner, 1993). Typically communicated by word of mouth—"through the grapevine"—these theories allege that crime, drug dealing, and other crime-related problems endured disproportionately by black communities are the result of a white effort to destroy those communities. In the discussion that follows, participants in one of the Boston focus groups charge police with intentionally "tunneling" drugs and guns into black neighborhoods as part of a genocidal plot:

Facilitator:	Who's doing these crimes [that concern us most]?
Lynette:	We are. Society.
Ertha:	But most of these crimes, a lot of these crimes, are provoked by—
Sandra:	Them—
David:	The White Man.
Ertha:	A lot of times it is those that wear the uniforms.
Sandra:	Yes! Them!
Ertha:	Not only—and not blaming the police themselves. But they are getting really careless [Ertha is referring to an incident in the news at the time of the interview in which a Black man was killed by a White police officer].
Sandra:	They're not being careless. It's *acceptable* to shoot us. Do you see what I'm saying? So it's not really carelessness— it's a *plan*. It's genocide.
David:	That's the way they get rid of you. . . .
Sandra:	Where do [the drugs] come from? Where do the guns come from?
Lynette:	Because the kids can get a gun since they were like day one.
Sandra:	Who's tunneling all this into our community?
Elaine:	The White man. The White man is tunneling and we've been the foolish ones buying.

Sandra: That's the point. They tunnel in the drugs. They tunnel in the guns. They're all coming our way.[19]

Such accounts are not always believed literally, even by those who tell them (Sasson, 1995a; Turner, 1993). Their popularity, however, is a good indicator of the alienation many African Americans feel from the criminal justice system. This alienation is one among many of the harmful consequences of the get-tough policies on crime and drugs.

Conclusion

In this chapter, we have argued that most Americans are not terribly worried about being struck by crime in the course of day-to-day life, although from time to time, Americans have become quite concerned about crime and drugs as social problems afflicting the country as a whole. But rising public concern about crime-related issues cannot be taken as support for a "democracy in action" thesis, which explains the get-tough policies of the 1980s and 1990s as a political response to public opinion. Instead, Americans have become most alarmed about crime and drugs on those occasions when national political leaders and, by extension, the mass media have spotlighted these issues.

Although mobilized by political elites, public concern about crime and drugs is valid and should be taken seriously. (Were Americans indifferent to the issue, elite efforts to mobilize popular concern would surely have fallen flat.) Although journalistic depictions of a bloodthirsty public are overdrawn, popular attitudes toward crime and criminal offenders did harden over the past three decades. But popular sensibilities are not of one piece: Most Americans also regard crime as a consequence of environmental and social factors, including family and community breakdown, and support a range of crime prevention initiatives. Most Americans also support rehabilitation efforts for offenders already serving time behind bars, as well as alternatives to incarceration and the death penalty. Indeed, support for these alternatives has grown in recent years. Politicians who believe that the public will respond only to get-tough appeals underestimate the complexity of popular sensibilities about crime and punishment.

7

Activism and the Politics of Crime

In the previous chapter, we argued that although many members of the public did become more punitive in the course of the war on crime, public views about and attitudes toward crime and punishment remain complex and ambivalent and there are signs that opposition to the get-tough approach is growing. We also argued that that the intensification of popular punitiveness (to the extent that it occurred) was largely a response to—rather than a cause of—political initiative on the crime issue. As a result, we treated the public as a largely reactive player in the war on crime. However, many members of the public have not merely responded to politicians' speeches about crime, but have actively attempted to shape crime policy. In this chapter, we discuss a number of social movements and organizations that have mobilized to influence crime policy. These include community-based crime prevention organizations; the victim's rights movement; and human rights campaigns against police brutality, the death penalty, and the drug war. Our goal in this chapter is to both describe these forms of activism and explain why some have been more successful in achieving their goals.

One of the most important conditions for the success of a social movement is its capacity to capitalize on opportunities created by the larger political environment. Thus, when powerful political leaders with strong views on particular issues ascend to office, new opportunities for political activists with complementary views rapidly materialize. For example, the election of Ronald Reagan in 1980 gave a dramatic boost to the antiabortion movement (Staggenborg, 1991; Tarrow, 1994). This dynamic also helps to explain the growth and direction of local anticrime activism and the victim's rights movement. Both have genuine grassroots support, but because most anticrime and victim's rights activists pursue goals that are largely compatible with those of political leaders and criminal justice agencies, they have also received a great deal of encouragement, guidance, and material support. By contrast, groups that oppose police brutality, capital punishment, and the drug war have been less able to form alliances with either criminal justice institutions or leading politicians, and have therefore had less success in achieving their goals.

This may be changing, however. Although prominent political leaders are particularly important resources for social movements, professional groups, civic organizations, international opinion, and local officials can also lend credibility to and generate resources for social movement organizations. Until recently, most such entities were reluctant to express more than mild opposition to the wars on crime and drugs. But over the course of the 1990s, more and more have begun to speak out. Today, it is not only progressive activists, but also judges, lawyers, doctors, human rights organizations, and even some law enforcement officials and conservative politicians who criticize crime and drug policies. As a result, grassroots opponents of the wars on crime and drugs have had a surprising degree of success in recent years, and a significant number of voters and local and state officials are rejecting some tough anticrime and antidrug policies—as well as the federal government's authority to determine policy in these areas.

Two issues have become particularly controversial: the death penalty and the war on drugs. In both cases, the federal government is increasingly at odds with state officials and others who challenge existing policies. How successful reform groups will ultimately be remains unclear, because the federal government is, at the time of this writing, refusing to budge. But before turning our attention to these recent developments, we begin with a discussion of less adversarial forms of activism, including community-based crime prevention efforts and the victim's rights movements.

Community-Based Crime Prevention Efforts

In the United States, community-based programs and organizations received a tremendous boost from the Kennedy administration, which increased federal financial aid for a variety of local endeavors in the early 1960s. As a result, the number of community organizations in the United

States increased rapidly, and many of these groups included crime on their list of concerns (Rosenbaum, 1988, p. 342). Surveys administered in the 1970s suggest that 11% to 20% of the public participated in local organizations that included crime prevention as one of their issues (Rosenbaum, 1988, p. 347).

Interestingly, most of these organizations did not treat crime as separate from other neighborhood issues. Instead, they sought to address the *social* causes of crime, such as insufficient job opportunities, poor educational facilities, and inadequate recreational activities for youth. The broad focus of this "social problems approach" to crime prevention reflects the then-prevalent belief that crime is a product of social conditions and is often perpetrated by members of the community. These beliefs stand in sharp contrast to the now-common assumptions that crime is a problem caused by dangerous outsiders and can be addressed independently of other community issues and problems (Podolefsky & Dubow, 1981).

Government support for community anti-crime efforts increased significantly in the years following the Kennedy administration. In 1965, President Johnson created the President's Commission on Law Enforcement and Administration of Justice to make recommendations for enhancing the efficiency of the criminal justice system. In its report, the Commission identified criminal victimization and the fear it engendered as important national problems and suggested that local communities should receive greater support to organize effective responses (President's Commission, 1967). Over the next decade, several other national commissions also recommended expanding the citizens' role in the war on crime, and law enforcement agencies increased their crime prevention educational efforts. As a result, financial support for community-based crime prevention increased throughout the 1970s (Hope, 1995). These funds were further augmented with the passage of the Community Anti-Crime Program of 1977 and the Urban Crime Prevention Program of 1980, which provided funds directly to community organizations (rather than to law enforcement agencies) engaged in crime prevention activities (Rosenbaum, 1988).

In recent years, government funds have been allocated to both law enforcement agencies and community organizations, and the emphasis has been on the need for partnerships between the two (Rosenbaum, 1988; see also National Crime Prevention Council, 1994a, 1994b).[1] Although some community organizations remain committed to addressing the social conditions that cause crime, an increasing number have come to focus on enhancing the effectiveness of social control mechanisms in their communities—independent of other kinds of social and economic reforms. Some community-based anticrime groups remain independent of government authorities, but many have taken advantage of the opportunity to form partnerships with the police and local officials. Before exploring the various approaches to local crime prevention, though, we address a prior question: Why has the government made community involvement in crime prevention and control efforts such a priority over the past several decades?

The Appeal of Community Crime Prevention

The term *community* has become something of a buzzword in policy circles. We hear, for example, of the need for "community policing," "community health care," and "care in the community." In this context, both local governments and the national government have embraced the concept of community crime prevention (Cohen, 1985; Crawford, 1995; Walklate, 1991). The reasons for this policy development appear to be both practical and political. At the practical level, many of these programs are touted as cheaper alternatives to the criminal justice system (although many such programs would—if successful—funnel more people into the system) (Rosenbaum, 1988; Walklate, 1991). In addition, the focus on community serves to mobilize individuals to take direct action against crime and to identify particularly high-risk areas for more intensive police intervention (Hope & Shaw, 1988).

Political considerations may also have helped catapult community-based crime prevention efforts to the top of the policy agenda. Several analysts have suggested that by declaring a war on crime, government officials increased the public's expectations regarding the state's responsibility and capacity to fight crime (see especially Crawford, 1995; Garland, 1996).[2] Unfortunately, neither local governments nor the national government have been all that successful in this war. By emphasizing the need for community involvement, officials may be attempting to reduce public expectations and shift responsibility for dealing with crime back to the community.[3] The rhetoric surrounding community-based programs does indeed imply at least some crime-fighting responsibility for civilians: In the past, the public was told that policing "must be left to the professionals"; now, it is informed that "policing cannot be left to the police alone" (Crawford, 1995, p. 100). To the extent that this rhetoric becomes part of the political culture, the government reduces its responsibility for crime control.[4]

Approaches to Community Crime Prevention

Community-based crime prevention programs rest on two main, often competing visions of community:

Attitudinal: In this conception, community is defined primarily as a set of collective views and sentiments:

> Community, in brief, is in people's heads . . . if you wish to improve community conditions you are in essence in the business of changing attitudes, or altering the symbols of community, in the hope that improved personal relations will follow. (Currie, 1988, pp. 280-281)

Structural: In this conception, community is defined in institutional terms, "not just as a set of attitudes we can implant or mobilize, but as an interlocking set of long-standing institutions which in turn are deeply affected by larger social and economic forces" (Currie, 1988, pp. 282-283). As we made evident in Chapter 3, these larger socioeconomic forces are crucial to our understanding of the nature and distribution of serious crime in the United States.

In what follows, we discuss three main types of community anti-crime programs: order maintenance, opportunity reduction, and the social problems approach. Order maintenance and opportunity reduction efforts rest on the attitudinal conception of community, which, we suggest, helps to explain the limited success of these programs. Community anticrime programs based on the social problems approach draw on a structural conception of community and address the root causes of crime. Although this approach is more analytically sound, the capacity of community groups to alter the fundamental structural forces that they recognize as shaping community life is quite limited.

Order Maintenance

Many community-based crime prevention programs are primarily attempts to restore or maintain order. Disorderliness can take both physical and behavioral forms. Its physical manifestations include broken windows, graffiti, and other architectural symbols of neighborhood decline (see Wilson & Kelling, 1982; see also Skogan, 1990). Its behavioral manifestations include panhandling and sidewalk soliciting by individuals, which make some residents feel unsafe. By increasing fear, proponents argue, these manifestations of disorder weaken the informal community controls that prevent crime. According to this theory, reducing disorder will reduce fear and enable residents to take more pride in and responsibility for their communities—all of which will eventually result in a long-term reduction in crime.[5]

Order maintenance programs often seek to organize community members to "take back their communities" by painting over graffiti; maintaining and cleaning public spaces such as parks; and ensuring that structures that invite "trouble," such as abandoned buildings, are removed or made impenetrable. The object of these activities is ultimately to restore a sense of community, thereby strengthening both informal and formal social control mechanisms. Insofar as these programs emphasize the need to strengthen community morale and solidarity, they rest primarily on the attitudinal conception of community.

Sponsors of these programs do not explain why manifestations of disorder—such as homelessness, panhandling, abandoned buildings, and so forth—might increase in particular areas at particular times. A structural conception of community would suggest that these manifestations of neighborhood decline are related to much larger socioeconomic forces such as deindustrialization and residential segregation. In the absence of such an analysis, those who are victims of such structural developments (such as the homeless and prostitutes) tend to be identified as the cause rather than the symptom of neighborhood decline (Walklate, 1991).

Some of the more controversial aspects of order maintenance programs have been on display in New York City, which has adopted what is sometimes called "quality-of-life" or "zero-tolerance" policing. Under this approach, discussed in greater detail in Chapter 9, the authorities deal aggressively with those who supposedly cause fear in the citizenry—panhandlers, subway turnstile jumpers, the homeless—to help restore order and to empower "law-abiding citizens" to "take back their communities." Defenders of this strategy argue that urban disorder intensified in the 1970s after deinstitutionalization of the mentally ill and the decriminalization of their behavior (Kelling & Coles, 1996, p. 42). To counter this development, advocates of quality-of-life policing tout an aggressive and interventionist police strategy and criminalization of the behavior and lifestyles of "undesirables."

By contrast, critics of quality-of-life policing point out that, far from being decriminalized, public order and drug offenses are being dealt with in an increasingly draconian fashion, a development that has helped to produce in the United States one of the highest rates of incarceration in the world. Furthermore, critics blame the growth of urban disorder not on the mentally ill, but on neoliberal economic policies that have helped to realize a massive redistribution of wealth from the poor to the rich. According to these critics, structural conditions (such as the grossly inequitable distribution of wealth, inadequate housing, and racial segregation, both past and present) are causing the problems of disorder and crime in the first place.[6] Finally, critics note that rude or hostile treatment of citizens by the police provokes anger and resentment—reactions that increase the likelihood of future offending. For this reason, "flooding high crime communities with aggressive police could backfire terribly, causing more crime than it prevents, as it has in repeated race riots over the past quarter century" (Sherman, 1997b, p. 2-14).

Opportunity Reduction

"Opportunity reduction," another popular approach to community crime prevention, seeks to reduce the number of situations that invite or encourage crime by intensifying community members' surveillance activities. Surveillance—that is, watching out for and over one's community— may be promoted by social and community organizations or through the modification of the physical environment. In either case, the idea is that residents can be an effective self-policing force by observing one another's property, looking out for suspicious people and activities, and so forth. Like order maintenance programs, these programs do not seek to change offenders' motivation to commit crime or address the social conditions that give rise to crime.

Neighborhood Watch is the clearest example of a program seeking to reduce criminal opportunities by enhancing community surveillance. Although there is a significant degree of variation in the implementation of Neighborhood Watch programs, most groups are organized at the block or neighborhood level and are sponsored by a criminal justice agency, usually a police or sheriff's department. In fact, most local law enforcement agencies now have on staff "crime prevention specialists" who promote and organize Neighborhood Watch-type groups. Although these law enforcement organizers stress that community residents must take greater responsibility for crime through their daily activities, they also instruct members of the public not to intervene in potentially dangerous situations, but rather to "observe and report." For this reason, Neighborhood Watch groups function largely as the "eyes and ears" of the police (see Garofalo & McLeod, 1989). These groups are also encouraged to take household security measures, such as engraving their property, forming crime-tip hotlines, improving street lighting, and engaging in "block parenting."

Neighborhood Watch and other block-watch programs are more popular in mostly white, middle-class neighborhoods than in high-crime urban neighborhoods (Garofalo & McLeod, 1989; Hope, 1995; Rosenbaum, 1988; Skogan, 1990). This is perplexing: One might reasonably expect that people living in the most dangerous areas would be drawn to these crime prevention programs. There are several reasons why this is not the case. First, white residents of middle-class communities are likely to believe that crime is caused by outsiders rather than by members of their own community (Sasson & Nelson, 1996).[7] As a result, they appear to be more confident in their ability to identify suspicious people and to be more comfortable doing so (Sasson & Nelson, 1996). Second, in high-crime areas, residents report higher levels of fear and suspicion of their immediate neighbors, which makes it more difficult for them to organize collectively. Middle-class communities, in contrast, have higher proportions of homeowners and married people, are more homogeneous, and are therefore easier to organize (Hope, 1995; Rosenbaum, 1988).

Race and class influence not only levels of participation but also the meaning and hopes that participants bring to such programs as Neighborhood Watch. In an analysis of participants' motivations for joining Neighborhood Watch, researchers found both similarities and differences between the African American and white members. Participants of all races hoped to enhance their personal security and improve the quality of neighborhood life. However, African American (but not white) participants also saw crime watch groups as a way to restore the authority of older residents, whose ability to supervise youth is perceived to have diminished.[8] By contrast, white participants hark back to an era in which mothers were more vigilant and involved in their children's lives. These racially based differences appear to reflect the fact that kin networks have historically been more extensive and responsibility for children more diffuse in African American communities (Sasson & Nelson, 1996). This study reminds us that although the basic content and philosophy of crime watch programs has been determined by law enforcement and government agencies (Garofalo & McLeod, 1989), participants bring to these programs their own meanings and intentions.

Rates of participation in Neighborhood Watch programs remain quite low in most cities, and efforts to raise them have not been fruitful (Skogan, 1990). Research also suggests that crime watch programs have not been terribly effective. Contrary to what supporters of the programs claim, the most methodologically rigorous studies show that crime watch programs do not reduce either rates or fear of crime. Nor do these programs have the desired effect on social cohesion; they do not activate social behaviors that are presumed to reduce crime (Skogan, 1990, p. 362).

Civilian or citizen patrols are an alternative for those inclined to be more actively involved in neighborhood surveillance. Civilian patrols first emerged in the 1960s, mostly in minority communities hoping to reduce police brutality by "policing the police." Not surprising, these patrols tended to have quite adversarial relationships with law enforcement (Harrington, 1992). Other kinds of patrols, such as the Guardian Angels, focus more on preventing conventional street crime. The Angels' tactics have sometimes been of dubious legal propriety, and some argue that the organization is part of the American vigilante tradition. Nevertheless, these patrols have typically been on much more favorable terms with the police than those seeking to monitor police behavior. Still other neighborhood patrol groups have been founded by white communities hoping to "defend" their communities from "invading" minorities. In Brooklyn, for example, white residents created the Civilian Observation Patrol to keep watch over the neighborhood—and to deny information about housing availability to inquiring Latinos (Harrington, 1992, p. 181).

Although neighborhood patrols report some crime incidents to the police, they do not have any clear effect on the overall crime rate. And although these patrols have been credited with reducing levels of fear among some residents, they make other residents nervous about the nature of their activities (Rosenbaum, 1988, p. 360).

The Social Problems Approach

The social problems approach to community crime prevention rests on the theory that crime is caused by and related to a number of different social problems, especially conditions that encourage youth to engage in delinquent activities (Podolefsky & Dubow, 1981; Rosenbaum, 1988). Groups adopting this approach therefore endeavor to create positive opportunities for young people, including athletic activities, employment services, drug prevention programs, social and academic clubs, and literacy programs. Other common activities include efforts to improve the social, economic, and physical environment in which community members live (Podolefsky & Dubow, 1981).

Whereas crime watch programs are most popular in predominantly white, middle-class neighborhoods—whose residents tend to believe that crime is perpetrated by outsiders—the social problems approach is most popular in racially heterogeneous and working-class communities (Podolefsky & Dubow, 1981). In such communities, those who get into trouble with the law could well be friends or family members (Podolefsky & Dubow, 1981; Sasson & Nelson, 1996). As a result, community members are less interested in merely detecting and reporting crime than in preventing it from occurring in the first place. Insofar as community groups adopting the social problems approach recognize the ways in which larger social forces influence the crime problem, they draw much more heavily on a structural conception of community.

The fate of community organizations adopting a social problems approach to community crime prevention is quite different from the fate of those focused on order maintenance and opportunity reduction. On one hand, groups with multi-issue agendas are much more likely to sustain high levels of participation than are groups that focus exclusively on crime (such as Neighborhood Watch) (Hope, 1995, p. 38). However, these multi-issue groups are often considered radical and are less likely to receive government support (Tonry & Morris, 1987). Indeed, federal aid to urban areas has declined sharply since 1980, and most of the funds that are available to such communities are attached to programs that do not attempt to redistribute urban resources in any significant way.

Despite anecdotal accounts of communities that have successfully reduced crime by adopting the social problems approach, little hard evidence of such success can be found. Some analysts suggest that this lack of evidence is not due to ineffectiveness but rather to the lack of "strong evaluations" of such programs (Rosenbaum, 1988, p. 354). Others argue that, try as they might, community activists simply do not have control over the larger social forces (such as the labor and housing markets) that so profoundly influence local crime problems:

> The scientific literature shows that the policies and market forces causing criminogenic community structures and cultures are beyond the control of neighborhood residents, and that "empowerment" does not include the power to change those policies. . . . While programs aimed

at linking labor markets more closely to high crime risk neighborhoods and individuals could have substantial crime prevention benefits . . . no program has yet shown success in tackling the unemployment rates of high crime neighborhoods. Yet of all the dimensions of neighborhood life, this one may have the most pervasive influence on crime. (Sherman, 1997a, p. 3-20)

Assessment of Community Efforts

Studies evaluating community crime prevention programs are aimed primarily at determining whether or not these programs work—that is, whether they reduce crime and fear of crime (Crawford, 1995; Walklate, 1991). As we have mentioned, such studies indicate that none of the community-based crime prevention efforts has been particularly success-ful, and they have been least successful in communities that need them the most. But ineffectiveness is not the only reason to worry about com-munity crime prevention efforts, particularly the order maintenance and opportunity reduction varieties now favored by government agencies.

Another concern centers on their ideological effects: To the extent that these programs draw on an attitudinal conception of community, their rhetoric helps to obscure the ways in which structural forces shape community life. This tendency is exacerbated by government funding programs that encourage communities to define and treat such issues as homelessness, prostitution, AIDS, and drug abuse as security rather than social problems (Crawford, 1995; Walklate, 1991). In short, the rhetoric and philosophy of order maintenance and opportunity reduction pro-grams encourage people to identify those affected by these conditions as "people who make trouble" rather than "people in trouble" (Gusfield, 1967).

A related concern has to do with the ways in which at least some community crime prevention programs may actually encourage social divisiveness. Although the goal of many of these programs is to promote a sense of community—and, hence, promote informal social control— many also encourage communities to unite in opposition to "strangers" and "people who do not belong." This understanding of the source of crime is more pronounced in predominantly white, middle-class com-munities, and the fact that programs like Neighborhood Watch focus almost exclusively on the kinds of crimes that are more likely to be com-mitted by "outsiders" exacerbates this tendency. Some researchers have argued that these programs are less popular in African American and working-class communities precisely because they require that people adopt a sort of oppositional stance against criminals, a stance that troubles those worried that their own children might one day get into—or be in—trouble.

The focus on the threat posed by invading "outsiders" and the need to "defend our neighborhoods" against them is highly controversial. Social critic Mike Davis, for example, argues that this mentality has led to a dramatic transformation of the urban built environment. Gated communities, restrictions on access to public spaces, and ubiquitous signs warning of a potential "armed response" indicate, he argues, a new "fortress mentality"; they are the architectural embodiment of intensified racial and class warfare. Indeed, Davis suggests that "'security' has less to do with personal safety than with the degree of personal insulation . . . from 'unsavory' groups and individuals" (Davis, 1992, p. 224). The fact that some community crime prevention programs actually increase residents' fear of crime (presumably because their constant focus on the local crime problem undermines participants' sense of security) (Hope, 1995, pp. 49, 54) suggests that crime prevention programs may indeed contribute to this fortress mentality. Other critics worry about the extent to which the rhetoric of "community empowerment" and "self-help" may encourage vigilantism and other zealous efforts to establish community control over local crime problems.

In sum, although many of the stated goals of the movement for community-based crime prevention are laudable, these efforts—particularly those types now favored by government agencies—are largely ineffective and raise many complex moral and political questions. Similar questions have been raised in response to the growth and transformation of the victim's rights movement.

The Victim's Rights Movement

What is now called the "victim's rights movement" first emerged in the United States in the 1960s. Although complex, the origins of this movement clearly lie in President Johnson's declaration of war on crime. Indeed, using the term *movement*—which implies both cohesiveness and a grassroots foundation—may not be the most accurate way of naming the complex of social forces and actors that have worked to put victims at the center of criminal justice policy. Many grassroots organizations have been involved in this campaign, but the goals and ideals that now characterize the victim's rights movement have been profoundly shaped by government policies and funding opportunities. In this section, we describe the emergence of the victim's rights movement in the United States and analyze the process by which the mainstream of this movement came to accept and promote policies associated with the government's war on crime.

The Origins of the Victim's Rights Movement

The idea of providing greater support to crime victims was a response to the growing perception that criminals were being coddled by the courts. Throughout the 1960s and 1970s, conservatives argued that Supreme Court decisions protecting defendants' rights had unfairly tipped the balance in favor of criminals. The courts had become so concerned with procedure and technicalities, conservatives argued, that they were regularly letting violent criminals off the hook. These critics also suggested that measures designed to protect the rights of the accused were a direct attack on crime victims. Defenders of the Warren Court counterargued that the Constitution and the Bill of Rights offer protection to *all* individuals from a potentially overzealous and intrusive state, and pointed out that a victim of crime may very well be accused of a crime at another time.

This debate over the "rights revolution" of the 1960s was an important impetus for the victim's rights movement and shaped the nature of the demands it eventually made (Weed, 1995). On the other hand, not all of the actors who set the stage for the victim's rights movement had the same motivations. President Johnson and other liberals hoped to undercut the Republican "ownership" of the crime issue, and one of their tactics was to create the President's Commission on Law Enforcement and Administration of Justice in 1965. In its final report, the Commission raised concerns about the reluctance of many crime victims to cooperate with prosecutors and testify in the courts. This report attributed what it saw as a low conviction rate—a sign of inefficiency—largely to this reluctance (Weed, 1995). The Commission's concern was echoed in the first National Crime Surveys (administered in the late 1960s by the Law Enforcement Assistance Administration [LEAA]). These surveys revealed that because many victims did not even bother to report their victimization to the police, the true prevalence of criminal victimization had been greatly underestimated (Weed, 1995, p. 9).

These concerns led the LEAA to create a number of "victim-witness assistance" programs (operated mainly out of prosecutors' offices) in the early 1970s. The main goal of these programs was to increase the conviction rate by encouraging crime victims to cooperate with the police and prosecutors. By 1980, more than 400 such programs were operating in the United States (Tonry, 1991; Weed, 1995, p. 10). Although a few states had already created victim compensation programs (see Henderson, 1985, p. 944; Mawby & Walklate, 1994, p. 77), the LEAA's victim-witness assistance program was the first nationally coordinated effort to provide material support to victims of crime. In addition to providing this financial aid, the LEAA employed a group of specialists whose main responsibility was to address the social and emotional needs of crime victims. The primary motivation for offering such counseling was to increase victims' cooperation with the state in criminal proceedings (Weed, 1995, p. 10).

Another important source of activity on behalf of victims came from feminists concerned about the plight of victims of rape and domestic violence. Feminist activists set up the first rape crisis centers in the early 1970s, which provided support and assistance to rape survivors. Initially, many of these centers were quite distrustful of the police and prosecutors, and they criticized the criminal justice system for revictimizing rape victims by treating them with disrespect, assuming that they were lying or "hysterical," and putting their sexual histories on trial. Feminist organizers also established emergency shelters for battered women and their children in the 1970s. As with rape crisis centers, these shelters initially were independent of the state and quite critical of its handling of domestic violence (Tonry, 1991; Weed, 1995, pp. 8-12).

In the late 1970s and into the 1980s, a variety of other voluntary organizations were created to fight on behalf of crime victims, usually victims of a particular type of crime. Many of these were initiated by family members of crime victims and sought to draw attention to the emotional pain such families endure. Some of the best-known examples of such organizations are Mothers Against Drunk Driving (MADD), Parents of Murdered Children, and the National Center for Missing and Exploited Children. Most of these organizations emphasize the need for grassroots efforts, but they have also been quite successful in attracting government support. These groups tend to combine a service orientation with a more political approach aimed at increasing public awareness and reforming criminal law and penal practices (Tonry, 1991; Weed, 1995, pp. 18-20). Increasingly, these organizations have come to identify enhanced victim rights—as opposed to victim services—as the best way to meet victims' needs (Weed, 1995, p. 21).

From Victims' Needs to Victims' Rights

The idea that crime victims should have unique legal rights is both very old and very new. In the early Middle Ages, crime victims primarily achieved justice by avenging their crimes through blood feuds. In those cases that did involve authorities, victims were sometimes awarded restitution—compensation for their pain and losses. Gradually, the notion that crimes are committed against society rather than against an individual led authorities to frown on private means of resolving disputes (feuds, duels, and so forth) and to replace the private legal system with a more public one. Increasingly, authorities (rather than the victim) took responsibility for initiating legal proceedings. The state was empowered to levy fines (which went into the Crown's purse) and to punish offenders who were found guilty of committing crimes against society (Henderson, 1985; Mawby & Walklate, 1994, pp. 66-68). Despite this shift, the victim was still the primary initiator of criminal proceedings under colonial law, and restitution—compensation for victims—was still the main rationale for doing so. Victims continued to play an important role throughout 19th-century Europe and America in determining whether or not a prosecution would take place (although they could be overruled by authorities).

Only with massive industrialization and urbanization did a fully public system of criminal law emerge in the United States. Under this system, the state began to play a more important role in protecting the rights of the accused; involving the victim in the legal process was thought to promote vigilantism and vengeance. Simultaneously, the goal of punishing the offender rather than producing justice for the offended began to take precedence in the criminal system. By contrast, the civil courts have retained more of the characteristics of earlier, private legal systems: Cases are initiated by one or both of the parties involved, and the goal is compensation rather than punishment.[9]

Today, some progressives complain that victims have been unfairly pushed out of the criminal justice process. According to this argument, state organizations have "stolen" conflicts from those actually involved, leaving both victims and offenders alienated from the dispute resolution process (e.g., see Christie, 1977, pp. 1-15). In most cases, they argue, justice is better served by restitution than by punishing offenders.[10] Conservatives also criticize the exclusion of victims from the criminal process, but they attribute this development to an unwarranted expansion of the rights of defendants. For example, the President's Task Force on Victims of Crime, created by President Reagan in 1982, suggested that the victim's role in the legal process should be "restored," that defendants' rights had been extended at the expense of victims, and that victims would be best served by enhancing the state's capacity to punish wrongdoers (Weed, 1995, pp. 13-14).

Many of those involved in the victim's rights movement have accepted the argument that victims should be more central to the criminal justice process, that the courts have gone too far in protecting the rights of the accused, that this protection comes at the expense of victims, and that punishment of the offender is a victim's right. As a result, some victim's rights measures promote a return to a more private and, critics would argue, vindictive legal system.

For example, some groups propose that suspects remain in custody after arrest (before conviction and despite the presumption of innocence); that delays be minimized between arrest and the preliminary hearing and between hearing and trial (despite the fact that defendants may need time to raise money for and organize a defense); that plea bargaining be eliminated or be victim-determined; that exclusionary rules regulating the way evidence is collected and presented in court be abandoned or weakened; that the *Miranda* rule protecting the rights of the accused be overturned; and that victims' testimony regarding their emotional experience be considered at the time of sentencing, especially in capital cases (see Henderson, 1985, pp. 967-968; Weed, 1995, pp. 24-26). Thus, although victims' groups continue to press for services and restitution for crime victims, the emphasis for many such groups has shifted to victims' legal rights.

Both political forces and pragmatic considerations appear to be fueling this trend. Over the past three decades, conservative political rhetoric has charged that excessive leniency on the part of the courts is responsible for much of the U.S. crime problem. Criticism of the Supreme Court's "rights revolution" during Chief Justice Earl Warren's tenure has been a centerpiece of this rhetoric. As we saw in previous chapters, the mass media have also emphasized criminal justice leniency. In this context, it is not surprising that many victim's rights activists believe that enhanced punishment is a "victim's right" (e.g., see Aynes, 1984).

A more practical reason for the emphasis on victims' rights rather than restitution and conflict resolution is that much of the available funding for victims' groups comes from the government—with strings attached. One of the main goals of the LEAA—the primary source of funding for victims' groups in the 1970s—was to increase the willingness of victims to cooperate with the police and prosecutors, thereby increasing rates of conviction. The LEAA (like other granting agencies) not only selected which organizations it would fund but also could stipulate which organizational activities its funds would support. In general, the LEAA (and the state governments that administered the block grants provided by the LEAA) opted to fund organizations that prioritized services for victims rather than those that engaged in suspect political activities or that criticized police, prosecutors, or judges (see Weed, 1995, p. 14).

Since the disbanding of the LEAA in 1980, the Crime Victim's Fund (created under the auspices of the Crime Victims Act) and state block grants have been the main sources of federal support for crime victims. These funds are not derived from tax revenues, but rather are generated from fines levied against those convicted of federal crimes (Elias, 1993, p. 32; Shapiro, 1997). This funding arrangement has had important consequences for the political orientation of the victims' movement. If, for example, drugs were decriminalized, the federal prison population—and the funds available for victims' organizations—would shrink dramatically (roughly 70% of all federal prisoners are drug offenders). Many state governments also fund victims' services at least in part through criminal fines, forfeited assets, and prisoner wages, and these funds would shrink if the war on crime were scaled back (Elias, 1993, p. 32).

Furthermore, because current compensation arrangements segregate crime victims from other recipients of social services, crime victims are less likely to see their cause as linked to efforts to improve schools, enhance employment opportunities, or reduce social inequality (Shapiro, 1997, p. 16). Many states also earmark specific surcharges (on divorce proceedings, for example) for crime victim groups, a practice that also isolates victim's organizations from other social service and welfare agencies (Weed, 1995, p. 18).

In sum, both the political climate and funding arrangements have contributed to the tendency of many victims' organizations to identify punishment as their primary "right." It is important to note, however, that these mainstream victim's rights organizations do not represent the views or desires of all crime victims. According to one study, those involved in the victims' organizations are overwhelmingly white, female, and middle-aged—a group demographic that is hardly representative of crime victims in general. These activist-victims tend to be more supportive of the death penalty and significantly more likely to believe that the sentences given their offenders are "much too lenient" than are victims of crime who are not involved in the movement. Somewhat more surprisingly, activist-victims are also more supportive of the police, prosecutors, and judges than their nonactivist counterparts (Smith, 1988).

Moreover, not all victims' groups are punitive. Indeed, some organizations—such as Murder Victims' Families for Reconciliation—explicitly reject the "politics of vengeance." Similarly, advocates of "restorative justice" challenge the idea that victims are best served by a punitive orientation, and seek instead to enhance the capacity of victims and offenders to reach mutually acceptable ways of resolving disputes and compensating victims for the pain they suffer.

Legal Reforms

The mainstream victim's movement has been quite successful in persuading legislatures to modify laws to promote what it sees as victims' interests. State statutes designed to protect and serve victims are now on the books in all 50 states, and as of 1996, 21 states had amended their state constitution to achieve these goals. Most recently, victim's rights activists have begun lobbying for an amendment to the U.S. Constitution aimed at balancing the protections offered to criminal defendants with provisions for victims' rights (Kleinknecht, 1996). Some critics of the movement point out that this very success belies the movement's claim that the criminal justice system favors criminals. Indeed, it is difficult to imagine associations of prisoners or criminal defendants exercising comparable influence.

As a result of this activism (and the government's desire to increase victims' cooperation), funding for victim services has increased sharply. These services come in a variety of forms, including financial aid, psychological support, and assistance in managing the criminal justice process. All but six states have also adopted statutes that enhance the courts' capacity to order restitution (although because criminal offenders are overwhelmingly poor and are paid very low wages for prison work, only about four cents on the dollar of every fine and restitution order is actually collected) (Shapiro, 1997, p. 18). Funding for victim services is more generous in the United States than in most other countries (Mawby & Walklate, 1994, p. 136). Nevertheless, the availability of these services varies significantly from state to state, and overall, only a small percentage of victims of violent crime actually receive them (Weed, 1995, p. 137).

Some newly recognized "rights" are also widely accepted, including the victim's right to be notified of court dates and other relevant judicial proceedings, the right to be present at these hearings, the right to be treated with dignity and respect, and the right to be free of intimidation and harassment by the defendant. As with orders of restitution, these rights are often difficult to ensure.

Reforms aimed at enhancing the role of the victim in judicial decision making have been far more controversial. About half the states now require that victims be consulted before any plea bargaining takes place, and many grant the victim veto power in these proceedings (Tonry, 1991). By the mid-1980s, 43 states had passed legislation allowing victims to make personal statements (Victim Impact Statements [VISs]) describing their experience of the crime in question. Inclusion of these statements in courtroom proceedings has been shown to produce more punitive sentences (Macleod, 1986), and parole boards appear to be less likely to grant parole when a VIS is presented to the board (Mawby & Walklate, 1994, p. 138). Research also suggests, however, that victims are not usually informed of their right to submit a VIS, and of those who are informed, only a small percentage actually file a VIS with the court (Weed, 1995, p. 136). Some states also allow victims to provide a "victim statement of opinion" regarding the appropriate sentence, especially in capital cases.

The idea that victims' feelings and experiences should be taken into account at the time of sentencing represents a significant challenge to the principle that crimes are committed against society rather than individuals. It also introduces a more personal—some would say vindictive—quality to the judicial process.

Also controversial are those reforms that undermine the rights of the accused. Some victim's rights measures, for example, have lowered evidentiary requirements, eliminated the insanity defense, and weakened exclusionary rules designed to block the introduction of illegally obtained evidence (Elias, 1993, p. 31). These reforms are based on the idea that the protection of defendants' rights comes at the expense of victims, and that more punishment would serve victims' interests. They are also predicated on the erroneous assumption that victims and accused offenders constitute distinctive and nonoverlapping groups.

The Politics of Vengeance

To the extent that the mainstream victim's rights movement defines its interests in terms of getting tough—demanding faster executions, longer sentences, and restrictions on defendants' rights—it has become part of the very powerful campaign to expand the penal system. In fact, the mainstream of the movement seems to have allied itself with other forces promoting the war on crime. In California, for example, the Doris Tate Crime Victim's Bureau obtains 78% of its funding from the California Correctional Peace Officers Association (the prison guard's union) and was the driving force behind California's three-strikes law. This union also provides more than 80% of the funding for a new political action committee called "Crime Victims United," an ally of former Governor Pete Wilson, one of the state's strongest and most influential advocates of penal expansion (Shapiro, 1997).

Ironically, crime victims will pay a significant price if the victim's rights movement succeeds in equating victims' interests with the war on crime: The policies associated with the war on crime actually undermine (rather than protect) what most see as the most fundamental right: the right not to be a victim. The war on crime does nothing to address the causes of serious crime discussed in Chapter 3. In fact, we will argue that its main effect is to exacerbate these conditions by creating a large pool of unemployable ex-cons and contributing to family and neighborhood disruption.

Furthermore, as the victim's rights movement has become a partner in the war on crime, it has come to define both crime and victimization very narrowly. The fact that the organized victim's rights movement is largely white and middle class has meant that many victims are not represented by the mainstream of this movement. Among those left out are the many victims of corporate and state crime. For example, victims of "environmental racism" are organizing to demand that corporations run manufacturing facilities and dispose of hazardous waste in a safer and more responsible fashion—but thus far, they have not been included in the victims movement.

An even broader conception of victimization would include victims of human rights abuses and those (such as the homeless) denied what the United Nations terms basic human rights—including the right to food, shelter, and clothing. In short, the victim's rights movement's growing tendency to equate victims' rights with greater punishment and its almost exclusive focus on street crime represents a very narrow interpretation of what it means to be a victim—and a similarly narrow sense of who is doing the victimizing. The same cannot be said of those protesting the aggressive policies and practices associated with the war on crime.

Adversarial Activism: Human Rights Campaigns Against Police Brutality, Capital Punishment, and the War on Drugs

Unlike many community crime prevention and victim's rights organizations, human rights groups confronting the criminal justice system seek to restrict the authority of state and criminal justice agencies. As a result, they are much less likely to receive government assistance or aid and have had a more difficult time establishing their credibility and achieving reform. On the other hand, these groups—particularly those fighting the death penalty and the drug war—are enjoying greater support from civic organizations, professional groups, and the international human rights community, and for that reason, they have enjoyed greater success in recent years. In this section, we discuss three main areas in which human rights organizations are most active in relation to criminal justice: police brutality, capital punishment, and the war on drugs.

Challenging the Cops: Fighting Police Brutality

The excessive use of force by police officers has long been a topic of concern, particularly in minority communities. Indeed, most of the major urban riots of the post-World War II period were triggered by allegations of police brutality. It is estimated that between 1% and 5% of police encounters with criminal suspects involve the excessive use of force, some of which is deadly (Walker, Spohn, & DeLone, 1996).

Recent legal reforms have reduced the number of people dying at the hands of the police. Until the 1970s, most police departments allowed officers to shoot anyone suspected of committing a felony (such as larceny) who attempted to flee. During this period, seven African American people were killed by the police for every white person killed. In 1985, however, the Supreme Court ruled this "fleeing felon rule" unconstitutional, and police departments were required to place greater restrictions on the circumstances under which officers are allowed to shoot. As a result, the number of people killed by police officers dropped significantly (from 559 in 1975 to 300 in 1987), and the ratio of African American to white suspects killed by police officers fell from 7 to 1 to 3 to 1.

Nevertheless, in high-crime communities, minorities continue to be subject to police brutality. Many large cities pay out millions of dollars each year to settle lawsuits over the excessive use of force by police officers. Minorities are also more likely to report being harassed, questioned, and frisked by the police than are whites (Walker et al., 1996). Each of these problems is aggravated by the new quality-of-life policing discussed previously (Amnesty International, 1998, chap. 3).

Some community groups have organized specifically around the issue of police brutality. These groups tend to have an adversarial stance: They see the government and police as the cause of the problem, and although they would like government institutions to respond to their concerns, they do not seek government support for their cause (Williams, 1995). Instead, these groups typically attempt to enhance the ability of community residents to oversee and regulate the police. In Los Angeles, for example, activists have attempted to create an independent civilian police review board to review complaints of police brutality and harassment, on the assumption that citizen-run review boards will provide more independent and meaningful oversight than police-run boards. (This is not always the case: Walker and Kreisel, 1996, found that in two thirds of all civilian review programs, police officers were primarily responsible for investigating complaints.)

Well-publicized cases of police brutality—such as the LAPD beating of motorist Rodney King—often trigger widespread protest. In the aftermath of the 1998 assault by New York police officers on Haitian immigrant Abner Louima, for example, activists from a number of different organizations (including Haitian, immigrant, and antiracist groups) joined together with anti-police brutality groups. Pointing out that in a recent 20-month period, more than 100 people had died while in the custody of the NYPD, these groups organized the Coalition Against Police Brutality and sponsored the National Day of Protest to Stop Police Brutality, in which thousands of people demonstrated (Dix, 1997, pp. 59-63).

Historically, the challenge for such groups has been to sustain this level of activism in the absence of well-publicized instances of police brutality and in the face of opposition from law enforcement and local officials. Human rights organizations have increasingly identified police brutality as a significant problem in the United States (and elsewhere) and hope that their educational efforts will raise awareness of the issue. In response to the videotaped police beatings of two unarmed African American men in 2002, for example, Amnesty International released a statement that read: "While some departments have introduced reforms following heightened scrutiny in recent years, this has not filtered down to all departments or all levels, and allegations of police brutality, particularly towards minority suspects, remain common in many areas" (Amnesty International, 2002).

Amnesty International was especially disturbed by remarks made by an Oklahoma City police spokeswoman, apparently justifying the officers' actions on the grounds that the suspect was "not compliant":

> International standards, such as those contained under the UN Code of Conduct for Law Enforcement Officials, state that force should be used only as a last resort and it must be proportionate to the threat posed. Repeatedly beating a barely resisting suspect, including while he is lying on the ground, appears in clear violation of these standards. (Amnesty International, 2002)

While public awareness and concern about the problem may increase as a result of these statements, the movement's main goal—true civilian-run review boards that have the power to oversee and regulate police conduct—remain few and far between.

Opposing Capital Punishment

In 1972, in *Georgia v. Furman,* the Supreme Court accepted the arguments of the National Association for the Advancement of Colored People and the American Civil Liberties Union and found capital punishment to be unconstitutional. This ruling was highly controversial and ignited an energetic campaign to reinstate the death penalty. In 1976, the Court overturned its own 1972 decision, declaring capital punishment to be constitutional after all.

Since the Court's reversal of *Georgia v. Furman,* capital punishment has been debated largely as a political rather than a legal issue. The death penalty has many quite vocal supporters, and public enthusiasm for it grew considerably between the 1960s and early 1990s (although much of this support disappeared when people were presented with the option of a sentence of life without parole as an alternative to death) (Haines, 1996). But capital punishment also has an increasing number of important opponents, including a growing number of religious bodies (such as the World Council of Churches, the American Friends Service Committee, the American Jewish Committee, and the U.S. Catholic Conference).

These and other death penalty opponents have been quite active in recent years. Several factors appear to have facilitated this revival, including the release of the well-known film *Dead Man Walking* and publicity surrounding the film's protagonist, anti-death penalty activist Sister Helen Prejean. Credit for sustaining the movement against the death penalty is also due to grassroots groups such as Murder Victims' Families For Reconciliation (MVFFR), a Virginia-based organization of relatives of murder victims with more than 4,000 members. MVFFR activists have been quite outspoken in opposing the argument that retribution serves victims' interests. Activist SueZann Bosler, for example, spent much of the 10 years following her father's murder working to prevent the execution of his murderer. She told the press that she cannot understand "why we kill people to show that killing people is wrong" (G. Anderson, 1998, pp. 10-11). This kind of opposition from those who have lost a loved one is especially powerful.

But the most significant development leading to the revival of anti-death penalty sentiment and activism has been the work of academics, activists, and journalists that have demonstrated the pervasiveness of wrongful convictions in the U.S. criminal justice system. Journalism students at Northwestern University in Chicago, for example, conducted investigations that revealed that at least two death row inmates were innocent. Other organizations, such as *The Innocence Project,* have also demonstrated the innocence of many convicts. As a result of these efforts, 102 death row inmates now known to have been wrongly convicted have been exonerated and released from prison.

In 12 of these death row cases, DNA testing provided conclusive proof of innocence (Death Penalty Information Center, n.d.). Overall, 115 inmates have been released from prison on the basis of exculpatory DNA evidence. Analysis of these cases suggests that inadequate defense counsel, widespread use of snitches, police and prosecutorial misconduct, false—and sometimes coerced—confessions, reliance on eyewitness testimony, fraudulent or "junk" science, and ongoing racism in the criminal justice system substantially contribute to the problem of wrongful conviction (Innocence Project, n.d.).

Indeed, it is evident that errors are rife throughout the criminal justice system as a result of these problems, and only some wrongful convictions are detected in the appeals process. A recent Columbia University study revealed that "two out of three [death penalty] convictions were overturned on appeal, mostly because of serious errors by incompetent defense lawyers or overzealous police officers and prosecutors who withheld evidence" (Liebman, 2000, p. 2030). But not all defendants can appeal their convictions. In Alabama and Georgia, for example, "there is no guarantee of a lawyer after the direct appeal of a conviction, and prisoners have only inconsistent access to a legal process that frequently overturns death sentences" (Goodstein, 2001, p. A12).

Nor is the appeals process, when available, foolproof: The convictions of many of the people who have been exonerated as a result of outside investigation were previously upheld by the appellate courts. Because DNA evidence is available in only a minority of cases, and because only some of the defendants involved in those cases are able to attract the attention of organizations like *The Innocence Project*, it is quite likely that many other innocent people remain behind bars. Worse, it is highly likely that some have been executed (Death Penalty Information Center, n.d.).

The stories of the wrongfully convicted men and women who have been released are heart-wrenching. On average, these wrongly convicted spent 8 years in prison before evidence proving their innocence emerged; one was freed from prison after 33 years of incarceration for a crime he did not commit. Wrongfully convicted death row inmates endure some of the most difficult of prison conditions, and their attempts to return to the lives they left behind are often fraught with difficulty (Earley, 1996).

As a result of these revelations, public discussions of the death penalty have become much more ambivalent, and levels of public support for capital punishment are declining. In 1997, the American Bar Association took the unprecedented step of calling for a moratorium on the death penalty, arguing that issues of racial inequality in capital sentencing, inadequate legal representation for capital defendants, and evidence of wrongful conviction necessitated a rethinking of the issue. In January 2000, the exoneration of 13 wrongfully convicted men led Illinois Governor Jim Ryan to declare a statewide moratorium on capital punishment. Despite allegations of corruption and plummeting levels of support for Governor Ryan personally, more than two thirds of state residents continue to support the moratorium, and only 26% oppose it (McDermott, 2002). Supreme Court Justice Sandra Day O'Connor—a swing vote on many death penalty cases—also publicly questioned the fairness of the death penalty that year: "If statistics are any indication, the system may well be allowing some innocent defendants to be executed" ("O'Connor Questions the Death Penalty," 2001, p. A9).

The questioning has continued. In 2002, Maryland Governor Parris Glendening imposed the second statewide moratorium, and federal district judge Jed Rakoff ruled that the death penalty was unconstitutional. Avoiding the question of whether or not the death penalty is racially discriminatory or constitutes cruel and unusual punishment (or both),

Judge Rakoff argued that the due process rights of capital defendants are violated because we now know that the inevitability of errors will lead to the execution of the innocent. The *New York Times* editorial praising this decision pointed out that "DNA testing is available only in a limited number of cases, and yet a number of executions have been overturned by DNA evidence. This suggests that the number of false convictions is higher than previously understood" ("The Death of Innocents," 2002, p. A20).

Even conservatives and long-time supporters of the death penalty are expressing reservations about capital punishment. Pat Robertson, the right-wing Christian celebrity and former presidential candidate, has called for a federal moratorium on the death penalty. George Will, the conservative columnist for *Newsweek* and the *Washington Post*, warns that "careless or corrupt administration of capital punishment" appears to be "intolerably common" ("Stop the Killing Machine," 2001, p. 8). Even President George W. Bush seems to be reconsidering the matter (in a limited way). As governor of Texas, Bush opposed bills that would have prohibited the execution of mentally retarded people, but in 2001, he stated, "We should never execute anybody who is mentally retarded" ("Stop the Killing Machine," 2001, p. 8). The majority of Supreme Court Justices have declared that they agree: In June 2002, the Court reversed its own 1989 ruling and banned the execution of mentally retarded convicts as unconstitutionally cruel. The Court explained this reversal in terms of a shift in public attitudes (Reinert, 2002).

Condemnation of the death penalty from outside the United States has also intensified. In April 2001, the United Nations Human Rights Commission called for a global moratorium "with a view to completely abolishing the death penalty" ("Stop the Killing Machine," 2001, p. 10). The vote was 27 to 18 in favor of the moratorium. That June, the Council of Europe, a human rights organization representing 43 countries, voted to remove Japan and the United States as observers unless they impose a moratorium on executions "without delay." U.S. human rights activists worry that the credibility of the United States on human rights issues is significantly diminished as a result of its refusal to halt executions. Others, noting that many European nations refused to extradite terrorism suspects to the United States in the aftermath of September 11, fear that international conflict over the issue may complicate cooperation on intelligence and security matters (Amnesty International, n.d.).

The long-term implications of recent developments remain unclear. Public support for the death penalty has declined from 77% in 1996 to

63% in 2001, and when life in prison is offered as an option, support drops to 46% ("Stop the Killing Machine," 2001). On the other hand, it is clear that the public remains divided and ambivalent, and there is no sign that Bush administration officials will moderate their support for capital punishment (other than for mentally handicapped inmates), even in the face of declining public support and international condemnation. Indeed, Attorney General John D. Ashcroft is aggressively pursuing the federal death penalty, frequently overruling his own prosecutors in the process (Eggen, 2002). Whether or not the political costs of continuing to do so will be great enough to deter current or future administration officials remains to be seen.

Seeking Truce in the War on Drugs

Like capital punishment, the drug war has become increasingly controversial. Grassroots opposition to the war on drugs takes a variety of forms. One arena of debate and resistance has been around the issue of access to clean needles. An increasing number of public health and community activists argue that needle exchange programs are necessary and effective. In June 2000, 36% of U.S. AIDS cases reported to the Centers for Disease Control and Prevention had occurred among injecting drug users, their sexual partners, and children. AIDS is the second leading cause of death among African Americans and the fourth leading cause of death of Latinos aged 25 to 44; half of these deaths were caused by injections with contaminated needles. Researchers have consistently found that improved access to sterile syringes is an effective method to reduce the spread of HIV and other infectious diseases (Drug Policy Alliance, n.d.-a).

But public health activists are stymied by drug war policies that criminalize the sale or possession of hypodermic needles. In 1998, the Department of Health and Human Services under President Clinton refused to lift a ban on federal funding for needle exchange programs.[11] In this context, activists around the country have been arrested for implementing their own needle exchange programs. In many areas, however, activists have forged alliances with local officials in order to implement such programs. By 1999, needle exchange programs exchanged 19 million sterile syringes. However, it is estimated that injection drug use involves 920 million to 1.68 billion injections annually in the United States (Drug Policy Alliance, n.d.-a). Clearly, many drug users lack access to clean needles, and this lack of access continues to harm public health.

Opposition to other antidrug laws—particularly mandatory minimum sentencing statutes—is also growing. These sentencing laws require that judges impose specified minimum penalties for drug offenders. Although ostensibly aimed at "drug kingpins," they predominantly affect low-level drug couriers ("mules") (Donziger, 1996). Most national-level politicians are opposed to scaling back the mandatory minimum drug laws. However, proposals to do just that are increasingly backed by police, judges, and attorneys, many of whom point out that the cost of incarcerating low-level, nonviolent drug offenders is quite high. Another catalyst for the campaign to repeal mandatory sentencing laws comes from grassroots organizations, especially Families Against Mandatory Minimums (FAMM). The membership of FAMM grew from a few dozen in 1991 to more than 33,000 in 1997. One of the main strategies of this group has been to publicize the nonviolent nature of the crimes committed by many individuals sentenced under these laws and to draw attention to the effects of harsh punishment on families and children. In the wake of much negative publicity (and in the context of a state budget deficit), Michigan repealed its mandatory minimum sentencing law that put some first-time, nonviolent drug offenders behind bars for as long as 25 years (Butterfield, 2001; Donziger, 1996; Kasindorf, 2002).

Other groups have targeted not just the laws, but the drug war's overarching goal—a "drug-free America." These activists argue that some drug use is inevitable, and that the goal of drug policy should be to reduce the harm associated with drug abuse rather than eradicating all drug use through criminalization. This "harm reduction" philosophy has attracted many supporters and may serve to unify academics, local officials, community activists, and others opposed to the war on drugs. In Washington, for example, the State Bar, Medical, and Pharmacy Associations all endorsed a King County Bar Association Report stressing that jail time—or the threat of it—does not address the problem of addiction, and calling for a new way of thinking about drugs (Kaiman, 2001).

Challenging the Feds

In recent years, this emerging drug reform movement has developed a new strategy: Rather than lobbying politicians who have supported the drug war in the past in an attempt to change their views, these activists decided to take the issue straight to the voters through the ballot initiative process. Funded by a number of wealthy philanthropists, as well as small group and individual donors, ballot initiative campaigns not only allow voters to directly express their views on particular subjects, but are also, in some states, veto-proof.

The first such initiative, California Proposition 215, legalizing the use of marijuana for medicinal purposes and was overwhelmingly approved by voters in 1996. (Similar laws had been passed by the California legislature in 1994 and 1995, but in each case, then-governor Pete Wilson had vetoed the legislation.) Since the passage of Proposition 215, seven additional states (Alaska, Colorado, Hawaii, Maine, Nevada, Oregon, and Washington) have adopted measures that remove state-level criminal penalties for growing and/or possessing medical marijuana. Several other states have passed bills that convey their support for the medical use of marijuana but do not remove state sanctions for its use.

Despite these clear expressions of voter preferences, and despite the fact that the Institute of Medicine ruled in 1999 that marijuana can be effective medicine for some patients, neither Congress nor federal administration officials have softened their opposition to the use of marijuana for medical purposes. Instead, federal officials seek to overturn these laws wherever possible. In 1998, when voters in the District of Columbia approved their medical marijuana initiative by 69%, Congress nullified the election results. (Congress is permitted to do so because DC is a federal district, not a state). To make their point even more clear, the U.S. House of Representatives also voted 311 to 94 for a nonbinding resolution condemning medical marijuana. The Justice Department, too, has declared that it opposes all marijuana use, medical or otherwise. Accordingly, it has sought to revoke the licenses of physicians who recommend medical marijuana to their patients, and federal law enforcement officials have "busted" those who provide medical marijuana to people who use it on the advice of their physicians.

According to federal officials, those who distribute marijuana—even to seriously ill people whose physicians have recommended marijuana— are in violation of the Controlled Substances Act. This law, passed by Congress in 1970, determined that marijuana had high potential for abuse, no currently accepted medical use in the United States, and was not safe for use under medical supervision. It therefore classified marijuana as a "Schedule I controlled substance" and provided for criminal penalties of up to 5 years' imprisonment and a $250,000 fine for possession of even a small amount of the drug.

Advocates of drug law reform, arguing that the marijuana provisions of the Controlled Substances Act do not apply to those distributing medical marijuana to patients living in states that allow for the medical use of marijuana, have taken their case to the courts. In 1999, the Ninth U.S. Circuit Court of Appeals ruled 3 to 0 that "medical necessity" is a valid defense against federal charges if a distributor can prove that the patients it serves are seriously ill, face imminent harm without marijuana, and have no effective legal alternatives. The Ninth Circuit Court also ruled that the federal government's attempts to revoke the licenses of doctors who recommend medical marijuana violate doctors' First Amendment rights. But in October 2001, the U.S. Supreme Court unanimously overruled the Ninth Circuit's ruling, arguing that "a medical necessity exception for marijuana is at odds with the terms of the Controlled Substances Act" (Slade, 2001, p. 56). Whether the federal government will appeal the Ninth Circuit Court's ruling regarding physicians' right to recommend marijuana remains to be seen.

Local, state, and federal officials have thus reached a standoff over medical marijuana. Despite the Supreme Court ruling, state and local officials in states with medical marijuana laws have declared that they will continue to support local medical marijuana distribution networks. Reports surfaced in fall of 2002 that a bipartisan coalition in Congress was developing legislation that would allow states to approve medical marijuana. If passed, such a bill would eliminate any conflict between state and federal law on the matter, but given recent federal action on the issue, its passage is far from assured. Federal and congressional opposition to the use of medical marijuana is somewhat puzzling, and certainly is not a response to popular opinion: A 2001 poll found that 73% of all Americans believe that doctors should have the right to recommend marijuana for their patients; only 21% did not (Maguire & Pastore, n.d., Table 2.85).

Perhaps pessimistic about Congress's willingness to support state laws allowing the medical use of marijuana, one group, The Coalition for Rescheduling Cannabis, has challenged the DEA's classification of marijuana as a Schedule I drug. As early as 1972, a petition was submitted to the Bureau of Narcotics and Dangerous Drugs (now called the Drug Enforcement Administration, or DEA) to reschedule marijuana so that it could be prescribed to patients. After much delay, the DEA's chief administrative law judge, Francis L. Young, ruled in 1988 that "marijuana, in its natural form, is one of the safest therapeutically active substances known. . . . It would be unreasonable, arbitrary and capricious for DEA to continue to stand between those sufferers and the benefits of this substance" (Oakland Cannabis Buyer's Cooperative, n.d.). Since then, however, the DEA has refused to implement this ruling and continues to classify marijuana as a Schedule I substance. In its rescheduling petition, the Coalition argues that all three of the government's claims—that marijuana has a high potential for abuse, has no currently accepted medical use in the United States, and is not safe for use under medical supervision—are contradicted by scientific research and medical convention (Oakland Cannabis Buyer's Cooperative, n.d.). Given Attorney General Ashcroft's position on the issue, however, it seems unlikely that a reclassification is forthcoming in the near future.

It is not just medical marijuana laws that have brought down the wrath of the feds. Many states have gone further, passing initiatives that decriminalize or legalize marijuana altogether. Like the medical marijuana laws, these efforts enjoy much public support: In 2001, 46% of all Americans opposed treating the possession of marijuana as a criminal offense, and 34% favored outright legalization. And when asked if drug abuse should be treated as a crime or a disease, 35% favored the former option, whereas 52% supported treating drug abuse as a disease (Maguire & Pastore, n.d., Table 2.85). Even among criminal justice officials, there is concern about current drug policies. A poll taken in 1996 found that more than 60% of police chiefs believe that antidrug strategies have been ineffective (Trebach, 1997), and more than 50 federal judges (many of whom are Reagan and Bush administration appointees) have refused to hear any more drug cases. As one retired judge explained, "I can't continue to give out sentences I feel . . . are unconscionable" (Bertram & Sharpe, 1997, p. 11).

At present, 12 states have decriminalization laws on the books, and at least until the 2002 elections, the momentum seemed to be moving very much in that direction. Several states have also passed initiatives that mandate treatment rather than jail for first- and second-time, nonviolent drug offenders. Arizona was the first to pass such a law in 1996; since then, California, Hawaii, and Washington, DC have followed suit. (In California, Proposition 36 diverted more than 12,000 individuals from prison into treatment within the first 6 months. According to the Drug Policy Alliance, the decline in incarceration of female nonviolent drug offenders has been so significant that lawmakers are considering closing one or two of the four women's prisons in order to help shrink California's enormous budget deficit) (Drug Policy Alliance, n.d.-b). Several other states have reformed sentencing laws in other ways in an effort to reduce the likelihood that nonviolent drug offenders will spend time behind bars, and many others are considering doing so in order to reduce correctional costs.

There appears, then, to be an ongoing and significant rethinking of the war on drugs, at least at the state and local levels. In November 2002, the drug reform movement's momentum slowed a bit when voters in Arizona and Nevada rejected marijuana decriminalization measures. However, since 1996, the drug reform movement has won 17 of 19 of its statewide ballot initiatives, as well as many local ordinances. The stage is now set for an unprecedented conflict between federal and state officials seeking to implement very different kinds of drug laws.

Conclusion

Far from being passive players in the wars on crime and drugs, some citizens have quite actively attempted to shape crime and drug policy. Most of this activism has been aimed at reducing crime through community-based crime prevention efforts or at providing for the needs and rights of crime victims. Because these forms of activism are largely consistent with the goals and philosophy of the federal government, they have received a great deal of state support. As a result, these movements have had a significant impact on criminal justice practices and policies.

By contrast, organizations whose goals are less compatible with the philosophy of the war on crime—such as community groups that adopt a social problems approach to crime prevention and victims' associations that do not advocate more punitive sentencing laws—have received significantly less government support. Groups that actively oppose aspects of the government's war on crime also have a more adversarial relationship to the government and receive very little support from it.

Increasingly, though, grassroots organizations, professional groups, academics, human rights organizations, billionaire philanthropists, and even some conservatives and law enforcement officials are supporting groups who challenge aspects of the wars on crime and drugs. As a result, these groups have recently affected public debate and had some success at the state and local levels. Nevertheless, most aspects of the wars on crime and drugs remain in place. In the chapter that follows, we examine these policies and their implications for American society.

8

Crime and Public Policy

Throughout this book, we have argued that the dramatic expansion of the U.S. penal system is primarily a consequence of the politicization of crime-related issues. Over the past three decades, politicians have kept the issues of crime and drug abuse at the top of the national agenda and framed them issues in ways that suggest a need for a harsher and more expansive system of criminal justice. This interpretation of crime and related issues has been amplified by the mass media and the victim's rights movement, and, at times, it has resonated with large segments of the American public.

The political obsession with crime and the spread of support for getting tough has precipitated a series of policy developments:

- Massive increases in drug arrests

- New, more punitive sentencing schemes

- Revival of capital punishment

- Retreat from juvenile justice

- Hardening of prison regimes

- Intensification of community surveillance

In this chapter, we take a closer look at these policies and practices, paying particular attention to their significance for criminal punishment and the dramatic expansion of the prison and jail populations. In the last section, we examine the implications of these changes for the control of crime and for the quality of social life more generally.

Drug Policing

Most of the public discussion about policing since the 1980s has focused on the kinds of collaborative, order maintenance, and quality-of-life initiatives discussed in the previous chapter. The image conveyed in these discussions has been that of the congenial beat cop of an earlier, gentler era. In reality, however, the most significant practical development in policing over the past two decades has been the crackdown on drugs.

Since the Reagan administration's Omnibus Crime Bill of 1984, police departments around the country have been encouraged to pursue drug offenders by the promise that they can confiscate any assets believed to be acquired with drug money—including cars, boats, houses, and bank accounts. Moreover, law enforcement agencies were allowed to keep a portion of seized assets, whether or not their owners were ever convicted of—or even formally charged with—a drug offense (Beckett, 1997; Gray, 1998). By 1990, more than 90% of police and sheriff's departments serving populations of at least 50,000 had received money or goods from a drug asset forfeiture program. Asset forfeiture receipts increased from $27.2 million in 1985 to $425.5 million in 2001; the assets and goods seized during the 1990s alone are worth more than $5 billion (Jensen & Gerber, 1996; Maguire & Pastore, 2002, Table 4.43; McAnany, 1992). As critics of these statutes point out, the lucrative nature of drug law enforcement means that law enforcement agencies may prioritize the prosecution of drug offenders over those who commit violent offenses (Rasmussen, 1994).

Thus, it is not surprising that the annual number of drug arrests has increased in recent years (see Exhibit 8.1). In 2001, nearly 1.6 million Americans were arrested on drug charges, roughly three times the number of annual arrests for aggravated assault and 15 times the number for robbery. Indeed, someone is arrested for a drug violation in the United States every 20 seconds (Egan, 1999; FBI, 2002, Table 29). Since the early 1980s, in any given year, the vast majority of drug arrests—between two thirds and four fifths of the total—have been for the crime of simple possession rather than trafficking (Maguire & Pastore, 1999, Tables 4.1, 4.29).

A popular interpretation of these numbers is that the drug problem in the United States worsened during the mid-1980s and mid-1990s. For

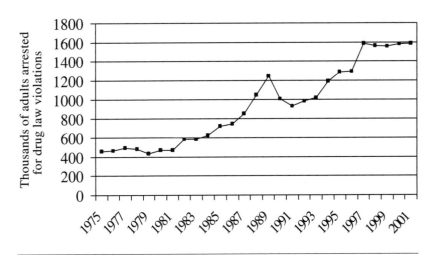

Exhibit 8.1   Drug Arrests

SOURCE: Bureau of Justice Statistics (2003), Drugs and Crime Facts. Available online at www.ojp.usdoj.gov/bjs. Accessed May 28, 2003.

example, in a special report on the explosion of drug arrests, researchers at the Federal Bureau of Investigation contend that "The Nation experienced its highest level of illicit drug activity in 1995 when measured by the total number of reported drug arrests since 1980" (FBI, 1997, p. 280). The problem with this interpretation is that the number of annual drug arrests may or may not reflect underlying drug activity. According to the National Institute of Drug Abuse's (NIDA) most recent National Household Survey, 11% of Americans used a prohibited drug during the past year—mainly marijuana, cocaine, or a hallucinogen such as LSD—and more than 6% used one in the past month.[1] Thus, the pool of potential drug offenders is huge.

In fact, among adults, the rate of illegal drug taking declined between 1980 and 1993 and has remained stable ever since (see Exhibit 8.2). Among high school seniors, the rate of drug use declined through 1993 but has since increased modestly due to rising use of marijuana (see Exhibit 8.3).[2] Thus, it appears that the surge in drug arrests does not reflect changes in drug taking so much as the political decision to fill the prisons with drug offenders.[3]

The crackdown on drug dealers and users has focused disproportionately on inner-city minority neighborhoods. According to the annual NIDA survey, African Americans make up about 13% of monthly users

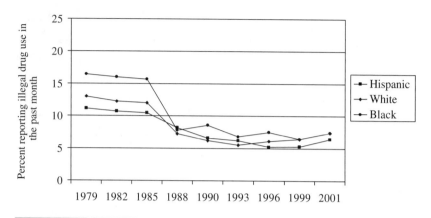

Exhibit 8.2   Share of Adult Population Reporting Illegal Drug Use

SOURCE: NIDA (1979, 1982, 1985, 1988, 1990, 1993, 1996, 1997); *Household Survey on Drug Abuse: Main Findings*; SAMSHA (1999, 2001); *National Household Survey on Drug Abuse*. Available online at www.samhsa.gov/oas/nhsda/2k1nhsda/vol3/Sect1v1_PDF_W_26-30.pdf Accessed May 23, 2003.

of illegal drugs, a number roughly proportionate to their share of the U.S. population.[4] During the 1980s, however, the proportion of drug possession arrests involving African Americans increased from about 1 in 4 to about 4 in 10—a ratio that remained stable throughout the 1990s (FBI, 1997, p. 282; 2002, p. 235). Some portion of this disparity may be due to the fact that some disproportionately poor and minority addicts slip through the cracks of national surveys. But as one research team concluded, "The degree of disparity between drug use and drug possession arrests is of such magnitude that it clearly points to disproportionate arrest practices" (Mauer & Huling, 1995, p. 9).

The police have focused their efforts in minority communities for several reasons:

- Drug dealing in predominantly minority inner-city neighborhoods, in contrast to middle-class areas, is more likely to occur in public places. "Open air" drug markets are more susceptible to police intervention through "buy and bust" undercover operations.

- The residents of inner-city neighborhoods tend to be politically powerless. Unlike their counterparts in upscale suburbs and on college campuses, they are unlikely to cause headaches for police and local politicians when arrested (Chambliss, 1994).

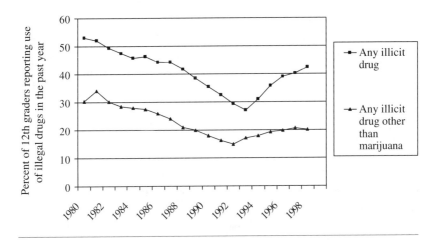

Exhibit 8.3   Illegal Drug Use Among High School Seniors

SOURCE: Johnston, L. D., O' Malley, P. M., & Bachman J. G. (1999). *National survey results on drug use from the Monitoring the Future Study, 1975–1998, vol. I: Secondary School Students* (NIH Publication No. 99-4600). Bethseda, MD: National Institute on Drug Abuse.

- Inner-city drug dealers fit the image of drug traffickers constructed in political discourse and in the news and entertainment media.

The surge in drug arrests has also brought a growing number of women into the criminal justice system. Between 1992 and 2001, the rate at which men were arrested for drug violations increased by 38%; the female rate increased by 51% (FBI, 2002, p. 239).

In and of itself, the dramatic growth in the number of annual drug arrests would have contributed to the growth of prison populations, female incarceration, and racial disparities among the incarcerated. But the impact of surging drug arrests has been compounded by harsh new mandatory sentencing laws and other new punitive sentencing practices, a topic to which we now turn.

Punitive Sentencing

Many politicians, neoconservative intellectuals, and members of the public are convinced that the sentences handed down by the courts are far too lenient. Their concerns have precipitated major changes in sentencing.

For most of the 20th century, a guilty verdict was followed by the proclamation of an open-ended, "indeterminate" sentence—5 to 20 years, in a typical case—with the precise release date to be determined by a parole board. This system honored, at least in principle, the notion that prisons ought to treat individual offenders on the basis of their particular situations and to release them once they have been rehabilitated.

Since the early 1980s, a new system of "determinate" punishment, founded upon a repudiation of rehabilitation, has been taking shape.[5] In the new regime, sentences are calibrated to punish offenders, deter would-be offenders, and incapacitate offenders who might pose a danger if free in society. The shift to determinate sentencing is taking shape primarily through three sentencing innovations: mandatory minimum sentencing laws, three-strikes legislation, and truth-in-sentencing requirements.

Mandatory Minimum Drug Sentences

Over the past two decades, mandatory minimum sentencing laws have become one of the most popular sentencing innovations. They have been adopted by state legislatures and Congress as a way of sending a message that particular offenses will be punished severely and limiting the discretion of judges to do otherwise. Between 1985 and 1991, Congress enacted at least 20 new mandatory sentencing laws, bringing to more than 100 the number of federal offenses governed by such laws (Tonry, 1996, p. 146).

Mandatory sentencing laws also proliferated at the state level. Massachusetts, for example, enacted mandatory penalties for unregistered firearms, drug law violations, drunk driving, and murder. By 1994, every U.S. state had adopted at least one new mandatory penalty, and most had adopted several (Tonry, 1996, p. 146). These laws typically apply to the most serious crimes, such as murder, rape, and felonies committed with a firearm. But they also frequently apply to drug offenses.

In fact, the mandatory penalty laws that have had the greatest impact on the nature and scope of criminal punishment have been those aimed at drugs. As with all laws of their type, mandatory minimum drug laws oblige judges to ignore information about an offender's job status, family obligations, history of victimization, and potential for rehabilitation. Moreover, because these laws punish according to the volume of the drug seized, they oblige judges to overlook even the particular details of the offense. Thus, it matters not whether the offender is a 17-year-old transporting drugs from one location to another (a "mule"), the battered girlfriend of a small-time distributor, or a genuine drug kingpin. In federal court, 1 gram of LSD, 5 grams of crack cocaine, and 100 grams of heroin each gets you 5 years (Donziger, 1996, p. 27). In Massachusetts, 200 grams of cocaine or heroin gets you 15 years, and 10,000 pounds of marijuana gets you 10 years (Massachusetts Sentencing Commission, 1996).

The results are sometimes surreal. Consider the following vignettes, culled from a *Boston Globe* "Spotlight" study of mandatory drug sentencing in Massachusetts:

> Rachel Acevedo, a poor mother of three, was caught with her former boyfriend selling four ounces of cocaine to an undercover police officer. Arrested in 1993, 22 years old, she is serving 10 years without any possibility of parole. She is a first-time offender with no criminal history.

> Victor B. Ramos, a 17-year-old high school student, was caught selling $40 worth of marijuana to a "pretty student" who turned out to be an undercover cop. "I was just trying to pick the girl up," Ramos explained to the *Boston Globe* reporter. He is serving a 2-year mandatory sentence without the possibility of parole for selling drugs within a school zone.

> Undercover agents ran Stanley Forrester, a novice with no prior criminal record, through five separate cocaine buys without arresting him. Their aim was to induce the 19-year-old father—a high school dropout employed in a dead-end job—to sell more than 100 grams of the drug and therefore trigger the 10-year mandatory minimum sentence. "I should do some time for what I've done. But show some mercy. Give me a chance to change. . . . There is much better treatment for those who do violent things to society. They come and go. I deserve punishment—just not 10 years." ("Overdosing on the Drug War," 1995, p. 1)

"Massachusetts has overdosed itself on the drug war—filling the state's prisons with hundreds of nonviolent, low-level offenders," conclude the *Boston Globe* reporters.

Globe reporters also discovered that high-level offenders, with "assets to forfeit and information to trade," have managed to evade the mandatory sentences. In such cases, prosecutors have used their discretion to either charge high rollers with lesser offenses or drop charges altogether. "An average payment of $50,000 in drug profits," the *Globe* calculated, "won a 6.3-year reduction in a sentence for dealers" ("Overdosing on the Drug War," 1995, p. 1).

The case of Massachusetts drives home one difficulty associated with mandatory minimum sentences. Such sentencing schemes turn judges into machines (input type of drug plus volume of drug, output sentence). Real sentencing power is shifted to prosecutors, who determine the original charge. Therefore, it is not surprising that in a 1993 survey of judges belonging to the American Bar Association, 82% of state judges and 94% of federal judges (many of whom are conservative appointees of the Reagan and Bush administrations) expressed opposition to mandatory minimum sentences (Tonry, 1996, p. 152).[6]

There is no evidence that the proliferation of mandatory drug sentences has deterred would-be users and dealers (Currie, 1993; Moore, 1990; Reuter & Kleiman, 1986; Tonry, 1996, pp. 139-142). Instead, the real impact of these laws has been to fill the prisons with drug addicts and small-time user-dealers. Between 1980 and 1999, the number of drug offenders serving time behind bars increased from 40,000 to 453,000—an increase of more than 1,000%. Of those now incarcerated in state prisons, three quarters have been convicted of drug and/or non-violent offenses only, and 58% have no history of either violence or high-level drug activity (King & Mauer, 2002a, p. 2).

Because the rate of incarceration for drug offenses has increased more rapidly than the rate for any other category of crime, the composition of the nation's prison population has shifted. Between 1985 and 1997, the percentage of state prison inmates serving sentences for violent crimes fell from 54% to 47%, and the percentage serving sentences for drug crimes rose from 9% to 21%. The shift was still more dramatic in the smaller federal system: The percentage of violent offenders declined from 28.1% to 15%, and the percentage of drug offenders increased from 33.3% to 63% (Bureau of Justice Statistics, 1997, pp. 10-11; Maguire & Pastore, 2002, Table 6.30).

Because mandatory drug sentences magnify the effects of high drug arrest rates of minorities and women, they are a key factor in the growing representation of these groups among the imprisoned. Thus, one study finds that drug enforcement during the 1990s accounts for 36% of increased female incarceration (compared with 18% of increased male incarceration) during that decade (American Society of Criminology, 2001, p. 17).

Moreover, some mandatory sentences have been written in ways that exacerbate racial disparities in incarceration. One example is the distinction made in the Federal Sentencing Guidelines and in most states between powder cocaine and crack cocaine. The two substances are pharmacologically similar, but the user populations of the two forms of cocaine are noticeably different. In the mid-1980s, when the federal government established its first mandatory penalty laws for drugs, powder cocaine was typically viewed as a recreational drug of upscale whites, and crack cocaine was depicted as the scourge of the ghetto poor (Reeves & Campbell, 1994). Around the time of the new federal law, about 9 out of 10 arrests for crack but only 3 of 10 arrests for powder cocaine involved an African American (Donziger, 1996, p. 119). Therefore, the decision by Congress to impose a 5-year mandatory prison term (with a statutory maximum of 20 years) for 5 grams of crack but for 500 grams of cocaine had a racially discriminatory impact.[7] In 2002, the U.S. Sentencing Commission recommended increasing the weight at which crack triggers a mandatory sentence (thereby reducing the disparity between crack and powder cocaine) and also urged that mandatory imprisonment for mere possession of the drug be scrapped (Coyle, 2002). These and similar prior recommendations have thus far been repudiated by Congress.

School zone laws are another example of mandatory sentences with discriminatory impact. These laws impose a mandatory penalty for drug sales within a specified distance—usually 100 yards—of a school. Schools, it turns out, are much more densely concentrated in inner-city neighborhoods than in suburbs and exurbs. Thus, the likelihood that an ordinary drug transaction (one not involving students or teachers) will be within the proximity of a school is much greater in largely minority neighborhoods.

Nearly three quarters of those admitted to state or federal prison for drug crimes in recent years were African American (FBI, 1996, p. 282). Between 1985 and 1995, the number of whites behind bars for drug crimes increased by 306%, whereas the number of blacks increased by 707% (Sentencing Project, n.d.-e). In 1997, among state prison inmates serving time for drugs, 56% were black, 23% were Hispanic, and 19% were white (see Exhibit 8.4) (Bureau of Justice Statistics, 1998c, pp. 11-12). The large and growing disparity between blacks and whites in the incarcerated population—like the growth of female incarceration—is, to a large extent, a product of the surge in drug arrests in combination with mandatory minimum penalties for drug offenders.

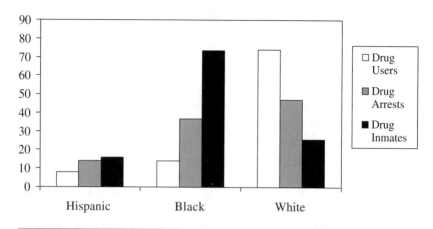

Exhibit 8.4   Race of Drug Users and Drug Offenders in the Criminal Justice System

SOURCE: Maguire, K., & Pastore, A. L. (1997). *Sourcebook of Criminal Justice Statistics 1996* (Table 4.10). Washington, DC: Bureau of Justice Statistics. NIDA, "Preliminary Results From the 1996 National Household Survey on Drug Abuse." National Corrections Reporting Program (1992). Table 1.13.

Note: Drug use data are for 1996; drug arrest data are for 1995. Drug inmates refers to those admitted to jail or prison for drug possession in 1992.

Three-Strikes Laws

The baseball metaphor "three strikes and you're out" refers to new laws aimed, at least in official pronouncements, at incapacitating dangerous repeat offenders. Since 1993, 25 states and the federal government have passed laws bearing the three-strikes slogan (Clark, Austin, & Henry, 1997). These laws typically oblige judges to increase penalties for second felony offenses and to sentence "three-time losers" to life in prison. Neither the particular circumstances, the seriousness of the crimes charged, nor the duration of time that has elapsed between crimes is given consideration. Moreover, like other mandatory penalties, three-strikes laws oblige judges to ignore mitigating factors in the background of offenders, as well as their ties to community, employment status, potential for rehabilitation, and obligations to children.

Under Washington State's new three-strikes law, 35-year-old Larry Fisher was sentenced to life in prison without the possibility of parole for robbing a sandwich shop of $151. At the time of the robbery, he was carrying a knife. Rather than display the knife, however, he jammed a finger in his coat pocket and pretended to have a gun. His previous two felony convictions were for stealing $360 from his grandfather and $100 from a pizza parlor. Fisher's lawyer argued that his client, who was raised in state custody after being pronounced "incorrigible" at age 12, is a product of the prison system: "We trained him that when he needs help to go out and commit a petty crime" ("Washington Case Is a Test," 1994, p. 1).

Fisher's case is not atypical of many "three-strikers." California's three-strikes law requires that the penalty for a second felony be doubled and that a third felony result in 25 years to life. To be convicted under the law, only the first two felony convictions must be for "strikeable" (serious but not necessarily violent) offenses; the third can be any offense, no matter how minor.[8] Among the more notorious three-strike cases in California have been individuals sentenced to serve 25 years to life for theft of a pizza slice (Slater, 1995), theft of meat from a grocery store (Donziger, 1996, p. 19), and theft of chocolate chip cookies from a restaurant (Elikann, 1996, pp. 112-113).

Thus, although three-strikes laws are typically represented as efforts to stem the tide of violent crime, in California, nonviolent property and drug offenders are the ones who have been most affected. As of 2001, nearly 70% of second-strike and 60% of third-strike cases did not involve violence against people (King & Mauer, 2001). Today, there are 344 California prisoners serving life sentences for crimes of petty theft (Greenhouse, 2002). Indeed, the majority of both second- and third-strike offenders are classified as either "minimum" or "low medium" security risks for purposes of incarceration—a further indication of their nonthreatening nature (Clark et al., 1997).

But the extent to which these laws are being used in the states where they have been adopted varies significantly. In some states, such as New Mexico, virtually no offenders have been sentenced under the new three-strikes laws. In a few states—especially California and Georgia—these laws have made a significant contribution to the expansion of the prison population (Dickey & Hollenhorst, 1998).

The long-term impact of three-strikes laws on prison populations and costs may be devastating in states where they are widely used. Imagine what prison populations would be like if we were still incarcerating octogenarians whose crimes consisted of bar fights and auto thefts they had committed in the 1940s! During the first 7 years of California's three-strikes law, nearly 45,000 offenders have had their sentences doubled under the second-strike provision, and nearly 7,000 have been sentenced to 25 years to life. At the current rate, by the year 2026, there will be 30,000 Californians serving life sentences at an annual cost of $750 million (King & Mauer, 2001). A 1996 study conducted by California's RAND Corporation concludes that a million dollars invested in the state's prisons would prevent 60 crimes a year, but the same amount invested in graduation incentive programs would prevent 258 crimes per year (Dickey & Hollenhorst, 1998, p. 6).

Despite such evidence, the legal basis of California's law is now firmly established. In February 2002, the U.S. Court of Appeals for the Ninth Circuit ruled that Leandro Andrade's life sentence for the theft of a few children's videos from Kmart constituted "cruel and unusual punishment" in violation of the Eighth Amendment. The ruling temporarily nullified provisions in California's law that make it possible to punish petty theft with a life sentence. In November, the U.S. Supreme Court heard arguments in Mr. Andrade's case, together with the case of Gary Ewing, a man sentenced to life for the theft of three golf clubs. In March 2003, the Supreme Court overturned the Court of Appeals. "To be sure," explained Justice Sandra Day O'Connor, "Ewing's sentence is a long one. But it reflects a rational legislative judgment, entitled to deference, that offenders who have committed serious or violent felonies and who continue to commit felonies must be incapacitated" ("Excerpts From Supreme Court Rulings," 2003, p. 1).

Truth-in-Sentencing

Like the other sentencing innovations discussed in this section, truth-in-sentencing reflects the underlying shift from indeterminate, rehabilitation-oriented sentences to determinate sentences aimed at administering punishment. The new truth-in-sentencing rules require that felony offenders serve most of their court-ordered sentence prior to parole eligibility. By 1993, several states and the federal government had adopted one or another version of truth-in-sentencing. In the 1994 Crime Bill, however, Congress mandated that states applying for $10.5 billion in federal assistance for new prison construction have laws on their books requiring that felony offenders serve at least 85% of their sentences.

"Truth" has a neutral ring to it, but its impact on prison populations has been anything but neutral. In principle, the shift to truth in sentencing would not necessarily entail longer sentences because judges would be free to order shorter terms. However, in the prevailing punitive environment, few judges have been willing to pronounce prison terms that are substantially shorter than in the past. And in some cases, their ability to do so has been constrained by the adoption of fixed or mandatory sentencing schemes. As a result, truth-in-sentencing laws have become another source of prison overcrowding, and average time served per offense continues to increase.

In summary, as a net result of mandatory sentences, three-strikes laws, and truth-in-sentencing requirements, as well as the generally punitive climate, offenders who once might have drawn probation are now going to prison, and prison-bound offenders are staying behind bars for longer stretches of time. Between 1980 and 1996, the number of new court commitments to state prison per 1,000 arrests grew by 29% for aggravated assault, 46% for burglary, 85% for larceny and motor vehicle theft, and 400% for drug offenses (see Beck, 1999, Table 11). Also, according to estimates compiled by the National Corrections Reporting Program, people committed to state prison in 1998 were expected to serve an average of 43 months behind bars, up from 38 months in 1990 and 31 months in 1985 (American Society of Criminology, 2001, p. 7; Beck, 1999, p. 62).

Return of Capital Punishment

The drive for tougher punishment has also prompted reinstatement of the death penalty. Since the 1976 U.S. Supreme Court decision in *Gregg v. Georgia* that ended the moratorium on executions, 38 states and the U.S. government have adopted death penalty laws, and nearly 5,000 offenders have been sent to death row. Between 1995 and 2003, prisoners in the United States were executed at an average rate of more than one per week. In 2002, 71 were executed, bringing the number executed since the return of the death penalty in the United States to 822.

The vast majority of executions are performed by a handful of southern states, led by Texas and Virginia. Most of the condemned are electrocuted or poisoned. A smaller number are gassed, shot with bullets, or hung by the neck. The condemned include mentally retarded prisoners and prisoners who committed their crimes as juveniles aged 16 or 17.[9] The United States is the only Western democracy that still executes convicted criminals.

Supporters of the death penalty contend that some crimes are so heinous that only execution can provide justice for the victim and healing for the victim's family. As discussed in the previous chapter, death penalty opponents respond with a number of arguments against judicial executions:

• Mistakes have been made in conviction and sentencing and inevitably will be made again in the future. Between 1973 and 2002, 102 prisoners were released from death row as a result of conclusive evidence of either innocence or wrongful conviction (Death Penalty Information Center, n.d.).

• The death penalty has never been shown to deter crime.[10] In fact, some evidence suggests that the opposite is true—that executions *encourage* violence among those already "ready to kill" (see Walker, 1994, pp. 102-103). Furthermore, states that execute in the largest numbers, such as Texas and Florida, also have the highest rates of homicide.[11]

• The death penalty is administered in a racially discriminatory fashion. Studies consistently show that prosecutors are far more likely to seek, and juries are more likely to vote for, death in cases involving black defendants and white victims (Baldus & Woodworth, 1998). In 13 death penalty states, significant race-of-offender bias has also been documented (Dieter, 1998).

• The death penalty is not cost-effective: It costs more to litigate capital cases and execute people than it would to incarcerate them for life (Bohm, 1998). This is the case because of the necessary safeguards that must be in place to diminish (though not eliminate) the risk that an error will be made.

• Finally, although a majority of Americans report that they support capital punishment, fewer than half favor the death penalty when they are given the option of a life sentence without the possibility of parole for convicted murderers (Sandys & McGarrell, 1995).

During the 1990s, New Hampshire, New York, and Kansas passed death penalty laws but joined the ranks of many states outside the southern "death belt" that have a death penalty on the books but rarely use it. On the other hand, several states have either debated repeal of the death penalty (New Hampshire) or adopted a moratorium on its use pending reform (Maryland, Illinois). Most dramatically, in January 2003, 2 days before the end of his term, Governor Jim Ryan commuted the death sentences of all 167 of Illinois's death row inmates. "Our capital system is haunted by the demon of error," declared the governor, "error in determining guilt and error in determining who among the guilty deserves to die" (Wilgoren, 2003, p. 1). The decision was decried by local prosecutors but hailed by a wide range of activists, academics, jurists, and representatives of foreign governments, including the European Union (which bans the death penalty). For the first time in decades, the wind has struck the sails of the movement for death penalty abolition (Wilgoren, 2003).

Retreat From Juvenile Justice

In the late 1980s and early 1990s, the mass media provided saturation coverage of a wave of juvenile violence. In Denver, Colorado, for example, the city's leading newspaper printed 44 front-page stories and 48 editorials on the topic of juvenile crime in the summer of 1993. During the previous summer, the paper had printed just two front-page stories and three editorials on the topic (Colomy & Greiner, 2001, p. 13). Several prominent criminologists provided fodder for the unfolding media spectacle by dubbing juvenile offenders "superpredators" and warning of an unprecedented wave of youth violence as the proportion of young people in the population increases (e.g., Bennett, DiIulio, & Walters, 1996).

A quick review of the actual data on crime patterns in the 1980s and 1990s reveals a more complicated picture. In fact, juvenile arrests have accounted for the same percentage of all violent crime arrests—about 20%—for the past 20 years. To the extent that a juvenile crime wave occurred, it consisted largely of a spike, from about 10% to 17%, in the juvenile share of all homicide arrests (see Exhibit 8.5) (Cook & Laub, 1998).[12] As we argued in Chapter 3, this jump in juvenile murder was largely a consequence of the arms race set in motion by the trade in crack cocaine.

The increase in juvenile violence has since subsided. Nevertheless, rising public concern about youth violence and declining faith in the capacity of the juvenile justice system to rehabilitate its charges fueled major changes. Most significantly, states have expanded the range of offenses for which juveniles can be tried in adult court and sentenced to prison. Many states have also lowered the age at which juveniles become eligible for waiver into adult court. For example, in 1996, without holding hearings and after only brief debate, Massachusetts adopted a juvenile justice law that automatically transfers juveniles 14 years old and older who are charged with murder to adult court. The law also features the equivalent of a juvenile "second strike": Prosecutors are empowered to charge any juvenile in adult court if he or she has already served time in juvenile detention on a previous charge.

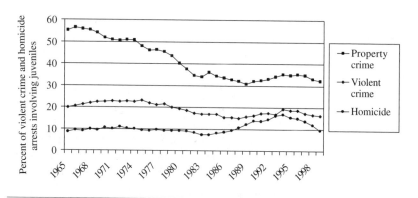

Exhibit 8.5   Juvenile Violent Crime and Homicide Arrests

SOURCE: Cook and Laub (2002), Figure A2.

Similarly, in 1998, New York expanded its juvenile code to allow trial in adult court and possible detention for up to 7 years for youngsters 14 and older who carry loaded guns to school ("Law Permits Trial," 1998). The net effect of these new laws has been a surge in the number of juveniles transferred to adult court and tried as adults. Over several decades leading up to the late 1980s, roughly 10,000 juveniles were transferred each year to adult court. During the 1990s, the annual number of juvenile transfers has been "upwards of 200,000" (Sentencing Project, n.d.-a).

Here's how *Time* magazine recently summed up the trend:

> In the past five years, most states have made it easier to charge and punish children as adults. Thirteen-year-olds are therefore getting mandatory life-without-parole sentences, and there's nothing appellate courts can do to help them. We have effectively discarded these lives. Should we make 11-year-olds eligible for life behind bars? Nine-year-olds? Seven-year-olds? We are inching closer and closer to a moral line. (Cloud, 1998)

Prisoner Warehousing

Over the past two decades, about 1,000 new prisons and jails have been built in the United States. Despite this fact, more than 30 state prison systems are operating at or above capacity, and 22 states are under court order to contain the size of their inmate populations (American Society of Criminology, 2001; Schlosser, 1998). Double bunking inmates in cells and cubicles designed for one has become the norm in prisons across the country. So, too, has the practice of housing inmates in prison gymnasiums and dayrooms or in county jails. In some states, such as Massachusetts, Hawaii, and Vermont, overcrowding has prompted prison authorities to ship inmates out of state to the small number of prison systems with surplus capacity. Texas, for example, incarcerates more than 5,000 inmates from 14 other states (Schlosser, 1998).

Prison overcrowding causes massive loss of privacy for inmates and has become a significant source of prison violence. Moreover, in combination with the voguish view that rehabilitation does not work and that prisons are country clubs, overcrowding has been accompanied by a wholesale retrenchment in programs for inmates. Educational, vocational, rehabilitation, drug treatment, and recreational programs have been dramatically cut back in many prison systems (Amnesty International, 1998a, p. 58; Butterfield, 1999). Nationwide, just 15% of prison inmates are currently enrolled in educational or rehabilitation programs (Butterfield, 2002b). Growing numbers of inmates are confined to their cells for 23 hours a day in "lockdown." One journalist described the consequences, based on an encounter with inmates at New Folsom maximum security prison in California:

> Behind the need to blame others for their predicament and the refusal to accept responsibility, behind all the denial, lay an enormous anger, one that seemed far more intense than the typical inmate complaints about the food or the behavior of certain officers. Shirtless, sweating, unshaven, covered in tattoos, one inmate after another described the rage that was growing inside New Folsom. The weights had been taken away; no more conjugal visits for inmates who lacked a parole date; not enough help for the inmates who were crazy, really crazy; not enough drug treatment, when the place was full of junkies; not enough to do—a list of grievances magnified by the overcrowding into something that felt volatile, ready to go off with the slightest spark. (Schlosser, 1998, p. 72)

In the words of two notable scholars, contemporary prisons represent a "new penology" that seeks not to deter or rehabilitate individual offenders but merely to warehouse a segment of the so-called urban underclass (see Feeley & Simon, 1992).

Indeed, prison design increasingly expresses an overriding concern with the facilities' strictly custodial function. The new "supermax" prisons for hard-to-handle inmates are designed to minimize all human contact among prisoners and between prisoners and their guards. Prisoners are held for long stretches of time in states of virtual sensory deprivation. During their one daily hour of exercise, supermax inmates are released into narrow chain-linked cages resembling dog runs. In 1997, there were 57 supermax prisons spread across 36 states, housing more than 13,000 prisoners (Amnesty International, 1998a, p. 74; see also Porter, 1998; Stern, 1998).

At the less serious end of the spectrum are the new mass-produced, prefabricated ("cookie-cutter"), medium security prisons popping up in rural communities across the country. These new facilities are designed around huge dormitories that house 80 or more inmates in tiny cubicles, often double bunked. In the words of two industry insiders, these prisons reflect "the most critical factor in contemporary correctional facility design: low cost" (Beilein & Krasnow, 1996, p. 129).

The cutback in prison programs and the emergence of a more custodial approach to punishment has occurred as general inmate populations have become increasingly female, black, and brown. Between 1980 and 1997, the proportion of women, blacks, and Hispanics in the state inmate population increased, whereas the proportion of white males declined.[13] Over the same period, the annual share of new prison commitments for nonviolent (including drug) offenses increased from about half of all new prison commitments to nearly three quarters (Miller, 1996).[14] The share of inmates addicted to drugs or suffering from serious mental illness also increased markedly.[15] In short, although prisons continue to house many serious, dangerous offenders, they have increasingly become "dumping grounds" for nonviolent petty offenders, drug addicts, and the mentally ill.

As in the past, U.S. prisons continue to be violent and degrading places. In the words of the international human rights organization Amnesty International (1998a):

> Every day in prisons and jails across the USA, the human rights of prisoners are violated. In many facilities, violence is endemic. In some cases, guards fail to stop inmates assaulting each other. In others, the guards are themselves the abusers, subjecting their victims to beatings and sexual abuse. Prisons and jails use mechanical, chemical and electroshock methods of restraint that are cruel, degrading and sometimes life-threatening. The victims of abuse include pregnant women and the mentally ill. (p. 55)

And in the wake of September 11, 1,500 to 2,000 immigrants have been detained (but not charged) as suspected terrorists. Many of these detainees have been denied their rights to legal counsel, to family visitation, and even to knowing the grounds for their detention.

The routine violence and degradation of prison life are nothing new. However, they are worsened by current prison conditions, and the dramatic expansion of incarceration in the United States means that the number of persons subjected to these conditions is without precedent.

The Surveillance Society

Concern about crime, together with the technologies and interests that have grown around it, has fueled and legitimated new strategies for keeping tabs on people. Surveillance practices long associated with prison have spilled into communities, as law enforcers and security guards increasingly monitor public places—a trend captured in the phrase "the prisonization of society." Today, everyone is watched by security cameras and frisked electronically when entering and exiting stores and public facilities. Increasingly, we are subjected to drug testing, background checks, metal detectors, and security gates (Staples, 1997).

Schools are also increasingly deploying technologies once reserved for prisons:

> The sprawling new brick building next to the Dallas County Probation Department has 37 surveillance cameras, six metal detectors, five full-time police officers, and a security-conscious configuration based on the principles of crime prevention through environmental design. It is not the Big House. It is a schoolhouse: Dallas's $41 million state-of-the-art Townview Magnet Center, which has been touted as a model for high-tech school security since it opened for the new school year. (Applebome, 1995, p. B11)

The spate of school shootings in the late 1990s proved to be a powerful catalyst of the trend toward "maximum security" schools:

> Going to class will be a little more like boarding an airliner for many U.S. pupils this year as educators try to prevent another year of bloodshed in America's schools. They'll walk through metal detectors and past police or other guards. . . . [They'll] be wearing photo ID badges and toting book bags made of see-through materials, if they're allowed to carry book bags at all. They're being given hot-line numbers to report, anonymously, signs that a schoolmate could turn violent, and some will face punishment if they don't. . . . Principals in places like

Evansville, Ind., are getting handheld metal detectors for frisking students suspected of being armed. Each Evansville high school is getting a breath machine to test if students have been drinking. (Greene, 1998, p. 4A)

All Americans are experiencing stepped-up surveillance. Suspect populations, however, are kept under far tighter scrutiny. Black men, regardless of their involvement with the justice system, are routinely subjected to motor vehicle stops for the crime of DWB—Driving While Black (Bennett et al., 1996). Members of minority groups are often stopped in airports, bus terminals, and other public places and questioned about drugs, a practice legitimated by typically ambiguous "drug courier profiles," which open the door for unlimited police discretion (Davey, 1995). Since September 11, 2001, racial profiling of Arabs and people believed to have ties to the Middle East has become especially widespread (Koh, 2002).

For individuals of all races who have been sentenced by a court, forms of surveillance range from regular probation, which might entail nothing more than a notification requirement concerning change of address, to electronic monitoring, day reporting, halfway house residency, and house arrest. Probationers and parolees suspected of substance abuse problems must submit to regular drug and alcohol testing. Sex offenders must register with local police, who in turn, in many jurisdictions, notify area residents and prospective employers.

In the United States, on any given day, nearly 1 in 3 young black men is under one form or another of criminal justice supervision. In many U.S. cities, the proportion is even more dramatic. As noted in Chapter 1, in 1997, 50% of black males in Washington, DC, between 18 and 35 years old were in jail or prison, on probation or parole, out on bond, or wanted on an arrest warrant. In neighboring Baltimore, Maryland, in 1991, the comparable statistic was 56% (Lotke, 1997; Miller, 1992). In high-poverty, racially segregated neighborhoods, the percentage is still higher.

One unsurprising consequence of the expansion and intensification of community surveillance (e.g., probation and parole) is the burgeoning number of people sent to prison for violating the conditions of community release. In 1980, new court commitments were responsible for 82% of prison admissions; parole and probation violations were responsible for 17%. By 1997, the share of prison admissions from the courts had declined to 60%, and the share stemming from conditional release violations surged to 40%. Many of these violators are detected through drug tests (American Society of Criminology, 2001, p. 17). Although probation and parole were conceived, at least in part, as mechanisms for reintegrating offenders into community life, they now help to explain why U.S. prisons are bursting at their seams.

Criminal Justice and Democracy

In the previous section, we discussed the most important developments in criminal justice policies and practices over the past two decades. These innovations have dramatically expanded the scale and scope of institutions of criminal justice in the United States. Many are rightly asking whether such costly policies have been effective in reducing crime. Some are even more concerned about the effect of these policies on the health and vitality of American democracy.

Crime Control

Defenders of the get-tough approach point to dropping crime rates as evidence that this approach is effective. Indeed, the violent crime rate has declined significantly over the past decade, for older Americans and juveniles alike. But a closer look reveals a more complicated picture. If filling the prisons by itself reduces crime, then it ought to have begun to do so in the 1970s and 1980s. Although the average prison sentence per violent crime tripled between 1975 and 1989, there was no discernable impact on the overall rate of criminal violence during this period (Reiss & Roth, 1993).[16] The historical evidence also shows no correlation between patterns in incarceration and patterns in crime (Currie, 1998; Tonry, 1995; Zimring & Hawkins, 1995).

In addition to the problematic historical evidence, the get-tough faction's argument is inconsistent with the current cross-sectional (comparative) evidence. Between 1991 and 1998, for example, Texas increased its rate of incarceration by 144% and experienced a 35% decrease in crime. New York, on the other hand, increased its rate of incarceration by just 24% but experienced a 43% crime reduction. Nationwide, the states that increased their prison populations most (on average by 72%) experienced an average crime drop of 13%; the states that increased their prison populations least (on average by 13%) experienced an average crime drop of 17% (Gainsborough & Mauer, 2000). Thus, it appears that less punitive states have experienced more dramatic decreases in crime rates than their more punitive counterparts.

Several factors account for the limited impact of mass incarceration on crime rates:

• By the time offenders have accumulated enough charges to justify a long prison sentence, most of them are on the verge of "maturing out" of crime (Currie, 1985). Efforts to devise schemes to identify and incarcerate high-rate offenders before they have done much damage inevitably run the risk of false positives. In the United States, we still do not imprison people on the basis of what they might do in the future.

• Incarcerating offenders for participation in the underground economy—for example, drug dealing, gambling, or prostitution—often generates a "replacement effect": People who are otherwise law abiding are recruited to fill what amount to job vacancies in illegal trades (Tonry, 1996, p. 138).

• Many people fail to make risk-benefit calculations before engaging in criminal behavior—or, having done so, they determine the risks to be acceptable. As criminologist Alfred Blumstein puts it,

There are some people who simply do not respond when a threat is presented to them. . . . For people who see no attractive options in the legitimate economy, and who are doubtful that they will live another ten years in any event, the threat of an extended prison stay is likely to be far less threatening than it would be to a well-employed person with a family. (Butterfield, 2002b, p. A11)

• As we argue in the next section, the experience of incarceration typically has contradictory effects on prisoners: It may motivate them to "go straight" to avoid another stint behind bars, but it also socializes offenders in the "code of the street," diminishes their chances of finding decent work, severs their ties to family and law-abiding friends, and opens up new opportunities and contacts for criminal activities.

Recent research shows that the recidivism rate today is higher than in 1983, suggesting that mass incarceration has failed to enhance the deterrent effect of imprisonment (Butterfield, 2002b, p. 1). On the other hand, two studies have concluded that mass incarceration has made a modest contribution to the drop in crime by incapacitating crime-prone individuals. One analysis suggests that perhaps 25% of the reduction in violent crime and homicide during the 1990s is due to incapacitation (Spelman, 2000). Another finds that perhaps 15% to 20% of the decline in adult homicide since 1980 is due to incarceration (Rosenfeld, 2000). As the author of the latter study points out, however, we cannot be certain about even this modest incapacitation effect, since these studies cannot ascertain what portion of the high propensity for homicide in the U.S. is itself a consequence of mass incarceration. We return to this question in the next section.

If mass incarceration has had little or no effect on crime rates, what accounts for most of the drop in crime? As mentioned in Chapter 3, epidemiological research sponsored by the National Institutes of Health finds that drops in homicide by city are correlated with changes in drug markets, especially crack markets. These changes, in turn, are a consequence of the natural course of the drug epidemic and not law enforcement interventions (Golub & Johnson, 1997). Researchers seeking to explain the recent drop in serious crime have also cited declining opportunities in the illicit labor market, demographic changes, and declining levels of unemployment (Blumstein & Rosenfeld, 1998; Fagan, Zimring, & Kim, 1998).

In sum, mass imprisonment has, at best, made a modest contribution to the drop in violent crime over the past decade, but that contribution comes at a high social and economic price. In the next section, we discuss these costs and consider whether they are sustainable or justifiable.

Unintended Consequences

In his book *Search and Destroy: African American Males in the Criminal Justice System*, crime policy analyst Jerome Miller (1996) uses the term *social iatrogenesis* to describe the impact of the new get-tough policies on drug dealing and crime. Iatrogenesis refers to a cure that is actually responsible for the underlying illness. Miller uses the term in relation to crime policy to describe "a 'treatment' that maims those it touches and exacerbates the very pathologies which lie at the root of crime. It suggests that the criminal justice system itself has been a major contributor to breakdown in the inner cities" (p. 9).

For example, consider the war on drugs. Like alcohol prohibition in the 1930s, the contemporary prohibition on marijuana, cocaine, and other drugs is directly responsible for the black market and for the violence it has spawned. Moreover, crackdowns on drug dealers tend to drive up prices and profits and hence make the risk taking associated with the trade more rational. Similarly, massive drug arrests in effect create new "job openings" for dealers while setting the stage for battles over ever-shifting turf. Finally, prohibition has facilitated the formation of violent drug cartels, especially in Colombia, Peru, and Mexico, which have seriously destabilized those countries. In a word, drug prohibition has proved a boon for daring criminals but has done little to stem the tide of drug use and abuse.[17]

More generally, the get-tough approach to crime and drug dealing fuels the material, social, and cultural ills that are the root causes of crime and drug dependency. Crackdowns divert resources from education and social welfare initiatives. In California, for example, between 1985 and 2000, state spending on higher education declined by $1.059 billion while spending on corrections increased by $3.074 billion (Justice Policy Institute, 2002). As a percentage of the state budget, prisons now consume nearly as much as the state's vaunted system of universities and colleges. The same shift in resources from higher education to incarceration occurred in New York, a state which now spends $275 million per year *more* on its prisons than its state and city colleges (American Society of Criminology, 2001). In 2000, nationwide, more black men were behind bars (791,600) than were enrolled in colleges and universities (603,000) (Justice Policy Institute, 2002).

Spending on social welfare for the poor has also declined over the past two decades. In 2002, the federal government spent more money on the war on drugs alone ($18.8 billion) than on Temporary Assistance to Needy Families ($16.7 billion), the nation's premier social welfare program (ONDCP, 2002; U.S. Department of Health and Human Services, 2002).

Massive criminal justice interventions foster joblessness and family disruption. Most prisoners have unimpressive work histories. Having served time and earned the label "ex-con," former prisoners typically find it more difficult than ever to secure stable employment (Western & Beckett, 1999). Jobs and stable families are society's most important bulwarks against both poverty and crime (Currie, 1985). Jobless men and men currently behind bars are among the least likely to support children. Predictably, therefore, in high-poverty, inner-city neighborhoods, both the rate of out-of-wedlock births and the share of unmarried women have risen in tandem with the incarceration rate of minority men (Wilson, 1987, 1996). Female-headed households are also disrupted by incarceration: Three fourths of the 54,000 women incarcerated for drug crimes have children (Egan, 1999). Overall, nearly 2 million children have a parent in prison (Butterfield, 1997b). Thus, criminal justice interventions increasingly represent a major cause of, rather than cure for, contemporary social ills.

Massive criminal justice intervention in the lives of poor people and minorities also increases their social and political isolation. Today, ex-felons are typically denied access to a wide range of social services, including education loans, housing assistance, and poverty relief (Travis, 2002). In 13 states, ex-felons are denied the right to vote, a fact that translates into the disenfranchisement of nearly 4 million voters (Mauer, 2002). According to one study, the lifetime voting bans, insofar as they have disproportionately excluded minorities who tend to vote Democrat, caused Republican victories in seven Senate races between 1970 and 1998, shifting control over that legislative body to the Republican Party in both 1986 and 2000 (Mauer, 2002). In the state of Florida in 2000, where George W. Bush edged out Al Gore in the presidential election by just 537 votes, fully 600,000 Floridians, most of them minority men, were denied the ballot. Nationwide, ex-felon voting bans disenfranchise 13% of African American men (Mauer, 2002).

Finally, massive criminal justice intervention reinforces the "code of the streets." In big cities, imprisonment has become virtually a formal rite of passage for young minority men, signaling their transition into a new way of life. Sadly, what prison best prepares its visitors for is survival in a violent, predatory world—that is, for survival on the inside. Beyond the prison walls, the skills and beliefs cultivated within prisons frequently lead ex-cons back into lives of crime, addiction, and trouble.

In summary, get-tough policies are not merely inefficient strategies for crime reduction. To the extent that these practices contribute to social inequality, family and community breakdown, and a predatory street culture, they are, in the long run, increasingly significant causes of the very problems they purport to correct.

The Prison-Industrial Complex

As if the picture were not sufficiently grim, many analysts are now warning of the emergence of a "prison-industrial complex." These critics argue that the dramatic escalation of criminal justice spending has generated constituencies with vested interests in existing practices and perspectives. Police departments, for example, are political sacred cows, immune to budget cuts, and strong supporters of the war on drugs—an increasingly important source of revenue. The private prison industry is also rapidly expanding, profitable for investors, and politically well connected. More than 119,000 prisoners are currently held in private facilities, up from about 5,000 a little more than a decade ago (Sentencing Project, n.d.-f).

In several states, unions of prison guards are also well organized and politically influential. In California, for example, the guards' union played an instrumental role in funding the ballot initiatives for the state's three-strikes law and donated millions of dollars to the election campaigns of the state's two most recent tough-on-crime governors (Donziger, 1996). Depressed rural communities in places like upstate New York have become important constituencies for new prison construction (Schlosser, 1998). Finally, as any casual glance at one of the many new glossy magazines or Web sites dedicated to the prison industry reveals, businesses that provide prisons with goods and services are flourishing. These include the telephone companies AT&T and MCI, which compete for lucrative prison contracts, and firms that build prisons, supply medical services, and market electronic surveillance and security devices.[18]

In short, concomitant with the growth of spending on criminal justice has been growth in the number of players with financial, professional, and ideological interests in get-tough approaches to crime and drugs. The formation of this new prison-industrial complex makes it difficult (though not impossible) for state governors and lawmakers to cut prison budgets even as they reduce spending on vital social services. As *New York Times* columnist John Broder (2003) writes of California's budget for 2003,

> State subsidies for homeless shelters will be slashed. Artificial limbs will no longer be provided for impoverished amputees. Welfare payments to the blind will be cut. College students will pay higher fees. But the state's vast prison system emerged untouched. (p. 5)

Still, over the past few years, as costs and criticisms mount, signs of change are increasingly visible. Activists against the drug war sponsored successful ballot initiatives in Arizona, California, and Washington, DC, to mandate community-based treatment rather than imprisonment for low-level, nonviolent drug offenders. California's new law (known as Proposition 36, passed in 2000) will divert an estimated 36,000 petty drug offenders from prison to community-based treatment. The law sets aside $120 million annually—a portion of the savings on the costs of incarceration—to fund treatment centers. Other states, including Louisiana, Indiana, North Dakota, Connecticut, and Michigan, have modified their mandatory minimum drug laws in ways that restore judicial discretion and encourage treatment instead of incarceration for low-level offenders. These changes suggest that the prison-industrial complex, however influential it might be, does not constitute an insurmountable obstacle to change.

Conclusion

In this chapter, we have examined the policies that have grown out of the politicization of crime. These policies have dramatically increased prison populations and the scope of the criminal justice system. They have contributed only modestly, at best, to public safety. Indeed, the criminal justice system is increasingly a major source of the problems it is supposed to contain, and this will be even more true in the long run.

When we consider the criminal justice trends discussed in this chapter in connection with the simultaneous reduction in welfare programs, the contours of our general predicament become more clear. In the United States, we are increasingly substituting for the welfare state, based on the principles of mutual responsibility and common destiny, a neoliberal security state. In this emerging social formation, race and class inequalities harden, and social peace is accomplished not through the promise of full citizenship and a decent life but rather through social control and punishment. In the next and final chapter, we discuss the choices still potentially within our grasp if only we find the political will to act.

9

Alternatives

In the previous chapter, we described and critiqued many of the anti-crime policies adopted in the rush to get tough on crime. These policies are predicated on the view that crime and drug use are primarily the consequence of immoral individuals and a permissive criminal justice apparatus that fails to punish their immoral acts. As we have seen, this way of framing crime was initially promoted by conservative opponents of civil rights and the welfare state. For these political actors, the emotionally and racially charged crime issue provided a means of legitimating individualistic explanations of a range of social problems, explanations that implied the need for enhanced social control rather than social welfare. Although these political actors were not initially responding to clear expressions of popular sentiments about crime and punishment, some segments of the public—especially those most concerned about the pace and nature of social change—found in the discourse of law and order a way of expressing those fears and concerns. As a result, the rhetoric of "law and order" provided a means by which increasing numbers of white, swing voters were wooed by the GOP and, later, by Democrats as well.

In short, political elites have framed crime-related issues as a product of excessive state lenience in an attempt to realign the electorate and mobilize support for a conservative political agenda. Over the years, liberal politicians have largely accepted the premise that the best way to deal with social problems such as crime, delinquency, drug abuse, and even poverty and homelessness is to "get tough." As a result, the wars on crime and drugs have enjoyed strong, bipartisan support, and the vast majority of our national politicians continue to accept the basic reorientation of domestic policy from social welfare to social control.

We believe that this policy shift is based on unsound evidence and is an ineffective response to crime. Furthermore, many of the new get-tough policies are unjust and reflect a disturbing tendency to scapegoat, exclude, and stigmatize those now seen as members of an underclass. The logical consequence of the war on crime—the incarceration of huge and growing numbers of people, especially young minorities—is, at least in political and moral terms, a crime of the state, the significance of which is far greater than the petty crimes committed by many of today's offenders.

It was political activism that led us down this path, and it is through political activism (of a very different sort) that the current crime and social policies will be transformed. Many people are mobilizing for such change, and there is substantial evidence that a variety of criminal justice reforms would be popular among many members of the public. As we discussed in Chapter 7, a variety of grassroots, religious, human rights, and political organizations are challenging practices and policies associated with the war on crime, including police brutality, capital punishment, and the war on drugs. There is also evidence of more general opposition to the prioritization of social control over social welfare. In Concord, California, for example, more than 2,000 high school students recently marched to protest declining educational funds, calling for "Education, Not Incarceration!" (Shaylor, 1998, p. 19).

This type of activism is needed to raise awareness of the costs of the war on crime and to pressure politicians to adopt more sensible and just anticrime policies. In what follows, we identify some alternative policies and programs that, if implemented, would not only address crime and drug abuse in a more effective and humane fashion, but also reduce the enormous human, social, and fiscal costs of incarcerating more than 2 million people. Our discussion of these policies is informed by our belief that lethal and domestic violence are the primary U.S. crime problems, that current policies do not address the causes of these problems, and that massive incarceration is an ineffective and inhumane solution to the problems associated with social marginality.

Social Investment

One of the most effective ways we can reduce crime—especially the very serious problem of lethal violence—is to reduce poverty and inequality.

As we saw in Chapter 3, serious interpersonal violence is concentrated in very poor, racially segregated communities. Studies consistently report that these areas are characterized by "resource deprivation," including high levels of poverty, joblessness, and single-headed households.[1] It is not surprising that cities with more generous welfare programs have less poverty (especially among children) and *lower* levels of crime, including homicide (Hannon & DeFronzo, 1998).

Comparative studies provide further evidence of the association between poverty, inequality, and crime: Countries with higher levels of poverty and inequality are also characterized by greater levels of serious violence (Currie, 1998, pp. 125-126). Thus, there is ample evidence that it is not welfare dependency but inequality and poverty that fuel high levels of interpersonal violence. There is also evidence that social investments such as education, job training, and drug treatment programs are cost-effective. For example, researchers found that every dollar invested in Job Corps (a federal program aimed at helping high-risk youth obtain employment) returned $1.46 to society in reduced prison and income support costs and increased tax contributions (see Donziger, 1996, p. 216).

Despite this, our politicians have systematically adopted policies that have exacerbated inequality and increased poverty, reversing the gains won earlier by welfare and civil rights activists. As a result of tax breaks for corporations and the rich, low minimum wage standards, and other policies that favor the wealthy, income and wealth inequality have grown steadily since the 1960s. The pace of this pattern intensified in the 1980s: Between 1983 and 1998, the bottom 40% of the nation's households saw their wealth diminish by more than 70%, whereas those in the top 1% enjoyed a more than 40% increase in their total assets (U.S. Bureau of the Census, n.d.-a, Table IE-6; Wolff, 2000, Table 3).

The welfare state retrenchment of the 1980s and 1990s has been particularly devastating for poor people in this country. Efforts to reduce social spending and remove families from welfare resulted in a 33% decline in per-child welfare spending between 1979 and 1993 ("Citing Drop," 1999, p. A12; Currie, 1998). More recent revisions to the welfare system (contained in the 1996 Personal Responsibility and Work Opportunity Act) further tightened eligibility requirements. As a result, the number of families receiving Aid to Families with Dependent Children (AFDC) in the United States declined by 52% between 1996 and 2001 (U.S. Department of Health and Human Services, 2002), and child poverty rates in the 1980s and 1990s were about one third higher than in the 1970s (Danziger & Gottschalk, 1995, p. 67).[2] The severity of poverty also increased during this period: The average payment required to lift the poor above the poverty line was more than 20% higher in the 1980s and early 1990s than in the 1970s (Danziger & Weinberg, 1994, p. 33). Although rates of poverty began to decrease in the late 1990s as a result of economic expansion, there is evidence that they are on the rise once again (U.S. Bureau of the Census, n.d.-b).

In sum, as a result of economic and policy developments, more children and their families in this country are poor and living in communities characterized by extreme and concentrated poverty. As we have seen, this kind of poverty encourages serious violence. To begin to address these problems, we need to adopt policies that invest in communities and families and that reduce high levels of inequality. Examples of such policies include "living wage" legislation (laws that require employers to pay their workers enough to support a family above the poverty line); increased social support and services, especially for those raising children; universalization of child and health care; increased support for high-quality public housing; investment in mental health care; and job creation programs that provide work and needed services for the unemployed. These and other policies aimed at reducing poverty, inequality, and unemployment would not only ameliorate criminogenic social conditions, but also be a first step in the creation of a more just and inclusive society.

Harm Reduction

Current drug control laws are aimed at eradicating all illegal drug use through punishment. This zero-tolerance approach treats the official distinction between legal and illegal drugs as entirely rational (which many believe it is not) and refuses to acknowledge any difference between recreational, experimental, or occasional drug use and chronic, uncontrolled, personally harmful, or socially disruptive drug abuse. The zero-tolerance approach also depicts drug use as an immoral, individual choice that is unrelated to larger social conditions (Beckett, 1997, p. 55; Reinarman & Levine, 1997b). The costs of this approach to drug use are alarmingly high: These policies have made a significant contribution to the expansion of prisons and jails, and, by causing family and community disruption and siphoning resources away from social services and programs, aggravated the social conditions that give rise to the worst forms of drug abuse.

Our drug policies should, we believe, be reoriented toward the goal of *harm reduction*. The harm reduction approach begins from the premise that consciousness-altering substances have been used in all known societies in which they are available, and that some drug use is inevitable. Furthermore, this approach suggests that not all drug use is personally or socially harmful. To the extent that it is, it may be the social context in which drugs are used or the policies that prohibit drugs that are responsible for at least some of this harm. The goal of drug policy should be to minimize the harm associated with drug abuse, not to punish those who use them.[3] This perspective has a number of important policy implications.

First, reorienting drug policy toward harm reduction would encourage policymakers to differentiate between drug use and drug abuse—to recognize, for example, that recreational use of some drugs does not constitute a major social problem. It would also imply the need to distinguish between drugs that pose a higher risk of serious harm and drugs that are relatively safe. Toward that end, we recommend that marijuana be legalized. Of the approximately 60 million Americans who have used marijuana in their lifetime, not one has died of an overdose.[4] And although smoking marijuana does pose certain health risks, so do many legal practices such as eating fast food and smoking tobacco. There is no evidence that marijuana is physically addictive or necessarily leads to the use of harder drugs (Nadlemann, 1997; see also Zimmer & Morgan, 1995). Furthermore, legalization of marijuana would lead to the separation of the cannabis and hard drug markets so that, in the course of buying marijuana, people would not also gain access to harder drugs. Finally, legalizing marijuana would reduce the prison, jail, and probation populations and decrease law enforcement costs considerably. In 2000, 46% of all drug abuse arrests involved marijuana, nearly 90% of which were for possession rather than distribution (Maguire & Pastore, n.d., Table 4.29).[5]

Orienting drug policy toward harm reduction would also require that we think critically about the origins of the harm that is associated with drug abuse. Toward this end, advocates of the harm reduction approach distinguish between *primary* and *secondary* drug problems. Primary drug problems are those that result from the use of the substance itself, such as liver damage caused by alcohol use or lung damage that results from smoking tobacco and marijuana. By contrast, secondary drug problems are the consequence of the social context in which drugs are used or of drug prohibition itself. Turf wars, for example, are a consequence of the criminalization of drugs that increases their profitability—as well as of the poverty-induced desperation that leads many to turn to the illegal drug market. Other examples of secondary drug problems include the spread of infectious diseases through the use of dirty needles (a consequence of a ban on needle exchange programs and other policies that restrict access to clean needles) and drug users' unwillingness to seek medical help for fear of detection (Egan, 1999).

One of the most effective ways of minimizing both the primary and secondary harm associated with drugs is by addressing the social conditions that underpin our most serious drug problems. A substantial body of sociological research demonstrates that the distribution, seriousness, and consequences of drug abuse are shaped by social conditions. It is clear, for example, that those who have a stake in "conventional life" are much better able to establish control over their drug use (Reinarman & Levine, 1997a; Waldorf, Reinarman, & Murphy, 1991)[6] and are more likely to benefit from treatment programs (Currie, 1993). There is also evidence that the impact of drug use by pregnant women on fetal health is mediated by diet, prenatal care, and other factors associated with social class.[7] In other words, ensuring that all pregnant women have access to health care and sound nutrition during their pregnancies would help to minimize the potentially adverse effects of drugs on their babies.

Dramatically reducing our reliance upon the criminal justice system in dealing with drug abuse would also reduce both primary and secondary drug problems. Making drug treatment more available and getting drug users out of the criminal justice system would not only reduce the size and expense of the system, but also encourage people with drug problems to seek help rather than go underground. According to one authoritative study, investment in drug treatment is 15 times more cost-effective than spending on federal mandatory minimum drug sentences.[8] Nevertheless, health researchers estimate that fewer than 1 in 10 individuals in need of drug treatment receives it (Drug Policy Alliance, n.d.-c).

The most common argument against the harm reduction approach is that the threat of punishment is a significant deterrent, and that removing it would result in dramatically higher rates of drug use. Drug warriors also argue that the war on drugs makes narcotics more difficult to obtain and raises the price of drugs, both of which, they believe, deter their use (e.g., see Walters, 2002). In fact, it is difficult to predict whether drug use would increase or decrease if the state took a hands-off approach to drug law enforcement. In some instances, decriminalization has led to an increase in rates of use; in others, it has not (see Nadlemann, 1997, p. 304). We think it is possible that experimental and recreational drug use would increase, perhaps temporarily, under such a decriminalization scheme.[9] But it is drug abuse—the uncontrolled and destructive use of drugs (legal and illegal)—that worries us, and there is significant evidence that harm reduction policies and decriminalization are a more effective and humane approach than punishing drug users while creating the very social conditions that encourage drug abuse. In fact, making the kinds of social investments discussed earlier—including health care, clean needles, drug treatment, and medical services—significantly reduces the harm that is associated with drug abuse and may reduce the incidence of drug abuse as well.

The Dutch experience provides support for this argument. In the Netherlands, the use of cannabis is largely ignored, and the use of hard drugs is treated as a social and health problem. Under this decriminalization model, the government ensures that the appropriate services are available to those with serious drug problems. Furthermore, through their more developed welfare state, the Dutch provide basic housing, nutritional and medical services to all, thereby addressing the social conditions that exacerbate drug problems and reducing the incentive to get involved in the drug trade (Cohen, 1997). Decriminalization has not given rise to high rates of drug use or abuse in the Netherlands. In fact, the consumption of cannabis products declined following their decriminalization in the 1970s. Although the incidence of marijuana smoking subsequently increased some, the percentage of people ever having used marijuana is still lower in the Netherlands than it is in the United States. More importantly, the incidence of heroin use remains quite low, and crack is nearly absent in that country. Finally, the Dutch government's efforts to ensure that those who inject drugs use clean needles means that rates of infectious disease remain quite low (Cohen, 1997; Nadlemann, 1997; Reinarman & Levine, 1997a, pp. 288-315).

Opponents of decriminalization argue that the Dutch experience is unique and does not apply to the United States (e.g., see Wilson, 1993). It is true that the historical evidence from our own experience is contradictory. On one hand, alcohol use did increase after the repeal of Prohibition, suggesting that the ban on alcohol consumption had some deterrent effect. On the other hand, the incidence of marijuana use did not increase in states that decriminalized marijuana in the 1970s (Nadlemann, 1997, p. 304; see also D. Anderson, 1998).

It is also true that important differences between the United States and the Netherlands exist, and that the precise impact of decriminalization on rates of drug use cannot be predicted. Nevertheless, there is strong evidence that such a policy would reduce the harm associated with drug abuse without leading to unacceptable levels of drug use. The alternative is not an attractive one: The zero-tolerance approach has not reduced serious drug abuse, has led to the incarceration of many whose main problem is their addiction to drugs, has left many of these individuals without access to treatment and services that might enable them to establish control over their drug habit (and their lives), and has cost the states millions of dollars in the process. The harm reduction model, including the decriminalization of drug use, offers a more humane and effective way of addressing the problem of drug abuse and reducing our nation's overcrowded prisons and jails. This approach would also provide a useful framework for rethinking the criminalization of prostitution, gambling, and other consensual crimes.

Alternative Sentencing

The enormous and ever-increasing cost of incarcerating over 2 million people—the majority of whom have committed nonviolent offenses—has led some to advocate the use of intermediate sanctions, such as boot camps, house arrest, intensive supervision, and electronic monitoring. Advocates of such programs point out that they are significantly cheaper than incarceration and offer judges a wider range of options when making sentencing decisions (Tonry, 1997). Unfortunately, most of these programs only provide new ways of supervising and controlling offenders, and it is not surprising that they do not lower rates of recidivism (Cullen, Wright, & Applegate, 1996). Nor do these programs challenge the notion that by depriving offenders of their liberty, the wrongs they committed have been redressed and justice has been done.

More promising, from our perspective, are programs aimed at "restoring justice." Restorative justice programs derive their theoretical inspiration from early European and indigenous procedures for resolving disputes. In these systems, crimes are treated as wrongs against individuals rather than against the state. Restorative justice programs therefore stress making amends to victims rather than retribution for offenders. In the words of one proponent, restorative justice emphasizes "the importance of elevating crime victims and community members, holding offenders directly accountable to the people they violate, restoring emotional and material losses of victims, and providing a range of opportunities for dialogue, negotiation, and problem solving" (Umbreit, 1998). Toward these ends, restorative justice conferences allow victims a meaningful role in the dispute resolution process and are aimed at allowing offenders to make amends to those they harmed and identifying offenders' needs (Umbreit, 1998).

Interest in restorative justice has grown tremendously in recent years. Programs based on its ideals have spread throughout Europe and are especially popular in Australia and New Zealand. In the United States, victim-offender mediation (a component of restorative justice programs) is being practiced in more than 290 communities. In 1994, the Vermont Department of Corrections identified 50% of their probation caseload that they believed should be dealt with by Reparative Probation Community Boards made up of citizen volunteers. As of 1998, 15 states had drafted or proposed legislation promoting restorative justice programs within their juvenile justice systems (Umbreit, 1998).

Although most of these programs are quite new, some early results of the first evaluation studies are trickling in. Preliminary results from the Reintegrative Shaming Experiments in Australia, for example, suggest that restorative justice conferences were more satisfying to victims, more emotionally intense for offenders, and perceived as more fair by both victims and offenders than traditional court procedures (Sherman, 1998). Analyses of outcomes in other locales are also positive, reporting victim and offender satisfaction, reduced victim fear and anxiety, more successful completion of restitution agreements, and reduced offender recidivism (Umbreit, 1998).

Thus, the available evidence suggests that restorative justice programs offer an attractive alternative to traditional criminal justice solutions to a variety of crimes and, if adopted, would help to reduce our nation's overcrowded prisons and jails. However, it is important to keep in mind that, in and of themselves, restorative justice programs do not reduce the scope of criminal law (only decriminalization of consensual crimes can do this). Nor do these programs do anything to alter the social conditions (especially concentrated poverty in racially segregated communities) that underlie our most serious crime problems. Still, with these caveats in mind, restorative justice programs appear to provide a promising means of settling disputes while reducing our reliance on institutions that incarcerate.

Rehabilitating Reintegration

Not all offenders can or should be dealt with in alternative venues such as restorative justice programs. But for those who serve terms in prison, we need to place greater emphasis on reintegration into society after release. Despite the fact that most of those in prison will eventually leave, very little emphasis is now placed on the need to facilitate their reintegration into society. The current tendency to ignore the reintegration process marks a significant shift in penal policy.

For much of the 20th century, a philosophy called "penal welfarism" served as the foundation of our penal system (Garland, 1985; Rothman, 1980). According to this philosophy, deviant behavior is at least partially caused by factors beyond the control of individual actors, but the nature of these factors varies from case to case. Criminal justice practitioners therefore identified rehabilitation—defined as the use of "individualized, corrective measures adapted to the specific case or the particular problem"—as the most appropriate response to deviant behavior (Garland, 1995, p. 187). The rehabilitative paradigm certainly did not preclude the use of incarceration, but juvenile justice, probation, and parole institutions were aimed at keeping those deemed "reformed" or "reformable" out of prison. And although efforts to "treat" or "correct" inmates were often underfunded and misguided, the possibility that offenders might be rehabilitated served as the primary ideological justification for incarceration (Garland, 1995, p. 187).

The situation is quite different today. Rehabilitation is no longer the primary rationale for incarceration, probation, or parole, and this is why relatively little emphasis is now placed on reintegrating prison inmates back into society (Donziger, 1996, pp. 191-193; Irwin & Austin, 1997, chap. 5). The rehabilitative approach was flawed in many ways, but it is also clear that the new approach does not work well. Despite increased efforts to supervise and control offenders in the community, rates of recidivism remain quite high for probationers, and they are even higher for those released from prison, whether directly into society or onto parole (Irwin & Austin, 1997, pp. 118-125; Simon, 1993; Walker, 1994, pp. 210-216). In addition, the new emphasis on supervision and surveillance has meant that more and more parolees are being readmitted to prison for violating the technical conditions of their parole programs. These high rates of revocation for technical violations have made an important contribution to the expansion of the prison population.[10]

So many ex-prisoners, parolees, and probationers are rearrested primarily because the social circumstances that led them to stray from the straight and narrow in the first place have not improved—and in many cases, have worsened. In addition, because employers are reluctant to hire ex-cons, incarceration makes it even more unlikely that ex-offenders will obtain legal work and, therefore, more likely that they will reoffend.[11] High rates of recidivism may also reflect the propensity of the police to "round up the usual suspects," that is, people known to have a criminal record (Irwin & Austin, 1997). Therefore, addressing the social conditions into which offenders are released and reducing our reliance on the criminal justice system as a way of dealing with minor offenders might lower rates of recidivism.

There is also reason to suspect that programs aimed at improving the reintegration of former prisoners would lower rates of recidivism. Ex-convicts face what has been called the "reentry problem": the task of surmounting the psychological, social, and financial consequences of incarceration and reintegrating into mainstream society (Irwin & Austin, 1997, pp. 125-131). Providing needed social services (including drug treatment, counseling, education, and vocational training) to inmates, parolees, and some probationers would facilitate the reentry process.[12] A study of people sentenced to intensive probation, for example, found that offenders who received drug treatment and other social services had lower rates of recidivism than those who were subjected to intensive supervision but did not receive such services (Petersilia & Turner, 1990).[13] Because the ability to find stable, legal work is a crucial component of the reintegration process, services aimed at helping ex-offenders find decent jobs and policies that encourage employers to hire them would also reduce rates of recidivism. For example, one experimental program—the Violent Juvenile Offender program—was aimed at reintegrating violent young offenders by strengthening their ties to family and work, and it was quite successful in reducing recidivism.[14]

In sum, the current emphasis on surveillance and rule enforcement in probation and parole offices increases the likelihood that offenders will be reincarcerated but fails to address the causes of their offending. Significant declines in spending on education,[15] vocational training, and drug treatment[16] within prisons also leaves many ex-convicts without the resources and capacities to deal effectively with the challenge of reentering society. Providing job training for prisoners, creating and locating jobs for probationers and ex-prisoners, subsidizing low wages, and providing incentives for employers to hire probationers and former prisoners would all increase the ability of ex-cons to sustain themselves through legal employment.[17]

Toward Disarmament

As was discussed in Chapter 3, the extraordinary availability of guns has made a significant contribution to high rates of homicide in the United

States. Americans fight, rob, and attack each other about as often as people living in other industrialized countries. But when we do, we often use guns, especially handguns.[18] And although we do not necessarily intend to kill, the ubiquity of guns and our willingness to use them means that, often, we do.[19]

The National Rifle Association spends millions of dollars every year representing the interests of gun owners (and, some would argue, the gun industry) (Hornblower, 1998, p. 45). These advertising, public relations, and lobbying efforts result in the dissemination of a great deal of anti-gun control propaganda. Much educational and political work is needed to heighten the public's awareness of the role of guns in producing distinctively high rates of lethal violence in the United States. People need to be informed, for example, that more than 75% of all murders in the United States involve guns, and that many of these are the unintended consequence of fights and assaults, often between acquaintances and family members. Heightening popular awareness of these basic facts about gun violence would be a first step in changing cultural attitudes and public policy about guns.

In the long term, getting as many guns out of circulation as possible is one of the best ways we can reduce lethal violence.[20] The question is how to do this. Scholars in the field distinguish between laws that regulate the sale, possession, and use of guns, and laws that ban the possession of handguns altogether. Laws regulating guns by restricting their sale, purchase, and ownership are common but vary tremendously across the United States. Most of these laws are designed to keep guns out of the hands of juveniles or people with a history of mental illness or criminal records. The 1993 Brady Bill, for example, requires a 5-day waiting period so that officials can check the records of all prospective gun buyers.

This strategy clearly has not kept guns out of the hands of the "bad guys." Between 500,000 and 750,000 illegal gun transactions occur every year (Walker, 1994, p. 189; see also Zimring & Hawkins, 1997, pp. 200-201), and studies report that only one sixth of all gun-using felons acquired their guns through legal transactions (Walker, 1994). Furthermore, restrictions on the sale and ownership of guns have not reduced overall gun ownership. Thus, even if gun regulations did keep guns out of the hands of the "bad guys," they would not do anything to prevent the many unplanned and unintended homicides committed by people without criminal records or histories of mental illness.

Some have responded to the obvious failure of existing gun regulations by arguing for more intensified enforcement of these regulations and more severe punishment of those who violate gun laws. Evaluations of such efforts report mixed results. For example, the Kansas City Gun Experiment, which involved intensive police efforts to locate and seize illegal firearms, reportedly led to a decline in serious violence (Sherman & Rogan, 1995).[21] In other cities, however, it is not clear that such efforts have reduced violence (Walker, 1994, pp. 191-194).

Recognizing the limited effectiveness of gun restrictions and regulations, some cities have banned handguns altogether. In 1975, for example, the District of Columbia banned the purchase, sale, transfer, and possession of most handguns. The city of Chicago also bans the sale and ownership of handguns. The evidence from follow-up studies suggests that these citywide bans have not appreciably reduced lethal violence. Opponents of gun control use these findings to argue that bans on gun ownership do not work (Walker, 1994, p. 185). Another interpretation of the failure of the citywide gun bans is that, to be effective, a ban would have to be federal (otherwise, people can simply buy their guns in neighboring jurisdictions).

But calls for a federal ban on handgun ownership are quite controversial. Opponents point out that even if a federal ban on handguns were adopted, there would still be nearly 200 million guns in circulation, and many gun owners would not turn in their weapons simply because a ban was passed. Both illegal gun ownership and the black market in guns would continue to exist. A federally funded gun "buy-back" campaign appears to be the most promising way to address these problems. City-sponsored buy-backs have been implemented and been somewhat successful in reducing the number of guns in circulation.[22] Although even a federally funded, enthusiastically promoted buy-back campaign would not get all guns out of circulation, it would significantly reduce their numbers and, as a result, the number of people killed by firearms would diminish (Skolnick & Bayley, 1986).

Community Policing

In recent years, "community policing" has received a great deal of attention. Although not well defined, the label generally refers to efforts to increase interaction between officers and citizens, including foot patrols, community substations, and sponsorship of block clubs and neighborhood watches. The hope is that such interactions will increase the amount of information officers receive, which will, in turn, help them to locate and address criminal wrongdoing. To varying degrees, community policing also aims to increase the ability of citizens to direct police activity. In its most progressive versions, community policing aims at "coproduction," a situation in which citizens and officers are coequal partners in planning crime control and neighborhood improvement activities (Skolnick & Bayley, 1986).

Coproduction has proven to be an elusive goal. Even when community policing is officially adopted, officers prefer to view citizens as simply their "eyes and ears": sources of information about what occurs in neighborhoods when the patrol cars are not around. Citizens, in other words, are seen not as coequal partners, but as junior deputies in police-sponsored crime control efforts (Sadd & Grinc, 1994). To the extent that this is the case, the potential for democratic oversight of the police is eliminated.

The emergence and popularity of three other developments in policing threaten to further reduce the potential democratizing impact of community policing. The first is known as "problem-solving policing." Here, the goal is to transform the police from a reactive force—one that simply responds to 911 calls after incidents have already occurred—to a proactive one. Proactive police officers attempt to discern patterns of criminal activity and eliminate them. For example, if officers analyze crime data and learn that many cars are being stolen in a particular neighborhood, they might saturate the area with patrols to deter criminals and catch more suspects. Despite the popularity of this approach, research suggests that the number of patrol officers and proactive policing strategies have little effect on crime rates (see Walker, 1994, p. 77).

The second major reform movement goes by several names—broken windows, order maintenance, quality of life, and zero tolerance. The origins of this movement can be traced to the influential argument that broken windows and other instances of disorder are important causes of crime. According to this view, signs of disorder—like unfixed broken windows—diminish residents' responsibility for their neighborhood, which leads to a progressive growth of wrongdoing. This theory, which has been challenged by recent research (Harcourt, 1998), implies that policing should focus on maintaining order and preserving a high quality of life to reduce crime. In New York City, this emphasis led to zero tolerance for any behaviors and people classified as disorderly, such as the streetside "squeegie men" who clean windshields for cash.

NYPD officials and former New York City Mayor Rudolph Giuliani have argued that these tactics are responsible for declining crime rates in New York City. Although these declines have been significant, studies suggest that a number of factors have contributed to the drop in crime that has occurred in New York City and elsewhere. As noted in Chapter 8, these include demographic changes and declining unemployment levels (National Institute of Justice, 1997). A study sponsored by the Justice Department provides further evidence that the decline of the crack cocaine market has also been important, a finding that helps to explain why the homicide rate has dropped in Los Angeles and other cities that have not adopted the zero tolerance approach but whose crack markets have shrunk, and increased in cities that have not experienced a decline in crack use and sales (Butterfield, 1997a).

There are also political problems with problem-oriented and zero tolerance policing. Unlike the more democratic versions of community policing, neither of these police strategies allows for citizen oversight of the police. In addition, these strategies continue to emphasize arrests and the threat of punishment as solutions to crime. This is most obvious with zero tolerance policing, which sets officers loose on any number of (potential) troublemakers. In New York City, order maintenance has meant a 50% increase in misdemeanor arrests. A disproportionate number of those arrested for petty crimes (such as vagrancy, disorderly conduct, and loitering) are black and Latino (Butterfield, 1997a). And it is no surprise that complaints about overaggressive officers increased significantly in zero tolerance New York (Butterfield, 1997a).[23]

Finally, one of the most significant changes in policing has been the addition of paramilitary (SWAT) teams in police departments around the country. Encouraged by federal grants and asset forfeiture laws, many police departments formed paramilitary units. The initial impetus for this development was the war on drugs. The deployment of paramilitary units has increased tenfold since the early 1980s. A recent survey found that 90% of police departments in cities with populations greater than 50,000 and 75% of those in cities with populations under 50,000 now have paramilitary units. Many of these units are known to be particularly aggressive. Critics also argue that the widespread use of paramilitary units for drug arrests, suicide threats, and even the serving of warrants symbolizes the fact that the war on crime is a war on our own citizens (Egan, 1999a).

In sum, despite all the talk about community policing, policing practices have become more aggressive and often keep the community in a very passive position vis-à-vis the police. The more democratic versions of community policing that enhance citizen oversight of the police, combined with independent, civilian-run police review boards, offer a more promising alternative than the aggressive tactics of the NYPD and the paramilitary units that now operate around the country.

Conclusion

The policies just described offer alternative ways of addressing crime in the United States. Ultimately, whether or not these and other policy alternatives are explored and implemented will depend on political action. In the current context, many politicians—especially at the federal level—are reluctant to challenge get-tough policies for fear of being labeled "soft on crime." This fear prevents any rational discussion or criticism of current anticrime policies and is a significant obstacle to change.

The only way politicians will reconsider the policies associated with the war on crime is if they are convinced that there is popular support for doing so. As was discussed in previous chapters, there are growing signs that this is the case. Groups and organizations across the country are challenging the policies and priorities of the war on crime, and a more careful analysis of public opinion polls shows that many Americans favor policies that address the social causes of crime. There are also signs that the elite consensus favoring current crime policies is breaking down. Many federal judges, for example, have registered their opposition to mandatory sentencing laws for drug offenders, and some prominent conservatives are openly critical of the war on drugs. These developments are quite promising, for it is only political opposition to the war on crime and drugs that will lead policymakers to rethink their conviction that enhancing punishment is the best solution to social problems such as crime and drug use.

Notes

Chapter 1

1. The quotations from Harold Richard and Derrick Ross are verbatim from this article; the rest of Sabrina's story is paraphrased.
2. For white males, the lifetime likelihood of incarceration is 4.4%.
3. In 2001, in addition to those serving time in state and federal prisons, 73,000 women were locked away in local jails. Thus, the total number of women behind bars in that year was more than 167,000 (Bureau of Justice Statistics, 2002a).

Chapter 2

1. Neither the NCVS nor the UCR measures the kinds of crimes that are committed by the rich or powerful, such as embezzlement, fraud, violations of health and safety regulations, and so forth.
2. The percentage of victims of violent crime who reported their victimization to the police increased from 44.2% in 1978 to 49.8% in 1992. See McCord (1997).
3. For a review of this literature, see O'Brien (1996). Although most agree that homicide statistics are fairly reliable, there are a significant number of missing persons whose fate is never determined, and some unknown number of these people are undoubtedly murder victims (Windelsham, 1998).
4. However, some scholars still use the UCR data to support their argument that crime—especially violent crime—is far more common today than in previous decades. See especially Currie (1998).
5. See Kurki (1997), p. 4. Of the five countries that participated in all three surveys administered since 1988, only the United States shows consistent decreases in the crime rate.
6. See Currie (1998) for a critique of this argument.

Chapter 3

1. In 2001, average black family income was 62% of average white family income; average Hispanic family income was 64%. U.S. Census Bureau, "Historical Income Tables–Families." www.census.gov/hhes/income/histinc/incfamdet.html.
2. James Gilligan (1996), however, provides a rather compelling account of the unmediated role of relative deprivation in the production of violence.
3. For an explication of this type of approach, see Sampson (1997), pp. 31-77.

4. For a discussion of the relevance of Shaw and McKay's work for contemporary research, see Sampson and Wilson (1995).

5. Sullivan defines high poverty areas as neighborhoods in which at least 30% of residents are poor.

6. Significantly, Sampson found that the percentage of households headed by a female was also significantly related to serious crime among whites.

7. Because segregation concentrates disadvantage, shifts in black poverty rates comparable with those observed during the 1970s have the power to transform the socioeconomic character of poor black neighborhoods very rapidly and dramatically, changing a low-income black community from a place where welfare-dependent, female-headed families are a minority to one where they are the norm, producing high rates of crime, property abandonment, mortality and educational failure. (Massey, 1990, p. 329)

8. The authors point out that New York City and Washington, DC, have larger-than-average drug industries. They estimate that, nationwide, drug-related homicides comprise 10% to 25% of all homicides (p. 144).

9. "Dissed" as in "disrespected."

Chapter 4

1. Civil rights activists did break southern state laws, but they did so to draw attention to the unconstitutionality of those laws. Thus, it is not clear that these civil rights tactics can be described accurately as "criminal," or even as "civil disobedience."

2. Quoted in Baker (1983), p. 245. On the stump, Wallace often concluded with the more baldly racist formulation, "[He] didn't get any watermelon to eat when he was 10 years old" (quoted in Carter, 1995, p. 313).

3. On the "culture of poverty," see Lewis (1969).

4. Katz and others show that the focus on the alleged misbehaviors of the poor has been central to their reconstruction as an undeserving underclass. See also Gans (1995); Morris (1994); and Schram (1995).

5. Nixon, no less than his strategists, understood the significance of symbolic communication. Looking ahead to the 1972 campaign, he instructed his aides to "scrape away all the crap and just pick three issues that will give us a sharp image." The aides "shouldn't be concerned if it is something we will actually accomplish. . . . Rather, we should look in terms of how we create issues. We need an enemy" (Carter, 1995, p. 398).

6. See also Wright (1985), pp. 35-37, for a discussion of other innovative techniques used by the Nixon administration to create the impression that the rate of crime was decreasing.

7. As Zimring and Hawkins point out, the traditional allocation of crime control responsibilities "is one in which the federal government plays a distant

secondary role to that of the states and local governments." But because the Harrison Narcotics Act established federal responsibility for the enforcement of narcotics laws, the federal government has played an important role in drug control throughout the 20th century (see Zimring & Hawkins, 1992, pp. 160-161). Heymann and Moore also note that the regulation of alcohol and other drugs has played an important role in expanding the scope of federal criminal jurisdiction (Heymann & Moore, 1996, p. 105).

8. The adoption of this line of reasoning helps to account for the Nixon administration's somewhat surprising support for methadone maintenance programs, aimed largely at reducing the likelihood that addicts would steal to finance their habit.

9. In fact, the resources of federal drug enforcement agencies increased from $65 million to $719 million between 1969 and 1975 (Baum, 1996, p. 75).

10. Only when faced with "exigent circumstances"—a situation in which a suspect may have concealed a weapon or been able to easily destroy evidence— were law enforcement agents permitted to seize evidence without a warrant (Davey, 1995).

11. However, Bertram et al. (1996) point out that although Presidents Ford, Carter, and (later) Clinton did not emphasize the crime and drug issues, neither did they attempt to reverse the expansion of the criminal justice system or issue any fundamental challenge to the logic of the wars on crime and drugs. Drug law enforcement budgets, for example, continued to increase and reached $855 million by 1980 (Bertram et al., 1996, p. 110). The fact that criminal justice institutions continued to expand during these times of relative political quiet, they argue, reveals the ability of those bureaucracies with law enforcement responsibilities to influence the political agenda:

> When Presidents such as Nixon, Reagan and Bush wanted to escalate drug enforcement, this drug control apparatus provided them with a firm basis and allies. . . . But even during times of relative calm . . . the drug control bureaucracy has exerted pressures to sustain and even expand the drug war. (Bertram et al., 1996, p. 126)

12. For a review of this literature, see Hannon and DeFronzo (1998).

13. For an extended discussion of the "crack panic" of 1986, see Reinarman and Levine (1989) and Beckett and Sasson (1997).

14. According to one study, despite the fact that assault weapons are used in only a fraction of all gun murders, the Crime Bill's ban on these weapons contributed to an estimated 6.7% decline in total gun murders between 1994 and 1995 (The Urban Institute, cited in Windelsham, 1998, p. 123).

15. Windelsham further argues that ultimately, the Congressional Black Caucus's main accomplishment was to sustain funding for prevention efforts, minimal as it was.

16. A copy of this unpublished survey may be obtained from the authors.

17. For example, a *Washington Post*-ABC News Poll found that 39% of those polled trusted the Democrats to handle the crime problem; 32% had more faith in the Republicans. See Poveda (1994), p. 76.

18. A small group of liberal Democrats in the Senate did propose an alternative package aimed at improving police training, abolishing mandatory sentencing statutes, and tightening gun restrictions. Members of the Congressional Black Caucus also criticized this proposed legislation, especially its rejection of the Racial Justice Act, which would have allowed defendants to use evidence of racial bias to challenge their death sentences. Neither of these efforts was ultimately successful.

Chapter 5

1. On crime coverage in Denver, Colorado, see Colomy and Greiner (n.d.); on Boston, Massachusetts, see Sasson (1998); on crime waves in general, see Fishman (1978).

2. The local news study examined three stations in Chicago, Illinois, between December 1989 and May 1990 (see Entman, 1992). The network news study examined 30 days of coverage on ABC, CBS, and NBC in 1990 (see Entman, 1994).

3. For example, one study examined opinion columns published in six metropolitan newspapers from 1990 through 1991. The frame that attributed crime to failures of the criminal justice system was expressed in 55% of the columns. The frames that attributed crime to either poverty or family breakdown were each visible in about one third of the columns (see Sasson, 1995b). Studies of news weeklies report coverage that is even more one-sided in favor of the "faulty system" perspective (see Barlow, 1998; Elias, 1993).

4. Indeed, Ericson et al. (1991) estimate that the proportion of news stories that focused on "deviance and control" was about 45% in newspapers, between 47% and 60% on television, and between 64% and 71% on the radio (pp. 239-242).

5. Lichter and his colleagues base their findings on a random sample of 620 prime-time television shows broadcast between 1955 and 1986. Comparisons to real-world crime draw upon the highly problematic Uniform Crime Reports of the FBI (see Chapter 2). Estimates of real-world crime that draw upon victimization surveys are higher, but even when these data were used as points of comparison, the "television rate for violent crimes was fifteen times higher" (Lichter et al., 1994, p. 276).

6. For example, roughly 1% of all felony arrests are rejected due to violations of the exclusionary rule (see Currie, 1985, pp. 66-67).

7. Of the series *NYPD Blue, Homicide: Life on the Streets,* and *Law and Order,* the UCLA team comments as follows: "The three series . . . are

commendable because they achieve a high level of grittiness and excitement without overemphasizing violence."

8. Reality-based police shows were popular in other countries before their introduction to the United States (see Cavender & Fishman, 1998).

9. On voyeurism in relation to reality-based programs, see also Andersen (1995), pp. 174-210, and Donovan (1998).

10. Several researchers have failed, in part or entirely, to replicate Carlson's findings (see Jeffres & Perloff, 1997).

11. In these studies, "light viewers" are those who watch up to 2 hours per day of television (see Morgan & Signorielli, 1990).

Chapter 6

1. Copyright 1994, Time Inc. Reprinted by permission.

2. For a discussion of the rationality of fear of crime, see Sparks (1992a).

3. For general discussions of the public's propensity to name crime as the nation's most serious problem, see Chambliss (1994), Roberts and Stalans (1997), and Warr (1995).

4. Because levels of public concern about crime and drugs vary with levels of elite political initiative on those issues, sorting out which side is leading and which is following is quite difficult. In this study, four case studies of month-by-month shifts in political initiative and public concern show that sudden drops in political attention to the crime and drug issues cannot be explained by prior shifts in levels of public concern but are followed by declining levels of public concern (see Beckett, 1994).

5. On the crush of political and media attention to crime in 1993-1994, also see Poveda (1994).

6. Participants in the focus group discussions were drawn from neighborhood crime watch groups. For a description of the sample and research methodology, see Sasson (1995b), especially Chapter 2.

7. On individualism and self-reliance as core values in American political culture, see Bellah, Madsen, Sullivan, Swidler, and Tipton (1985); Carbaugh (1988); de Tocqueville (1981); Gamson (1992); and Gans (1988).

8. Zimring and Hawkins (1997) describe the consequences of "categorical contagion" in this way: "The fear generated by the kidnap and murder of Polly Klaas in California provokes long sentences for residential burglars because the burglar in the citizen's scenario has acquired the characteristics of Polly Klaas's killer" (pp. 12-13).

9. See discussion in Chapter 5. News exposés on the failures of the justice system probably contribute to the public's tendency to overestimate rates of recidivism and underestimate the justice system's propensity to incarcerate (see Roberts, 1992, pp. 109-121).

10. In a comparison between sentencing preferences of jurors and judges in Chicago, researchers found jurors more willing than judges to assign probation alone, or probation and jail, as alternatives to prison time (see Diamond &

Stalans, 1989). For a thorough review of the evidence on the relative severity of the public versus the courts, see Roberts and Stalans (1997), pp. 210-212.

11. For a more detailed discussion of popular slogans and catch-phrases as instances of media discourse, see Gamson (1992) and Sasson (1995b).

12. The researchers performed multiple regression analyses on the survey data to test the possibility that the correlation between punitiveness and opposition to civil rights might be spurious, that is, a consequence of some third variable (such as region or political orientation) associated with both racial prejudice and punitiveness. The correlation, however, survived all statistical controls.

13. "Crime prevention" in this case included "community education" and "youth programs."

14. Interestingly, this "social breakdown" perspective is also widespread in England; see Loader, Girling, and Sparks (1998).

15. In response to the question, "Once people who commit crimes are in prison, which of the following do you think should be the most important goal of prison?" 48.4% chose "rehabilitation," 14.6% chose "punishment," and 33.1% chose "crime prevention/deterrence" (see Maguire & Pastore, 1997, Table 2.6).

16. The national survey is cited in Ellsworth and Gross (1994). The statewide surveys, administered between 1985 and 1989, posed the following question: "Suppose convicted first-degree murderers in this state could be sentenced to life in prison without parole and also be required to work in prison for money that would go to the families of their victims. Would you prefer this as an alternative to the death penalty?" Evidence from these surveys also suggests that the public would be willing to accept parole of first-degree murderers after at least 25 years if an offender has fully met the restitution requirement (see Bowers, 1993).

17. On the importance of symbolically communicating societal disapproval, see also Gaubatz (1995) and Kahan (1996).

18. Black and white punitiveness do not necessarily stem from the same sources. One statistical analysis finds that black punitiveness correlates with fear of crime, whereas white punitiveness correlates with racial prejudice (see Cohn et al., 1991). On the slight convergence of black and white attitudes on crime control, see Secret and Johnson (1989).

19. This is an expanded version of the transcript of the same session found in Sasson (1995a), pp. 268, 271.

Chapter 7

1. By contrast, the Kennedy administration's "War on Poverty" programs of the 1960s allocated federal funds to groups attempting to ameliorate the social conditions—especially "blocked opportunities"—that were believed to give rise to crime and delinquency (see Rosenbaum, 1988, p. 352).

2. Others argue that the ascendance of the crime issue on the local political agenda is a product of the increasing crime rate. To support this argument, researchers point out that the Uniform Crime Reports (UCR) data do indeed

show an increase in crime at the same time that urbanites became more likely to identify crime as an important problem in their communities (see Jacob & Lineberry, 1983). As was discussed in Chapter 2, however, this argument becomes more difficult to sustain if one looks at victimization survey data rather than the estimates provided by the UCR.

3. For slightly different versions of this argument, see Crawford (1995) and Garland (1996).

4. For this reason, Garland refers to such appeals to community as part of the process of "responsibilization"—an effort to shift the responsibility for the crime problem away from the state (see Garland, 1996).

5. A more recent iteration of this theory appears in Kelling and Coles (1996).

6. For an extended discussion of these and other criticisms of the "broken windows" approach, see Herbert (in press).

7. This perception may be fairly accurate in the case of burglary, which is emphasized in the Neighborhood Watch literature, but it is a less accurate view for crimes such as homicide, domestic violence, and child abuse.

8. Research suggests that these perceptions are accurate: Because of increased unemployment, the expansion of the drug trade, and massive levels of incarceration in black communities, kinship networks and community authority figures have been substantially weakened (see Anderson, 1990; Wilson, 1996).

9. As Shapiro (1997) points out, the existence of this alternative to the criminal justice system is often ignored by victim rights activists, who seek to expand the rights of the victim in criminal proceedings.

10. Many "restorative justice" programs, for example, seek to replace the current emphasis on punishment with the goal of compensating the victims for the harm done to them.

11. This announcement came as something of a surprise. In February 1997, following the completion of a sixth federally funded study of needle exchange programs (NEPs) concluding that NEPs helped to prevent the spread of HIV and other blood-borne diseases and do not increase drug use, Health and Human Services Secretary Donna Shalala had announced her support for NEPs. Apparently, concerns about being labeled "soft on drugs" led the administration to refuse to lift the federal ban at the last minute (see "Flat Earth AIDS Policy," 1998; "Inside the Beltway," 1997).

Chapter 8

1. Among high school seniors, more than 1 in 3 reported marijuana use and 1 in 12 reported use of either PCP (angel dust) or LSD (see Maguire & Pastore, 2002, Tables 3.72, 3.91, 3.92).

2. The NIDA surveys are of households and thus ignore institutionalized people and the homeless, among whom are a disproportionate number of drug addicts. Therefore, it may be the case that during the 1980s, drug dealing and

using became more flagrant or destructive among the hard-core addict population. A rise in the number of cocaine-related emergency room visits coinciding with the 1980s crack epidemic suggests this possibility (see Currie, 1993; Tonry, 1995). The drug war, however, was not a "surgical strike" aimed at this relatively small portion of the population of a handful of major cities. Instead, it was aimed more or less indiscriminately at all users and dealers, especially, as we shall see, at those who reside in minority, inner-city neighborhoods.

3. Tonry (1995, chap. 3) reviews a wider range of surveys and arrives at the same conclusions.

4. In recent survey years, for example, cocaine use during the past 30 days was reported by 0.8% of white, 1% of black, and 1.1% of Hispanic respondents. Similarly, marijuana use during the past 30 days was reported by 3% of white, 3.5% of black, and 2.8% of Hispanic respondents (Maguire & Pastore, 1997, Tables 3.72, 3.76). Among high school students, ethnic differences are somewhat more pronounced, with black students less likely than their white and Hispanic counterparts to be regular users of cocaine and several other illegal drugs (e.g., see Maguire & Pastore, 1999, Table 3.68).

5. Notably, the conservatives and civil libertarians converged in their critiques of rehabilitation. Libertarians, however, believed a system of "just punishment" would imprison fewer people for shorter stretches, whereas conservatives viewed "just punishment" as a way to end what they perceived to be the permissiveness of a rehabilitation-oriented prison system. For a discussion of these issues, see Tonry (1996).

6. Fifty federal judges, many of them conservative Reagan administration appointees, have refused to hear drug cases (Elikann, 1996, p. 97).

7. Defenders of the harsh penalties for crack argued that the substance was peculiarly destructive, as discussed in Chapter 4. As numerous scholars have pointed out, however, drug prohibition laws have historically derived their impetus from popular anxieties about racial minorities (see Bertram et al., 1996).

8. To be convicted under the "second strike" provision, only the first felony need be serious (see Clark et al., 1997).

9. Between 1977 and 1999, 12 people who committed their crimes while they were children were executed in the United States. During the same period, at least 30 mentally retarded prisoners were put to death (Amnesty International, 1998b).

10. As Peterson and Bailey (1998) conclude in their comprehensive review of the literature,

> the empirical evidence does not support the belief that capital punishment was an effective deterrent for murder in past years. Nor is there any indication that returning to our past execution practices [e.g., executing people more often and more quickly] would have any deterrent effect on the current homicide problem. (p. 83)

11. For a review of the literature on deterrence and the death penalty, see Bailey and Peterson (1997).

12. Notably, as calculated by Cook and Laub (1998), the homicide commission rate for teenage African American males more than tripled between 1985 and 1991. Cook and Laub further point out that, although the share of violent crimes "cleared" by arrest of a juvenile was only slightly higher in 1994 (13%) than in 1975 through 1979 (12%), the proportion of young people in the population was significantly smaller. This observation implies a higher rate of juvenile offending in the late 1980s and early 1990s.

13. The female proportion of the state inmate population grew from 4% to 6%, the Hispanic proportion from 10% to 17%, and the black proportion from 47% to 51%. The proportion of state inmates who are white dropped from 52% to 47% (see Beck, 1999, pp. 47-48; see also Maguire & Pastore, 2002, Tables 6.29 and 6.3).

14. On annual prison census days, the percentage of state prisoners serving time for violent crimes dropped from 59% in 1980 to 47% in 1995 (see Beck, 1999, p. 49). The difference between these two measures of prison populations is due to the tendency of violent offenders to serve longer terms and therefore to accumulate within prisons.

15. "On any day, almost 200,000 people behind bars—more than 1 in 10 of the total—are known to suffer from schizophrenia, manic depression or major depression, the three most severe mental illnesses" (Butterfield, 1998, p. A1). Similarly, Elliott Currie (1998) notes that 7% to 15% of California jail inmates and 8% to 20% of prison inmates are seriously mentally ill.

16. Comparable findings have been reported by government-sponsored panels of social scientists in both Canada and Great Britain; for details, see Tonry (1996), p. 137.

17. On the war on drugs, see Baum (1996); Bertram et al. (1996); Currie (1993); Gray (1998).

18. For more on the "prison-industrial complex" perspective, see Chambliss (1994); Christie (1993); Donziger (1996).

Chapter 9

1. This is true not just in the United States but in other industrialized countries as well. For further evidence of this association, see Currie (1998), pp. 125-130.

2. It is sometimes argued that poor children in the United States are poor compared to their middle- and upper-class counterparts, but not all that poor. In fact, poor children in the United States are considerably worse off than poor children in other industrialized countries (see Currie, 1998, p. 121).

3. See Chapters 15-17 in Reinarman and Levine (1997a).

4. By contrast, alcohol is involved in about 10,000 overdose deaths annually (see Nadlemann, 1997, p. 302).

5. Since 1965, state and local authorities have made more than 11 million marijuana arrests. Federal authorities also make marijuana arrests, and although the exact number is unknown, there may be as many as 10,000 of these per year. The precise number of marijuana offenders who are currently incarcerated is also unknown. Estimates are that between 12% and 15% of the federal prison population—about 15,000 people—are serving time for marijuana violations, and another 21,000 are serving time in state prisons or jails for such offenses (see Schlosser, 1994; Thomas, 1998).

6. Similarly, a recent study published by the National Center on Addiction and Substance Abuse found that although higher-income women were more likely to try illegal drugs, poorer women were more likely to be unable to control their use of illegal substances (Califano, 1996, p. A19).

7. For example, the incidence of Fetal Alcohol Syndrome (FAS) among children of chronically alcoholic mothers is strongly influenced by the social class of the mother—4.5% of the children of upper-middle-class alcoholics, versus 71% of those of poor alcoholic mothers, were diagnosed with FAS (see Bingol et al., 1987).

8. The RAND Corporation study is reported in Sentencing Project (n.d.-h).

9. Decriminalization is not the same thing as legalization. With the former, the state reduces the official penalties for drug law violations, deemphasizes drug law enforcement, and focuses on dealers rather than users. By contrast, legalizing drugs would involve repealing the laws that prohibit the use or sale of controlled substances. Each of these options offers certain advantages and disadvantages. If a policy of decriminalization (combined with the legalization of marijuana) were adopted, the many people whose main problem is drug addiction would not be incarcerated, and the money currently spent to imprison them could be spent on drug abuse prevention and treatment programs. However, under decriminalization, the drugs themselves would remain illegal, and their price would therefore remain artificially high. This means that the drug trade would continue to be regulated through the use of violence (although addressing the complex array of social and economic problems facing urban communities might reduce the numbers of people who are drawn into the drug trade). Furthermore, because drugs other than marijuana would remain illegal, they would be impossible to regulate, and the secondary problems this causes—accidental overdoses, poisonings—would continue. By contrast, the legalization of drugs would eradicate the black market for drugs and, presumably, the violence it spawns. By legalizing drugs, the government would also make possible their regulation (just as alcohol is currently regulated by state and local governments). Furthermore, under legalization, drugs could be taxed, which would generate revenues that could be used to fund drug treatment and prevention (see Nadlemann, 1997; Reinarman & Levine, 1997a, pp. 214-224).

10. Nationwide, parolees returned to prison comprised 12% of all state prison admissions in 1974 but 29% of state prison admissions in 1989 (see Irwin & Austin, 1997, chap. 5; Simon, 1993, p. 210).

11. Both experimental and statistical studies suggest that the employment prospects of job applicants with no criminal record are far better than those of people who were convicted and incarcerated. See Western and Beckett (1999) for a review of these studies. There is also evidence that offenders who are incarcerated are more likely to reoffend than are similar offenders who are convicted but sentenced to probation (see Petersilia & Peterson, 1986).

12. Studies reporting that rehabilitation does not work often group all rehabilitation programs together and, as a result, do not differentiate between successful and unsuccessful programs. By contrast, studies that examine the impact of particular rehabilitation programs suggest that some of these are successful in reducing recidivism (see Cullen, Van Voorhis, & Sundt, 1996).

13. This study also found no correlation between technical violations and new criminal offenses, a finding that challenges the widespread practice of incarcerating those who violate the technical conditions of probation.

14. This success was contingent on the program being fully implemented (see Currie, 1998, p. 168).

15. In 1994, more than half of all states reported that they had made cuts in or eliminated inmate education programs. The 1994 Crime Bill eliminated federal funding for prisoner education. As a result, the number of state prison inmates enrolled in postsecondary education declined from 38,000 to 21,000 (in a population of nearly 1 million) (see Currie, 1998, p. 169).

16. Between 1990 and 1997, the proportion of state prison inmates who received drug treatment declined from 24.5% to 9.7%. Over the same years, the proportion who had been drug users at the time of arrest increased from 50% to 57% (Butterfield, 1999).

17. There is evidence that the ex-convicts' ability to find work or obtain economic assistance reduces rates of recidivism (see Berk & Rauma, 1987).

18. About 70% of all homicide cases known to the police involve firearms. And although only about one third of all guns in circulation are handguns, handguns are used in about three fourths of all deaths caused by firearms (see Zimring & Hawkins, 1997, p. 199).

19. Although serious assaults with knives and other cutting instruments occur about as frequently as serious assaults with firearms, the latter are about five times as likely to result in death (see Zimring & Hawkins, 1997, p. 199).

20. On the importance of guns in the production of high homicide rates and the need for effective gun control, see Zimring and Hawkins (1997). Of course, there are those who argue that widespread gun ownership reduces crime and violence by deterring would-be criminals. One study purporting to demonstrate this examined crime rates in 10 states that passed legislation allowing people to carry concealed weapons between 1977 and 1992. According to this study,

the rate of murder, rape, and aggravated assault dropped in these 10 states after the passage of these laws. The author argues that these drops are a result of would-be criminals being deterred from committing crimes when the would-be victim just might have a pistol in her purse (see Lott, 1998). However, critics point out that very few people actually carry concealed weapons in these states and that the deterrent effect of this practice would therefore be minimal. Furthermore, cross-cultural research suggests that rates of lethal violence are lower in societies characterized by few—not many—guns (see Zimring and Hawkins, 1997). Thus, there is reason to suspect that the reported correlation between right-to-carry laws and declining levels of crime is a spurious one.

21. In Boston, police efforts to seize guns were combined with community outreach programs aimed at enhancing opportunities for youth and diffusing gang violence. Shortly after this program was adopted, levels of violence declined significantly—although other cities in Massachusetts also experienced declining levels of violence (see Currie, 1998, p. 179).

22. In 1974, the city of Baltimore offered $50 for handguns and eventually bought about 8,400 handguns—about one fourth of the number estimated to exist in the city (see Walker, 1994, p. 187).

23. According to Harcourt (1998), the number of complaints of police brutality received by the New York City Civilian Complaint Review Board rose from 3,580 in 1993 to 5,550 in 1997.

References

Alderman, J. (1994). Leading the public: The media's focus on crime shaped sentiment. *Public Perspective, 5,* 26-28.

Allen, J., Livingstone, S., & Reiner, R. (1998). True lies: Changing images of crime in British postwar cinema. *European Journal of Communication, 13,* 53-75.

American Society of Criminology. (2001). *The use of incarceration in the United States.* Retrieved from http://www.asc41.com/policypapers.html

Amnesty International. (1998a). *United States of America—Rights for all.* New York: Amnesty International Publications.

Amnesty International. (1998b, December 3). *USA: The conveyor belt of death continues* [Press release].

Amnesty International. (2002, July 12). *USA: Racist police brutality remains endemic in many areas* [Press release].

Amnesty International. (n.d.). *International human rights standards: The death penalty is a violation of human rights.* Available online at http://www.amnestyusa.org

Andersen, R. (1995). *Consumer culture and TV programming.* Boulder, CO: Westview.

Anderson, D. (1998). *Sensible justice: Alternatives to prison.* New York: New Press.

Anderson, E. (1990). *Streetwise: Race, class and change in an urban community.* Chicago: University of Chicago Press.

Anderson, E. (1994, August). The code of the streets. *Atlantic Monthly,* pp. 82-94.

Anderson, E. (1999). *Code of the streets.* New York: Norton.

Anderson, G. (1998, January 2). Organizing against the death penalty. *America, 178,* 10-11.

Applebome, P. (1995, September 20). For the ultimate safe school, eyes turn to Dallas. *New York Times,* p. B11.

Aynes, R. (1984). Constitutional considerations: Government responsibility and the right not to be a victim. *Pepperdine Law Review, 11,* 63-116.

Bailey, W., & Peterson, R. (1997). Murder, capital punishment, and deterrence: A review of the literature. In H. A. Bedau (Ed.), *The death penalty in America.* New York: Oxford University Press.

Baker, L. (1983). *Miranda: Crime, law and politics.* New York: Atheneum.

Baldus, D., & Woodworth, G. (1998). Race discrimination and the death penalty: An empirical and legal overview. In J. Acker, R. Bohm, & C. Lanier (Eds.), *America's experiment with capital punishment: Reflections on the past, present and future of the ultimate penal sanction.* Durham, NC: Carolina Academic.

Bank, D. (2002, February 13). Poll shows support for crime prevention is rising as tough approach loses favor. *Wall Street Journal,* p. B8.

Barak, G. (1994). Between the waves: Mass-mediated themes of crime and justice. *Social Justice, 21,* 133-147.

Barkan, S., & Cohn, S. (1994). Racial prejudice and support for the death penalty for whites. *Journal of Research in Crime and Delinquency, 31,* 202-209.

Barlow, M. H. (1998). Race and the problem of crime in *Time* and *Newsweek* cover stories, 1946-1995. *Social Justice, 25,* 149-183.

Baum, D. (1996). *Smoke and mirrors: The war on drugs and the politics of failure.* New York: Little, Brown.

Bayer, R. (1981). Crime, punishment and the decline of liberal optimism. *Crime & Delinquency, 27,* 169-190.

Beck, A. (1999). Trends in U.S. correctional populations. In K. Haas & G. Alpert (Eds.), *The dilemmas of corrections* (4th ed.). Prospect Heights, IL: Waveland.

Becker, H. (1967). Whose side are we on? *Social Problems, 14,* 239-247.

Beckett, K. (1994). Setting the public agenda: Street crime and drug use in American politics. *Social Problems, 41,* 425-447.

Beckett, K. (1995). Media depictions of drug use: The impact of official sources. *Journal of Research in Political Sociology, 7,* 161-182.

Beckett, K. (1996). Culture and the politics of signification: The case of child sexual abuse. *Social Problems, 43,* 57-76.

Beckett, K. (1997). *Making crime pay.* New York: Oxford University Press.

Beckett, K., & Sasson, T. (1998). The media and the construction of the drug crisis in America. In E. Jensen & J. Gerber (Eds.), *The new war on drugs.* Cincinnati, OH: ACJS/Anderson.

Beilein, T., & Krasnow, P. (1996, April). Jail prototype leads to faster construction, lower costs. *Corrections Today,* 128-131.

Beirne, P., & Messerschmidt, J. (1991). *Criminology.* New York: Harcourt Brace Jovanovich.

Bellah, R., Madsen, R., Sullivan, W., Swidler, A., & Tipton, S. (1985). *Habits of the heart.* New York: Harper & Row.

Bennett, S. E., & Tuchfarber, A. (1975). The social structural sources of cleavage on law and order policies. *American Journal of Political Science, 19,* 419-438.

Bennett, W., DiIulio, J., & Walters, J. (1996). *Body count.* New York: Simon & Schuster.

Berk, R., & Rauma, D. (1987). Remuneration and recidivism: The long-term impact of unemployment compensation on ex-offenders. *Journal of Quantitative Criminology, 3,* 3-27.

Bertram, E., Blachman, M., Sharpe, K., & Andreas, P. (1996). *Drug war politics: The price of denial.* Berkeley: University of California Press.

Bertram, E., & Sharpe, K. (1997). War ends, drugs win. *The Nation, 264,* 11.

Best, J. (1999). *Random violence.* Berkeley: University of California Press.

Bingol, N., Schuster, C., Fuchs, M., Iosub, S., Turner, G., Stone, R., & Gromisch, D. (1987). The influence of socioeconomic factors on the occurrence of Fetal Alcohol Syndrome. *Advances in Alcohol and Substance Abuse, 105,* 105-118.

Blamed in crime rise: Civil rights excesses. (1967, February 27). *U.S. News & World Report,* p. 15.

Blumstein, A., & Cork, D. (1996). Linking gun availability to youth gun violence. *Law and Contemporary Problems, 59,* 5-24.

Blumstein, A., & Rosenfeld, R. (1998). Assessing the recent ups and downs in U.S. homicide rates. *National Institute of Justice Journal, 237,* 9-11.

Boggess, S., & Bound, J. (1997). Did criminal activity increase during the 1980's? Comparisons across data sources. *Social Science Quarterly, 78,* 725-736.

Bohm, R. M. (1998). The economic costs of capital punishment. In J. R. Acker, R. M. Bohm, & C. S. Lanier (Eds.), *America's experiment with capital punishment: Reflections on the past, present and future of the ultimate penal sanction.* Durham, NC: Carolina Academic.

Bourgeois, P. (1995). *In search of respect: Selling crack in el barrio.* New York: Cambridge University Press.

Bourgeois, P. (1997). In search of Horatio Alger: Culture and ideology in the crack economy. In C. Reinarman & H. Levine (Eds.), *Crack in America: Demon drugs and social justice.* Berkeley: University of California Press.

Bowers, W. (1993). Capital punishment and contemporary values: People's misgivings and the court's misperceptions. *Law and Society Review, 27,* 157-176.

Box, S., Hale, C., & Andrews, G. (1988). Explaining fear of crime. *British Journal of Criminology, 28,* 340-356.

Broder, J. (2003, January 19). No hard time for prison budgets. *New York Times,* p. 5.

Bureau of Justice Statistics. (1995). *Correctional populations in the United States 1990.* Washington, DC: Author.

Bureau of Justice Statistics. (1997). *Prisoners in 1996.* Washington, DC: Author.

Bureau of Justice Statistics. (1998a). *Crime and justice in the United States and in England and Wales, 1981-1996: Executive summary.* Washington, DC: Author.

Bureau of Justice Statistics. (1998b). *National Criminal Victimization Survey, crime trends, 1973-1997.* Washington, DC: Author.

Bureau of Justice Statistics. (1998c). *Prisoners in 1997.* Washington, DC: Author.

Bureau of Justice Statistics. (2001). *Prisoners in 2000.* Washington, DC: Author.

Bureau of Justice Statistics. (2002a). *Prison and jail inmates at midyear 2001.* Washington, DC: Author.

Bureau of Justice Statistics. (2002b). *Prisoners in 2001.* Washington, DC: Author.

Bureau of Justice Statistics. *Criminal offender statistics.* www.ojp.usdoj.gov/bjs/crimoff.htm

Bush, G. (1990). Address to students on drug abuse." *Public papers of the President 1989* (Vol. 1, pp. 746-749). Washington, DC: U.S. Government Printing Office.

Butterfield, F. (1997a, April 7). As inmate population grows, so does focus on children. *New York Times,* p. 1.

Butterfield, F. (1997b, October 27). Drop in homicide rate linked to crack's decline. *New York Times,* p. A10.

Butterfield, F. (1998, March 5). Asylums behind bars. *New York Times,* p. A1.

Butterfield, F. (1999, January 6). Drug treatment in prisons dips as use rises, study finds. *New York Times,* p. A10.

Butterfield, F. (2001, September 2). States ease laws on time in prison. *New York Times,* p. A1.

Butterfield, F. (2002a, December 29). Freed from prison, but still paying a penalty. *New York Times,* p. A19.

Butterfield, F. (2002b, June 3). Study shows building prisons did not prevent repeat crimes. *New York Times,* p. A11.

Califano, J. (1996, August 24). Welfare's drug connection. *New York Times,* p. A19.

Caplan, G. (1973). Reflections on the nationalization of crime, 1964-8. *Law and the Social Order, 3,* 583-638.

Carbaugh, D. (1988). *Talking American.* Norwood, NJ: Ablex.

Carlson, J. M. (1985). *Prime time law enforcement: Crime show viewing and attitudes toward the criminal justice system.* New York: Praeger.

Carter, D. (1995). *The politics of rage.* New York: Simon & Schuster.

Cavender, G. (1998). In the shadow of shadows: Television reality crime programming. In G. Cavender & M. Fishman (Eds.), *Entertaining crime: Television reality programs.* Hawthorne, NY: Aldine.

Cavender, G., & Fishman, M. (1998). *Entertaining crime: Television reality programs.* Hawthorne, NY: Aldine.

Chambliss, W. (1994). Policing the ghetto underclass: The politics of law and law enforcement. *Social Problems, 41,* 177-194.

Chermak, S. (1994). Crime in the news media: A refined understanding of how crimes become news. In G. Barak (Ed.), *Media, process and the social construction of crime: Studies in newsmaking criminology.* New York: Garland.

Chermak, S. (1995). *Victims in the news: Crime and the American news media.* Boulder, CO: Westview.

Chesney-Lind, M. (2002). Imprisoning women: The unintended victims of mass imprisonment. In M. Mauer & M. Chesney-Lind (Eds.), *Invisible punishment: The collateral consequences of mass imprisonment*. New York: New Press.

Chiricos, T., Eschholz, S., & Gertz, M. (1997). Crime, news, and fear of crime. *Social Problems, 44,* 342-357.

Christie, N. (1977). Conflicts as property. *British Journal of Criminology, 17,* 1-15.

Christie, N. (1993). *Crime control as industry.* London: Routledge.

Citing drop in welfare rolls, Clinton to seek further cuts. (1999, January 25). *New York Times,* p. A12.

Clark, J., Austin, J., & Henry, D. A. (1997, September). *"Three strikes and you're out": A review of state legislation* [Occasional paper]. Washington, DC: National Institute of Justice.

Clinton nurtures high hopes. (1993, November 20). *National Journal,* pp. 2794-2795.

Cloud, J. (1998, August 24). For they know not what they do? *Time Magazine.*

Cohen, P. D. A. (1997). Crack in the Netherlands: Effective social policy is effective drug policy. In C. Reinarman & H. Levine (Eds.), *Crack in America: Demon drugs and social justice*. Berkeley: University of California Press.

Cohen, S. (1985). *Visions of social control.* Cambridge, MA: Polity.

Cohn, S., Barkan, S., & Halteman, W. (1991). Punitive attitudes toward criminals: Racial consensus or racial conflict? *Social Problems, 38,* 287-296.

Cole, D. (2002, September 23). Enemy aliens and American freedoms. *The Nation, 275,* 20-30.

Coleman, C. (1993). The influence of mass media and interpersonal communication on societal and personal risk judgements. *Communication Research, 20,* 611-628.

Colomy, P., & Greiner, L. R. (2001, August). *Ideal victims, inviolate spaces, and the youthful offender: News media representations of street violence and the recriminalization of delinquency*. Paper presented at the annual meeting of the Society of the Study of Symbolic Interaction.

Colomy, P., & Greiner, L. R. (n.d.). *Innocent blood: Ideal victims and the summer of violence*. Manuscript submitted for publication.

Cook, P., & Laub, J. (1998). The unprecedented epidemic of youth violence. In M. H. Moore & M. Tonry (Eds.), *Crime and justice: A review of research* (Vol. 24). Chicago: University of Chicago Press.

Cook, P., & Laub, J. (2002). After the epidemic: Recent trends in youth violence in the United States. *Crime and Justice: A Review of Research, 29,* 1-27.

Corbett, M. (1981). Public support for "law and order": Interrelationships with system affirmation and attitudes toward minorities. *Criminology, 19,* 328-343.

Courtright, D. (1996). *Violent land.* Cambridge, MA: Harvard University Press.

Coyle, M. (2002). *Race and class penalties in crack cocaine sentencing* [Brief]. Washington, DC: Sentencing Project.

Crawford, A. (1995). Appeals to community and crime prevention. *Crime, Law and Social Change, 22*, 97-126.

Crew, B. K. (1990). Acting like cops: The social reality of crime and law on TV police dramas. In C. Sanders (Ed.), *Marginal conventions*. Bowling Green, OH: Bowling Green State University Popular Press.

Crime and Justice Foundation. (1991). *Shifting the debate on crime: A study of public opinion and new approaches to fighting crime*. Boston, MA: Author.

Cronin, T. E., Cronin, T. Z., & Milakovich, M. (1981). *The U.S. versus crime in the streets*. Bloomington: Indiana University Press.

Cullen, F., Skovron, S. E., Scott, J. E., & Burton, V. S., Jr. (1990). Public support for correctional treatment: The tenacity of rehabilitative ideology. *Criminal Justice and Behavior, 17*, 6-18.

Cullen, F., Van Voorhis, P., & Sundt, J. L. (1996). Prisons in crisis: The American experience. In R. Matthews & P. Francis (Eds.), *Prisons 2000: An international perspective on the current state and future of imprisonment*. London: Macmillan.

Cullen, F., Wright, J. P., & Applegate, B. K. (1996). Control in the community: The limits of reform? In A. Harland (Ed.), *Choosing correctional options*. Thousand Oaks, CA: Sage.

Currie, E. (1985). *Confronting crime: An American challenge*. New York: Pantheon.

Currie, E. (1988). Two visions of community crime prevention. In T. Hope & M. Shaw (Eds.), *Communities and crime reduction*. London: Her Majesty's Stationery Office.

Currie, E. (1993). *Reckoning: Drugs, the cities, and the American future*. New York: Hill & Wang.

Currie, E. (1998). *Crime and punishment in America*. New York: Holt.

Danielman, L. H., & Reese, S. D. (1989). Intermedia influence and the drug issue: Converging on cocaine. In P. Shoemaker (Ed.), *Communication campaigns about drugs: Government, media and the public*. Hillsdale, NJ: Lawrence Erlbaum.

Danziger, S. H., & Gottschalk, P. (1995). *America unequal*. Cambridge, MA: Harvard University Press.

Danziger, S. H., & Weinberg, D. H. (1994). The historical record: Trends in family income, inequality and poverty. In S. H. Danziger, G. D. Sandefur, & D. H. Weinberg (Eds.), *Confronting poverty: Prescriptions for change*. New York: Russell Sage.

Davey, J. D. (1995). *The new social contract: America's journey from the welfare state to police state*. Westport, CT: Praeger.

Davis, D. (1983). The production of crime policies. *Crime and Social Justice, 20*, 121-137.

Davis, M. (1992). *City of quartz: Excavating the future in Los Angeles*. New York: Vintage.

The death of innocents. (2002, July 2). *New York Times*, p. A20.

Death Penalty Information Center. (n.d.). *Innocence: Released from death row*. Available online at http://www.deathpenaltyinfo.org/

Department of Health and Human Services, Administration for Families and Children. (n.d.). *Percent change in AFDC/TANF families and recipients.* Retrieved from http://www.acf.hhs.gov/news/stats.afdc.htm

de Tocqueville, A. (1981). *Democracy in America.* New York: Random House.

Diamond, S., & Stalans, L. (1989). The myth of judicial leniency in sentencing. *Behavioral Sciences and the Law, 7,* 73-89.

Dickey, W., & Hollenhorst, P. S. (1998, December). Three-strikes laws: Massive impact in California and Georgia, little elsewhere. *Overcrowded Times, 9,* 1-5.

Dieter, R. (1998). *The death penalty in black and white: Who lives, who dies, who decides.* Washington, DC: Death Penalty Information Center.

Dix, C. (1997, Spring). Police violence: Rising epidemic/raising resistance. *Black Scholar, 27,* 59-63.

Doble, J., Immerwahr, S., & Richardson, A. (1991). *Punishing criminals: The people of Delaware consider the options.* New York: Edna McConnell Clark Foundation.

Doble, J., & Klein, J. (1989). *Punishing criminals, the public's view: An Alabama survey.* New York: Edna McConnell Clark Foundation.

Donahue, J. J. (1997). Some perspectives on crime and criminal justice policy. In L. Friedman & G. Fisher (Eds.), *The crime conundrum.* Boulder, CO: Westview.

Donovan, P. (1998). Armed with the power of television: Reality crime programming and the reconstruction of law and order in the U.S. In G. Cavender & M. Fishman (Eds.), *Entertaining crime: Television reality programs.* Hawthorne, NY: Aldine.

Donziger, S. R. (Ed.). (1996). *The real war on crime: The report of the National Criminal Justice Commission.* New York: Harper Perennial.

Dorfman, L., & Schiraldi, V. (n.d.). *Off balance: Youth, race & crime in the news.* (Available from the Youth Law Center, 1010 Vermont Avenue, Suite 310, Washington, DC)

Dorfman, L., & Schiraldi, V. (2001, April). *Off balance: Youth, crime, and race in the news* (Online). Retrieved September 22, 2003 www.buildingblocksforyouth. org/media

Doyle, A. (1998). "Cops": Television policing as policing reality. In G. Cavender & M. Fishman (Eds.), *Entertaining crime: Television reality programs.* Hawthorne, NY: Aldine.

Drug Policy Alliance. (n.d.-a). *Reducing harm: Treatment and beyond: Needle exchange.* Available online at http://www.drugpolicy.org/reducingharm/ needleexchan/

Drug Policy Alliance. (n.d.-b). *State-by-state: Reform in California.* Available online at http://www.drugpolicy.org/news/

Drug Policy Alliance. (n.d.-c). *What's wrong with the drug war: Access to treatment.* Available online at http://www.lindesmith.org/rugwar/access/

Durkheim, É. (1951). *Suicide*. New York: Free Press.

Earley, P. (1996). *Circumstantial evidence: Death, life and justice in a southern town*. New York: Bantam.

Edelman, M. (1988). *Constructing the political spectacle*. Chicago: University of Chicago Press.

Edsall, T. B., & Edsall, M. (1991). *Chain reaction: The impact of rights, race and taxes on American politics*. New York: Norton.

Egan, T. (1999a, March 11). Soldiers of the drug war remain on duty. *New York Times*, pp. A1, A16.

Egan, T. (1999b, February 28). The war on drugs retreats, still taking prisoners. *New York Times*, p. 1.

Eggen, D. (2002, July 1). Ashcroft aggressively pursues death penalty. *Washington Post*, p. A1.

Ehrlichmann, J. (1970). *Witness to power: The Nixon years*. New York: Simon & Schuster.

Elias, R. (1993). *Victims still: The political manipulation of crime victims*. London: Sage.

Elikann, P. (1996). *The tough on crime myth*. New York: Insight.

Ellsworth, P., & Gross, S. (1994). Hardening of the attitudes: Americans' views on the death penalty. *Journal of Social Issues, 50*, 19-52.

Entman, R. (1992). Blacks in the news: Television, modern racism and cultural change. *Journalism Quarterly, 69*, 341-361.

Entman, R. (1994). Representation and reality in the portrayal of blacks on network news. *Journalism Quarterly, 71*, 509-520.

Epstein, E. (1977). *Agency of fear: Opiates and political power in America*. New York: Random House.

Ericson, R., Baranek, P., & Chan, J. (1991). *Representing order*. Toronto: University of Toronto Press.

Excerpts from Supreme Court rulings on California's "three strikes" law. (2003, March 6). *New York Times*, p. 1.

Executive Office of the President. (1990). *Budget of the U.S. government*. Washington, DC: U.S. Government Printing Office.

Fagan, J., Zimring, F., & Kim, J. (1998, October). Declining homicide in New York City: A tale of two trends. *National Institute of Justice Journal, 237*, 12-13.

FBI director weighs war on drug trafficking. (1981, February 26). *New York Times*, p. A27.

Federal Bureau of Investigation. (1950-2002). *Uniform crime reports*. Washington, DC: U.S. Department of Justice.

Federal Bureau of Investigation. (2001). *Crime in the United States 2000*. Washington, DC: U.S. Department of Justice.

Feeley, M., & Simon, J. (1992). The new penology: Notes on the emerging strategy of corrections and its implications. *Criminology, 30*, 449-474.

Ferraro, K. (1995). *Fear of crime: Interpreting victimization risk.* New York: State University of New York Press.

Ferraro, K., & LaGrange, R. (1987). The measurement of the fear of crime. *Sociological Inquiry, 57,* 70-101.

Feuerherd, J. (2002, September 6). September 11: A year later: Congress questions Patriot Act policies. Retrieved from http://natcath.org/NCR_Online/archives2/2002c/090602/090602e.htm

Fishman, M. (1978). Crime waves as ideology. *Social Problems, 25,* 531-543.

Fishman, M. (1998). Ratings and reality: The persistence of the reality crime genre. In G. Cavender & M. Fishman (Eds.), *Entertaining crime: Television reality programs.* Hawthorne, NY: Aldine.

Fiske, J. (1987). *Television culture.* New York: Routledge.

Flanagan, T. (1987). Change and influence in popular criminology: Public attributions of crime causation. *Journal of Criminal Justice, 15,* 231-243.

Flanagan, T., & Longmire, D. (Eds.). (1996). *Americans view crime and justice.* Thousand Oaks, CA: Sage.

Flat earth AIDS policy. (1998). *Progressive, 62*(6), 9-10.

Forman, A., & Lachter, S. B. (1989). The National Institute on Drug Abuse cocaine prevention campaign. In P. Shoemaker (Ed.), *Communication campaigns about drugs: Government, media and the public.* Hillsdale, NJ: Lawrence Erlbaum.

Frankel, B., & Weinstein, F. (1997, August 18). Crusader. *People,* p. 93.

Freeman, R. B. (1991). *Crime and the employment of disadvantaged youths.* National Bureau of Economic Research Working Paper no. 3875.

Furstenberg, F. (1971). Public reaction to crime in the streets. *American Scholar, 40*(4), 601-610.

Gainsborough, J., & Mauer, M. (2000, September). *Diminishing returns: Crime and incarceration in the 1990s* [Brief]. Washington, DC: Sentencing Project.

Gallup, G. (Ed.). (1990). *The Gallup poll.* Wilmington, DE: Scholarly Resources.

Gamson, W. A. (1992). *Talking politics.* New York: Cambridge University Press.

Gamson, W., & Lasch, K. E. (1983). The political culture of social welfare policy. In S. E. Spiro & E. Yuchtman-Yaar (Eds.), *Evaluating the welfare state: Social and political perspectives.* New York: Academic Books.

Gamson, W. A., & Modigliani, A. (1987). The changing culture of affirmative action. *Research in Political Sociology, 3,* 137-177.

Gans, H. (1979). *Deciding what's news.* New York: Vintage.

Gans, H. (1988). *Middle American individualism.* New York: Oxford University Press.

Gans, H. (1995). *The war against the poor.* New York: Basic Books.

Garland, D. (1985). *Punishment and welfare: A history of penal strategies.* Aldershot, UK: Gower.

Garland, D. (1990). *Punishment and modern society: A study in social theory.* Chicago: University of Chicago Press.

Garland, D. (1995). Penal modernism and postmodernism. In T. G. Blomberg & S. Cohen (Eds.), *Punishment and social control*. New York: Aldine.

Garland, D. (1996). The limits of the sovereign state: Strategies of crime control in contemporary society. *British Journal of Criminology, 36*, 445-471.

Garofalo, J., & McLeod, M. (1989). The structure and operation of Neighborhood Watch programs in the United States. *Crime & Delinquency, 35*, 326-344.

Gaubatz, K. T. (1995). *Crime in the public mind*. Ann Arbor: University of Michigan Press.

Georgia v. Furman, 408 U.S. 238 (1972).

Gerber, J., & Engelhardt-Greer, S. (1996). Just and painful: Attitudes toward sentencing criminals. In T. Flanagan & D. Longmire (Eds.), *Americans view crime and justice*. Thousand Oaks, CA: Sage.

Gerbner, G., Gross, L., Morgan, M., & Signorielli, N. (1980, Summer). The "mainstreaming" of America: Violence profile no. 11. *Journal of Communication, 30*, 10-29.

Gilliam, F. D., Jr., & Iyengar, S. (2000). Prime suspects: The influence of local television news on the viewing public. *American Journal of Political Science, 44*, 560-573.

Gilligan, J. (1996). *Violence*. New York: Vintage.

Gitlin, T. (1983). *Inside prime time*. New York: Pantheon.

Goldstein, P. L., Brownstein, H. H., Ryan, P. J., & Belluci, P. A. (1989). Crack and homicide in New York City, 1988: A conceptually-based event analysis. *Contemporary Drug Problems, 16*, 651-687.

Goldwater's acceptance speech to GOP convention. (1964, July 17). *New York Times*, p. A17.

Golub, A. L., & Johnson, B. D. (1997). *Crack's decline: Some surprises across U.S. cities*. Washington, DC: National Institute of Justice.

Goodstein, L. (2001, June 17). Death penalty falls from favor as some lose confidence in its fairness. *New York Times*, p. A12.

Gordon, M., & Riger, S. (1989). *The female fear*. New York: Free Press.

Gray, M. (1998). *Drug crazy*. New York: Random House.

Greene, R. (1998, August 31). Educators model airport security to prevent more bloodshed. *Buffalo News*, p. 4A.

Greenhouse, L. (2002, November 6). California's 3-strikes law tested again. *New York Times*, p. 1.

Gurr, T. R. (Ed.). (1989). *Violence in America* (Vol. 1). Newbury Park, CA: Sage.

Gusfield, J. (1967). Moral passage: The symbolic process in public designations of deviance. *Social Problems, 15*, 175-188.

Hagan, J. (1994). *Crime and disrepute*. Thousand Oaks, CA: Pine Forge.

Hagan, J., & Albonetti, C. (1982). Race, class and the perception of criminal injustice in America. *American Journal of Sociology, 88*, 329-355.

Haghighi, B., & Sorensen, J. (1996). America's fear of crime. In T. Flanagan & D. Longmire (Eds.), *Americans view crime and justice.* Thousand Oaks, CA: Sage.

Haines, H. H. (1996). *Against capital punishment: The anti-death penalty movement in America, 1972-1994.* New York: Oxford University Press.

Hall, S., Critcher, C., Jefferson, T., Clarke, J., & Roberts, B. (1978). *Policing the crisis: Mugging, the state and law and order.* New York: Holmes & Meier.

Haller, M. H. (1989). Bootlegging: The business and politics of violence. In T. R. Gurr (Ed.), *Violence in America* (Vol. 1). Newbury Park, CA: Sage.

Haney, C., & Manzolati, J. (1983). Television criminology: Network illusions of criminal justice realities. In E. Aronson (Ed.), *Readings on the social animal.* San Francisco: W. H. Freeman.

Hannon, L., & DeFronzo, J. (1998). The truly disadvantaged: Public assistance and crime. *Social Problems, 45,* 383-392.

Harcourt, B. E. (1998). Reflecting on the subject: A critique of the social influence conception of deterrence, the broken windows theory, and order-maintenance policing, New York style. *Michigan Law Review, 97,* 292-389.

Harrington, C. B. (1992). Popular justice, populist politics: Law in community organizing. *Social and Legal Studies, 1,* 177-198.

Heath, L., & Gilbert, K. (1996). Mass media and fear of crime. *American Behavioral Scientist, 39,* 379-386.

Heath, L., & Petraitis, J. (1987). Television viewing and fear of crime: Where is the mean world?" *Basic and Applied Social Psychology, 8,* 97-123.

Henderson, L. N. (1985). The wrongs of victim's rights. *Stanford Law Review, 37,* 937-1021.

Herbert, S. (2001). Policing the contemporary city. *Theoretical Criminology, 5*(4), 317-339.

Herman, E., & Chomsky, N. (1988). *Manufacturing consent.* New York: Pantheon.

Heymann, P. B., & Moore, M. H. (1996). The federal role in dealing with violent street crime: Principles, questions and cautions. *Annals of the American Academy of Political and Social Science, 543,* 103-115.

Hilgartner, S., & Bosk, C. L. (1998). The rise and fall of social problems: A public arenas model. *American Journal of Sociology, 94*(1), 53-78.

Hope, T. (1995). Community crime prevention. In M. Tonry & D. P. Farrington (Eds.), *Building a safer society: Strategic approaches to crime prevention.* Chicago: University of Chicago Press.

Hope, T., & Shaw, M. (1988). Community approaches to reducing crime. In T. Hope & M. Shaw (Eds.), *Communities and crime reduction.* London: Her Majesty's Stationery Office.

Hornblower, M. (1998, July 6). Have guns will travel. *Time.*

Idelson, H. (1993, August 14). Democrat's new proposal seeks consensus by compromise. *Congressional Quarterly, 51,* 2228-2289.

Idelson, H. (1994, January 29). Tough anti-crime bill faces tougher balancing act. *Congressional Quarterly Weekly Reporter,* pp. 171-173.

Idelson, H. (1995, February 18). Block grants replace prevention, police hiring in House bill. *Congressional Quarterly*, pp. 530-532.

Innocence Project. (n.d.). *Causes and remedies of wrongful conviction.* Available online at http://www.innocenceproject.org/

Inside the beltway: Clinton administration endorses needle exchange programs. (1997, Winter/Spring). *Drug Policy Letter*, p. 14.

Irwin, J., & Austin, J. (1997). *It's about time.* Belmont, CA: Wadsworth.

Iyengar, S. (1991). *Is anyone responsible?* Chicago: University of Chicago Press.

Iyengar, S. (1995). Effects of framing on attributions of responsibility for crime and terrorism." In R. V. Ericson (Ed.), *Crime and the media.* Aldershot, UK: Dartmouth.

Jacob, H., & Lineberry, R. L. (1983). Crime, politics and the cities. In A. Heinz, H. Jacob, & R. L. Lineberry (Eds.), *Crime in city politics.* New York: Longman.

Jeffres, L. W., & Perloff, R. M. (1997). *Mass media effects.* Prospect Heights, IL: Waveland.

Jenkins, P. (1994). *Using murder.* Hawthorne, NY: Aldine.

Jensen, E. L., & Gerber, J. (1996). The civil forfeiture of assets and the war on drugs: Expanding the criminal sanctions while reducing due process protections. *Crime and Delinquency*, 42, 412–434.

Johnson, B., Golub, A., & Dunlap, E. (2000). The rise and decline of hard drugs, drug markets, and violence in inner-city New York. In A. Blumstein & J. Wallman (Eds.), *The crime drop in America.* New York: Cambridge University Press.

Johnson, D. (2002). Review of *Corporate Crime, Law, and Social Control,* by Sally S. Simpson. *Law and Politics Book Review*, 12(8), 454-463.

Johnson, L. B. (1965). Remarks on the City Hall steps, Dayton, Ohio. In *Public papers of the presidents 1964* (Vol. 2). Washington, DC: U.S. Government Printing Office.

Johnson, L. B. (1966). Special message to the Congress on law enforcement and the administration of justice. In *Public papers of the presidents 1965* (Vol. 1). Washington, DC: U.S. Government Printing Office.

Johnston, L. D., O'Malley, P. M., & Bachman, J. G. (1999). *National survey results on drug use from the Monitoring the Future Study, 1975-1998, vol. I: Secondary School Students* (NIH Publication No. 99-4600). Bethseda, MD: National Institute on Drug Abuse.

Justice Policy Institute. (2002). *Cellblocks or classrooms? The funding of higher education and corrections and its impact on African American men.* Retrieved from http://www.justicepolicy.org

Kahan, D. (1996). What do alternative sanctions mean? *University of Chicago Law Review*, 63, 591-653.

Kaiman, B. (2001, December 13). State groups push drug reform. *Seattle Times,* p. B3.

Karst, K. L. (1993). *Law's promise, law's expression: Visions of power in the politics of race, gender and religion.* New Haven, CT: Yale University Press.

Kasindorf, M. (2002, February 28). Three-strikes laws fall out of favor. *USA Today*, p. A3.

Kasinsky, R. G. (1994). Patrolling the facts: Media, cops and crime. In G. Barak (Ed.), *Media, process and the social construction of crime: Studies in newsmaking criminology*. New York: Garland.

Katz, M. B. (1989). *The undeserving poor: From the war on poverty to the war on welfare*. New York: Pantheon.

Kaufman, J. (1998, October 27). Prison life is all around for a girl growing up in downtown Baltimore. *Wall Street Journal*. Retrieved from http://www.wsj.com

Kelling, G., & Coles, C. (1996). *Fixing broken windows*. New York: Free Press.

King, R., & Mauer, M. (2001). *Aging behind bars: "Three strikes" seven years later* [Brief]. Washington, DC: Sentencing Project.

King, R., & Mauer, M. (2002a). *Distorted priorities: Drug offenders in state prisons*. Washington, DC: Sentencing Project.

King, R. S., & Mauer, M. (2002b). *State sentencing and corrections policy in an era of fiscal restraint* [Brief]. Washington, DC: Sentencing Project.

Kitsuse, J., & Spector, M. (1973). Toward a sociology of social problems: Social conditions, value-judgements, and social problems. *Social Problems, 20,* 407-419.

Kleinknecht, W. G. (1996). Victim's rights advocates on a roll. *National Law Journal, 18,* A1, A8.

Klite, P., Bardwell, R., & Salzman, J. (1995). *Pavlov's TV dog: A snapshot of local TV news in America taken on September 20, 1995* (Rocky Mountain Media Watch Content Analysis 7). Denver: Rocky Mountain Media Watch.

Koch, N. (2002, December 25). Police shows thrive, cable is grabbing its share. *New York Times*, p. E1.

Koh, E. L. (2002, September 8). Groups playing against stereotype Muslim, Arab. *Boston Globe*, p. 1.

Kooistra, P., Mahoney, J., & Westervelt, S. (1998). The world of crime according to "Cops." In G. Cavender & M. Fishman (Eds.), *Entertaining crime: Television reality programs*. Hawthorne, NY: Aldine.

Krahn, H., Hartnagel, T., & Gartrell, J. (1986). Income inequality and homicide rates: Cross-national data and criminological theories. *Criminology, 24,* 269-293.

Kramer, M. (1994, February 21). From Sarajevo to Needle Park. *Time*, p. 29.

Kurki, L. (1997, October). International crime survey: America rates about average. *Overcrowded Times, 8,* 4.

Lacayo, R. (1994, February 7). Lock 'em up! *Time*, pp. 50-54.

LaFree, G. (1989). *Rape and criminal justice: The social construction of sexual assault*. Belmont, CA: Wadsworth.

Land, K., McCall, P., & Cohen, L. (1990). Structural co-variates of homicide rates: Are there any invariances across time and space? *American Journal of Sociology, 95,* 922-963.

Lane, R. (1989). On the social meaning of homicide trends in America. In T. R. Gurr (Ed.), *Violence in America* (Vol. 1). Newbury Park, CA: Sage.

Law permits trial of youths as adults for guns at school. (1998, August 19). *New York Times*, p. B4.

Lawrence, R. G. (1996). Accidents, icons and indexing: The dynamics of news coverage of police use of force. *Political Communication, 13,* 437-454.

Levine, H., & Harmon, L. (1993). *The death of an American Jewish community.* New York: Free Press.

Lewis, D., & Salem, G. (1986). *Fear of crime: Incivility and the production of a social problem.* New Brunswick, NJ: Transaction Books.

Lewis, O., with Butterworth, D. (1969). *A study of slum culture.* New York: Random House.

Lichter, S. R., Lichter, L., Amundson, D., & Butterworth, T. (2002). *Hollywood cleans up its act: Changing rates of sex and violence in entertainment media.* Washington, DC: Center for Media and Public Affairs.

Lichter, S. R., Lichter, L. S., & Rothman, S. (1994). *Prime time: How TV portrays American culture.* Washington, DC: Regnery.

Liebman, J. S. (2000). The overproduction of death. *Columbia Law Review, 100,* 2030.

Liska, A., Sanchirico, A., & Reed, M. (1988). Fear of crime and constrained behavior: Specifying and estimating a reciprocal effects model. *Social Forces, 66,* 827-837.

Living in fear. (1998, August 23). *Los Angeles Times*, p. B1.

Loader, I., Girling, E., & Sparks, R. (1998). Narratives of decline: Youth, dis/order and community in an English "middletown." *British Journal of Criminology, 38,* 388-403.

Logan, J., & Molotch, H. (1987). *Urban fortunes.* Berkeley: University of California Press.

Lotke, E. (1997). *Hobbling a generation: Young African American men in D.C.'s criminal justice system five years later.* Washington, DC: Sentencing Project.

Lott, J. R., Jr. (1998). *More guns, less crime: Understanding crime and gun control laws.* Chicago: University of Chicago Press.

Lynch, J. (1995). Crime in international perspective. In J. Q. Wilson & J. Petersilia (Eds.), *Crime.* San Francisco: Institute for Contemporary Studies.

Macleod, M. (1986). Victim participation at sentencing. *Criminal Law Bulletin, 22,* 501-517.

Maguire, K., & Pastore, A. L. (Eds.). (1980). *Sourcebook of criminal justice statistics 1979.* Washington, DC: Bureau of Justice Statistics.

Maguire, K., & Pastore, A. L. (Eds.). (1994). *Sourcebook of criminal justice statistics 1992.* Washington, DC: Bureau of Justice Statistics.

Maguire, K., & Pastore, A. L. (Eds.). (1995). *Sourcebook of criminal justice statistics 1994.* Washington, DC: Bureau of Justice Statistics.

Maguire, K., & Pastore, A. L. (Eds.). (1996). *Sourcebook of criminal justice statistics 1995.* Washington, DC: Bureau of Justice Statistics.

Maguire, K., & Pastore, A. L. (Eds.). (1997). *Sourcebook of criminal justice statistics 1996.* Washington, DC: Bureau of Justice Statistics.

Maguire, K., & Pastore, A. L. (Eds.). (1998). *Sourcebook of criminal justice statistics 1997* (online). Retrieved May 24, 1999 from www.albany.edu/sourcebook/

Maguire, K., & Pastore, A. L. (Eds.). (2002). *Sourcebook of criminal justice statistics 2001* (online). Retrieved September 22, 2003 from www.albany.edu/sourcebook/

Maguire, K., & Pastore, A. L. (Eds.). (2001). *Sourcebook of criminal justice statistics 2000.* Retrieved from http://www.albany.edu/sourcebook

Maguire, K., & Pastore, A. L. (Eds.). (2002). *Sourcebook of criminal justice statistics 2001.* Retrieved October 21, 2002, from http://www.albany.edu/ sourcebook/

Maguire, K., & Pastore, A. L. (Eds.). (n.d.). *Sourcebook of Criminal Justice Statistics* [Online]. Retrieved from http://www.albany.edu/sourcebook

Marion, N. E. (1994). *A history of federal crime control initiatives, 1960-1993.* Westport, CT: Praeger.

Marsh, H. L. (1991). A comparative analysis of crime coverage in newspapers in the United States and other countries from 1960-1989: A review of the literature. *Journal of Criminal Justice, 19,* 67-80.

Masci, D. (1994, August 27). $30 billion anti-crime bill heads to Clinton's desk. *Congressional Quarterly,* pp. 2488-2493.

Massachusetts Sentencing Commission. (1996, April 10). Report to the general court. Appendix A.

Massey, D. (1990). American apartheid: Segregation and the making of the underclass. *American Journal of Sociology, 96,* 329-357.

Matusow, A. J. (1984). *The unraveling of America: A history of liberalism in the 1960's.* New York: Harper Torchbooks.

Mauer, M. (2002). Mass imprisonment and the disappearing voters. In M. Mauer & M. Chesney-Lind, *Invisible punishment: The collateral consequences of mass imprisonment.* New York: New Press.

Mauer, M., & Huling, T. (1995). *Young black Americans and the criminal justice system.* Washington, DC: Sentencing Project.

Mawby, R. I., & Walklate, S. (1994). *Critical victimology.* London: Sage.

Mayhew, P., & Van Dijk, J. J. M. (1997). *Criminal victimization in eleven industrialized countries: Key findings from the 1996 International Crime Victims Survey.* The Hague: Dutch Ministry of Justice.

McAnany, P. (1992, November). *Assets forfeiture as drug control strategy.* Paper presented at the annual meeting of the American Society of Criminology, New Orleans.

McCord, J. (1997). Placing violence in its context. In J. McCord (Ed.), *Violence and childhood in the inner city.* New York: Cambridge University Press.

McCorkle, R. (1993). Punish or rehabilitate? Public attitudes toward six common crimes. *Crime & Delinquency, 39,* 240-252.

McDermott, K. (2002, August 25). Support holds for Gov. Ryan's moratorium on death penalty. *St. Louis Post-Dispatch*, p. A12.

Merton, R. K. (1938). Social structure and anomie. *American Sociological Review, 3*, 672-682.

Messner, S. (1989). Economic discrimination and societal homicide rates: Further evidence on the cost of inequality." *American Sociological Review, 54*, 597-611.

Messner, S., & Tardiff, K. (1986). Economic inequality and levels of homicide: An analysis of urban neighborhoods. *Criminology, 24*, 297-316.

Michelowski, R. (1993, May/June). Some thoughts regarding the impact of Clinton's election on crime and justice policy. *The Criminologist, 18*, 1, 5-7, 11.

Milakovich, M., & Weis, K. (1975, January). Politics and measures of success in the war on crime. *Crime and Delinquency, 21:* 1-10.

Miller, J. G. (1992). *Hobbling a generation: Young African American males in the criminal justice system of America's cities: Baltimore, Maryland.* Washington, DC: Sentencing Project.

Miller, J. G. (1996). *Search and destroy: African-American males in the criminal justice system.* New York: Cambridge University Press.

Minow, M. (2002, October 1). The USA Patriot Act. *Library Journal*, p. 1.

Monkkonen, E. (1981). *Police in urban America, 1860-1920.* New York: Cambridge University Press.

Moore, M. (1990). Supply reduction and drug law enforcement. In M. Tonry & J. Q. Wilson (Eds.), *Drugs and crime*. Chicago: University of Chicago Press.

Morgan, D. (1986). *The flacks of Washington: Government information and the public agenda.* New York: Greenwood.

Morgan, M., & Signorielli, N. (Eds.). (1990). *Cultivation analysis: New directions in media effects research.* Newbury Park, CA: Sage.

Morganthau, T. (1986, June 16). Crack and crime. *Newsweek*, pp. 16-22.

Morris, L. (1994). *Dangerous classes: The underclass and social citizenship.* New York: Routledge.

Moynihan, D. P. (1973). *The politics of a guaranteed income: The Nixon administration and the family assistance plan.* New York: Random House.

Myers, L. (1996). Bringing the offender to heel: Views of the criminal courts. In T. Flanagan & D. Longmire (Eds.), *Americans view crime and justice*. Thousand Oaks, CA: Sage.

Nadlemann, E. (1997). Drug prohibition in the U.S. In C. Reinarman & H. Levine (Eds.), *Crack in America: Demon drugs and social justice*. Berkeley: University of California Press.

National Crime Prevention Council. (1994a). *Partnerships to prevent youth violence* [Research brief]. Washington, DC: Office of Justice Programs, U.S. Department of Justice.

National Crime Prevention Council. (1994b). *Working as partners with community groups* [Research brief]. Washington, DC: Office of Justice Programs, U.S. Department of Justice.

National Institute of Justice. (1997, November). A study of homicide in eight U.S. cities: An NIJ intramural research project [Research brief]. Washington, DC: National Institute of Justice.

Nava, M. (1988). Cleveland and the press: Outrage and anxiety in the reporting of child sexual abuse. *Feminist Review, 28,* 103-121.

Nimmo, D. (1964). *Newsgathering in Washington: A study in political communication.* New York: Atherton.

Nixon, R. (1966, August 15). If mob rule takes hold in the US: A warning from Richard Nixon. *U.S. News & World Report,* pp. 64-65.

Oakland Cannabis Buyer's Cooperative. (n.d.). Press release from the Coalition for Rescheduling Cannabis. Available online at http://www.rxcbc.org/

O'Brien, R. M. (1996). Police productivity and crime rates: 1973-1992. *Criminology, 34,* 183-207.

O'Connor questions the death penalty. (2001, July 4). *New York Times,* p. A9.

OECD. (2000). *Income distribution in OECD countries.* Paris: Author.

Oliver, M. B., & Armstrong, G. B. (1998). The color of crime: Perceptions of Caucasians' and African Americans' involvement in crime. In G. Cavender & M. Fishman (Eds.), *Entertaining crime: Television reality programs.* Hawthorne, NY: Aldine.

Omi, M. (1987). *We shall overturn: Race and the contemporary American right.* Unpublished doctoral dissertation, University of California, Santa Cruz.

Omi, M., & Winant, H. (1986). *Racial formation in the United States.* New York: Routledge and Kegan Paul.

ONDCP. (1992). *National drug control budget: Executive summary.* Washington, DC: Author.

ONDCP. (1998). *National drug control budget: Executive summary.* Washington, DC: Author.

ONDCP. (1999). *National drug control budget: Executive summary.* Washington, DC: Author.

ONDCP. (2002). *National drug control budget: Executive summary.* Washington, DC: Author.

Orcutt, J., & Faison, R. (1994). Sex role attitude change and reporting of rape victimization, 1978-1985. In D. H. Kelly (Ed.), *Criminal behavior: Text and readings.* New York: St. Martin's.

Overdosing on the drug war. (1995, September 24). *Boston Globe,* p. 1.

Perez-Pena, R. (1997, December 17). New York's income gap largest in the nation. *New York Times,* p. A14.

Petersilia, J., & Peterson, R. (1986). *Prison versus probation.* Santa Monica, CA: RAND.

Petersilia, J., & Turner, S., with Peterson, J. (1986). *Prison versus probation in California: Implications for crime and offender recidivism.* Santa Monica, CA: RAND.

Petersilia, J., & Turner, S. (1990). Comparing intensive and regular supervision for high-risk probationers. *Crime & Delinquency, 36,* 87-111.

Peterson, R. D., & Bailey, W. C. (1998). Is capital punishment an effective deterrent for murder? An examination of the social science research. In J. R. Acker, R. M. Bohm, & C. S. Lanier (Eds.), *America's experiment with capital punishment: Reflections on the past, present and future of the ultimate penal sanction.* Durham, NC: Carolina Academic.

Phillips, K. (1969). *The emerging Republican majority.* New York: Arlington House.

Piven, F., & Cloward, R. (1969). *Poor people's movements: Why they succeed, how they fail.* New York: Arlington House.

Podolefsky, A., & Dubow, F. (1981). *Strategies for community crime prevention: Collective responses to crime in urban America.* Springfield, IL: Charles C Thomas.

Porter, B. (1998, November 8). Is solitary confinement driving Charlie Chase crazy? *New York Times Magazine,* pp. 52-58.

Potter, W. (1986). Perceived reality and the cultivation hypothesis. *Journal of Broadcasting and Electronic Media, 30,* 159-174.

Poveda, T. G. (1994). Clinton, crime and the Justice Department. *Social Justice, 21,* 73-84.

Powers, S., Rothman, D. J., & Rothman, S. (1996). *Hollywood's America.* Boulder, CO: Westview.

Prajean, Sr. H. (1993). *Dead man walking.* New York: Random House.

President's Commission on Law Enforcement and the Administration of Justice. (1967). *The challenge of crime in a free society.* Washington, DC: U.S. Government Printing Office.

Public Opinion Survey: National Issues (Survey #328). (1994, January). *Los Angeles Times.*

Rafter, N. (2000). *Shots in the mirror: Crime films and society.* New York: Oxford University Press.

Rand, M., Lynch, J. P., & Cantor, D. (1997). *Criminal victimization, 1973-1995.* Washington, DC: Bureau of Justice Statistics.

Rapping, E. (1994). *Mediations.* Boston: South End.

Rasmussen, D. W. (1994). *The economic anatomy of a drug war: Criminal justice in the commons.* Lanham, MD: Rowman & Littlefield.

Reagan, R. (1984a). Remarks at the annual convention of the Texas State Bar Association in San Antonio. In *Public papers of the presidents 1984* (Vol. 2). Washington, DC: U.S. Government Printing Office.

Reagan, R. (1984b). Remarks at the Conservative Political Action conference dinner. In *Public papers of the presidents 1983* (Vol. 1). Washington, DC: U.S. Government Printing Office.

Reagan, R. (1984c). Remarks at a fundraising dinner honoring former Representative John M. Ashbrook in Ashland, Ohio. In *Public papers of the presidents 1983* (Vol. 1). Washington, DC: U.S. Government Printing Office.

Reagan, R. (1989). Remarks to members of the National Governors Association. In *Public papers of the presidents 1988* (Vol. 1). Washington, DC: U.S. Government Printing Office.

Reeves, J. L., & Campbell, R. (1994). *Cracked coverage: Television news, the anti-cocaine crusade, and the Reagan legacy.* Durham, NC: Duke University Press.

Reinarman, C. (1995). Crack attack: America's latest drug scare, 1986-92. In J. Best (Ed.), *Images of issues.* New York: Aldine de Gruyter.

Reinarman, C., & Levine, H. (1989). Crack in context: Politics and media in the making of a drug scare. *Contemporary Drug Problems, 16,* 535-577.

Reinarman, C., & Levine, H. (Eds.). (1997a). *Crack in America: Demon drugs and social justice.* Berkeley: University of California Press.

Reinarman, C., & Levine, H. (1997b). Punitive prohibition America. In C. Reinarman & H. Levine (Eds.), *Crack in America: Demon drugs and social justice.* Berkeley: University of California Press.

Reiner, R. (1997). Media made criminality: The representation of crime in the mass media. In M. Maguire, R. Morgan, & R. Reiner (Eds.), *The Oxford handbook of criminology* (2nd ed.). Oxford, UK: Clarendon.

Reinert, P. (2002, June 21). Court bans executing retarded, justices cite shift in public attitude. *Houston Chronicle,* p. A1.

Reiss, A., Jr., & Roth, J. (Eds.). (1993). *Understanding and preventing violence.* Washington, DC: National Academy Press.

Reuter, P., & Kleiman, M. (1986). Risks and prices: An economic analysis of drug prices. In M. Tonry & N. Morris (Eds.), *Crime and justice: A review of research.* Chicago: University of Chicago Press.

Roberts, J., & Doob, A. (1990). News media influence on public views on sentencing. *Law and Human Behavior, 14,* 451-468.

Roberts, J., & Edwards, D. (1992). Contextual effects in judgements of crimes, criminals and the purpose of sentencing. *Journal of Applied Social Psychology, 19,* 902-917.

Roberts, J., & Stalans, L. (1997). *Public opinion, crime and criminal justice.* Boulder, CO: Westview.

Roberts, J. V. (1992). Public opinion, crime and criminal justice. In M. Tonry (Ed.), *Crime and justice: A review of research* (Vol. 16). Chicago: University of Chicago Press.

Rosenbaum, D. (1988). Community crime prevention: A review and synthesis of the literature. *Justice Quarterly, 5,* 323-395.

Rosenfeld, R. (2000). Patterns in adult homicide, 1980-1995. In A. Blumstein & J. Wallman (Eds.), *The crime drop in America.* New York: Cambridge University Press.

Rossi, P., & Berk, R. (1997). *Just punishments: Federal guidelines and public views compared.* Hawthorne, NY: Aldine.

Rothman, D. (1980). *Conscience and convenience: The asylum and its alternatives in progressive America.* New York: HarperCollins.

Sadd, S., & Grinc, R. (1994). *Issues in community policing: Problems in the implementation of eight innovative neighborhood-oriented policing projects.* Washington, DC: National Institute of Justice.

Sampson, R. J. (1987). Urban black violence: The effect of male joblessness and family disruption. *American Journal of Sociology, 93,* 348-382.

Sampson, R., & Wilson, W. J. (1995). Race, crime and urban inequality. In J. Hagan & R. Peterson (Eds.), *Crime and inequality.* Stanford, CA: Stanford University Press.

Sampson, R. J. (1997). The embeddedness of child and adolescent development: A community-level perspective on urban violence. In J. McCord (Ed.), *Violence and childhood in the inner city.* Cambridge, UK: Cambridge University Press.

Sandys, M., & McGarrell, E. F. (1995). Attitudes toward capital punishment: Preference for the penalty or mere acceptance? *Journal of Research in Crime and Delinquency, 32,* 191-213.

Sasson, T. (1995a). African American conspiracy theories and the social construction of crime. *Sociological Inquiry, 65,* 265-285.

Sasson, T. (1995b). *Crime talk: How citizens construct a social problem.* New York: Aldine de Gruyter.

Sasson, T. (1998, November). *Beyond agenda setting: The framing effects of "Nannygate" on a death penalty debate.* Paper presented at the annual meeting of the American Society of Criminology, Washington, DC.

Sasson, T., Beckett, K. (1997). The media and the construction of the drug crisis in America. In E. Jensen and J. Gerber (Eds.), *The New War on Drugs: Symbolic Politics and Criminal Justice Policy* (pp. 25-43). Cincinnati, OH: Anderson.

Sasson, T., & Nelson, M. K. (1996). Danger, community and the meaning of crime watch: An analysis of the discourses of African-American and white participants. *Journal of Contemporary Ethnography, 25,* 171-200.

Schlesinger, P. (1990). Rethinking the sociology of journalism. In M. Ferguson (Ed.), *Public communication: The new imperatives.* London: Sage.

Schlesinger, P., & Tumber, H. (1994). *Reporting crime: The media politics of criminal justice.* Oxford, UK: Clarendon.

Schlesinger, P., Tumber, H., & Murdock, G. (1991). The media politics of crime and criminal justice. *British Journal of Sociology, 42,* 397-420.

Schlosser, E. (1994, August). Reefer madness. *Atlantic Monthly,* pp. 45-63.

Schlosser, E. (1998, December). The prison industrial complex. *Atlantic Monthly,* pp. 51-77.

Schram, S. (1995). *Words of welfare: The poverty of social science and the social science of poverty.* Minneapolis: University of Minnesota Press.

Schudson, H. (1978). *Discovering the news: A social history of American newspapers.* New York: Basic Books.

Seagal, D. (1993, November). Tales from the cutting room floor. *Harpers,* pp. 50-57.

Secret, P., & Johnson, J. (1989). Racial differences in attitudes toward crime control. *Journal of Criminal Justice, 17,* 361-375.

Sentencing Project. (n.d.-a). *Children prosecuted in adult criminal court* [Brief]. Washington, DC: Author.

Sentencing Project. (n.d.-b). *Crime, punishment and public opinion: A summary of recent studies and their implications for sentencing policy* [Brief]. Washington, DC: Author.

Sentencing Project. (n.d.-c). *The expanding federal prison population* [Brief]. Washington, DC: Author.

Sentencing Project. (n.d.-d). *Felony disenfranchisement laws in the United States* [Brief]. Washington, DC: Author.

Sentencing Project. (n.d.-e). *National inmate population of two million projected by 2000* [Brief]. Washington, DC: Author. Retrieved June 3, 1999 from http://www.sentencingproject.org/pubs/tsppubs/prison1.htm

Sentencing Project. (n.d.-f). *New prison population figures: Crisis and opportunity* [Brief]. Washington, DC: Author.

Sentencing Project. (n.d.-g). *Prison privatization and the use of incarceration* [Brief]. Washington, DC: Author.

Sentencing Project. (n.d.-h). *Proposed changes in crack/cocaine sentencing laws would increase number of minorities in prison, have little impact on drug abuse* [Brief]. Washington, DC: Author.

Sentencing Project. (n.d.-i). *Rates of incarceration in selected nations* [Chart]. (Available from the authors.)

Shapiro, B. (1997, February 10). Victims and vengeance: Why the victims' rights amendment is a bad idea. *The Nation, 264,* 11-19.

Shaw, C., & McKay, H. (1942). *Juvenile delinquency and urban areas.* Chicago: University of Chicago Press.

Shaylor, C. (1998, Fall). Organizing resistance: Building a movement against the prison industrial complex. *Colorlines, 1.*

Sherizen, S. (1978). Social creation of crime news: All the news that's fitted to print. In C. Winick (Ed.), *Deviance and the mass media.* Beverly Hills, CA: Sage.

Sherman, L. (1997a). Communities and crime prevention. In L. W. Sherman, D. C. Gottfredwon, D. L. MacKenzie, J. Eck, P. Reuter, & S. D. Bushway (Eds.), *Preventing crime: What works, what doesn't, what's promising.* Washington, DC: National Institute of Justice.

Sherman, L. (1997b). Thinking about crime prevention. In L. W. Sherman, D. C. Gottfredwon, D. L. MacKenzie, J. Eck, P. Reuter, & S. D. Bushway (Eds.), *Preventing crime: What works, what doesn't, what's promising.* Washington, DC: National Institute of Justice.

Sherman, L. (1998, June 30). *Experiments in restorative policing: A progress report on the Canberra Reintegrative Shaming Experiments (RISE).* Canberra: Australian National University and Australian Federal Police.

Sherman, L., & Rogan, D. P. (1995). Effects of gun seizure on gun violence. *Justice Quarterly, 12,* 673-693.

Sherman, L. W., Gottfredwon, D. C., MacKenzie, D. L., Eck, J., Reuter, P., & Bushway, S. D. (Eds.). (1997). *Preventing crime: What works, what doesn't, what's promising.* Washington, DC: National Institute of Justice.

Shipley, W., & Cavender, G. (2001). Murder and mayhem at the movies. *Journal of Criminal Justice and Popular Culture, 9,* 1-14.

Sigal, L. (1973). *Reporters and officials: The organization and politics of newsmaking.* London: Heath.

Signorielli, N. (1990). Television's mean and dangerous world: A continuation of the cultural indicators perspective. In M. Morgan & N. Signorielli (Eds.), *Cultivation analysis: New directions in media effects research.* Newbury Park, CA: Sage.

Simon, J. (1993). *Poor discipline: Parole and the social control of the underclass.* Chicago: University of Chicago Press.

Simpson, S. S. (2002). *Corporate crime, law, and social control.* Cambridge, UK: Cambridge University Press.

Skidmore, P. (1995). Telling tales: Media, power, ideology and the reporting of child sexual abuse in Britain. In D. Kidd-Hewitt & R. Osborne (Eds.), *Crime and the media.* London: Pluto.

Skogan, W. (1990). *Disorder and decline.* Berkeley: University of California Press.

Skogan, W., & Maxfield, M. (1981). *Coping with crime.* Beverly Hills, CA: Sage.

Skolnick, J., & Bayley, D. (1986). *The new blue line.* New York: Free Press.

Slade, D. C. (2001). Taps for medical marijuana. *World and I, 16*(11), 56.

Slater, E. (1995, January 22). California's pizza bandit facing life in prison. *Philadelphia Inquirer,* p. 1.

Smith, B. L. (1988). Victims and victim's rights activists: Attitudes toward criminal justice officials and victim-related issues. *Criminal Justice Review, 13,* 21-28.

Solomon, A. (2002, September 11-17). Things we lost in the fire. *The Village Voice,* pp. 32-36.

Soothhill, K., & Walby, S. (1991). *Sex crimes in the news.* New York: Routledge.

Sparks, R. (1992a). Reason and unreason in "left realism": Some problems in the constitution of the fear of crime. In R. Matthews & J. Young (Eds.), *Issues in realist criminology.* London: Sage.

Sparks, R. (1992b). *Television and the drama of crime: Moral tales and the place of crime in public life.* Buckingham, UK: Open Unversity Press.

Spelman, W. (2000). The limited importance of prison expansion. In A. Blumstein & J. Wallman (Eds.), *The crime drop in America.* New York: Cambridge University Press.

Staggenborg, S. (1991). *The pro-choice movement: Organization and activism in the abortion conflict.* New York: Oxford University Press.

Stanko, E. (1985). *Intimate intrusions: Women's experience of male violence.* London: Routledge.

Stanko, E. (1990). *Everyday violence: How women and men experience sexual and physical danger.* London: Pandora.

Staples, W. (1997). *The culture of surveillance.* New York: St. Martin's.

Stark, S. (1987). Perry Mason meets Sonny Crockett: The history of lawyers and the police as television heroes. *University of Miami Law Review, 42,* 244.

Stern, V. (1998). *A sin against the future.* Boston: Northeastern University Press.

Stinchcombe, A., Adams, R., Heimer, C., Scheppele, K. L., Smith, T., & Taylor, D. G. (1980). *Crime and punishment in America: Changing attitudes in America.* San Francisco: Jossey-Bass.

Stojanovich, P. (Executive Producer). (1997, April 1). COPS [Television broadcast]. Los Angeles: Langley Productions.

Stop the killing machine. (2001). *The Progressive, 65*(8), 8.

Stutman, R. (1992). *Dead on delivery: Inside the drug wars, straight from the street.* Boston: Little, Brown.

Sullivan, M. (1989). *Getting paid: Youth crime and work in the inner city.* Ithaca, NY: Cornell University Press.

Surette, R. (1994). Predator criminals as media icons. In G. Barak (Ed.), *Media, process and the social construction of crime: Studies in newsmaking criminology.* New York: Garland.

Surette, R. (1998). *Media, crime and criminal justice: Images and realities* (2nd ed.). Belmont, CA: Wadsworth.

Tarrow, S. (1994). *Power in movement.* New York: Cambridge University Press.

Thomas, C. (1998, November). *Marijauna arrests and incarceration in the United States: Preliminary report.* Washington, DC: Marijuana Policy Project.

Tonry, M. (Ed.). (1991). *Crime and justice: A review of research* (Vol. 14). Chicago: University of Chicago Press.

Tonry, M. (1995). *Malign neglect: Race, crime and punishment in America.* Oxford, UK: Oxford University Press.

Tonry, M. (1996). *Sentencing matters.* New York: Oxford University Press.

Tonry, M. (1997). *Intermediate sanctions in sentencing guidelines.* Washington, DC: National Institute of Justice.

Tonry, M., & Morris, N. (Eds.). (1987). *Communities and crime, crime and justice: A review of research* (Vol. 10). Chicago: University of Chicago Press.

Travis, J. (2002). Invisible punishment: An instrument of social exclusion. In M. Mauer & M. Chesney-Lind (Eds.), *Invisible punishment: The collateral consequences of mass imprisonment.* New York: New Press.

Trebach, A. (1997, Winter/Spring). Arizona and California voters seize initiatives. *Drug Policy Letter,* pp. 23-24.

Tuchman, G. (1978). *Making news: A study in the construction of reality.* New York: Free Press.

Turner, P. (1993). *I heard it through the grape vine.* Berkeley: University of California Press.

Umbreit, M. S. (1998). Restorative justice through victim-offender mediation: A multi-site assessment. *Western Criminological Review, 1.* Retrieved from http://wcr.sonma. edu/v1n1/umbreit.html

University of California, Los Angeles. (1999). *U.C.L.A. Television Violence Monitoring Project.* Retrieved May 19, 1999, from http://media-aware-ness.ca/eng/med/home/resource/ucla.htm

U.S. Bureau of the Census. (1998). *Statistical abstract of the United States.* Washington, DC: Author. Retrieved June 4, 1999 from http://www.census.gov/statab/www/

U.S. Bureau of the Census. (n.d.-a). *Measures of income inequality, Table IE-6.* Retrieved from http://www.census.gov/hhes/income/histinc/ineqtoc.html

U.S. Bureau of the Census. (n.d.-b). *Poverty in the United States.* Retrieved from http://www.census.gov/hhes/www/poverty01.html

U.S. Bureau of the Census. (n.d.-c). *Historical income tables–Families.* Retrieved August 11, 2003 from www.census.gov/hhes/income/histinc/incfamdet.html, Table F-5.

U.S. Department of Commerce. (1974-2001). *State government finances, 1973-2000.* Washington, DC: U.S. Government Printing Office.

U.S. Department of Commerce. (1998-2001). *State and local finances, 1997-2000.* Washington, DC: U.S. Government Printing Office.

U.S. Department of Health and Human Services. (2002). Retrieved May 26, 2003 from www.hhs.gov/budget/docbudget.htm.

U.S. Department of Justice. (1981). *Attorney general's task force on violent crime: Final report.* Washington, DC: U.S. Government Printing Office.

Van Dijk, J. J. M., & Mayhew, P. (1991). *Experiences of crime across the world: Key findings of the 1989 International Crime Survey* (2nd ed.). Boston: Kluwer Law and Taxation.

Vleminckx, K., & Smeding, T. (Eds.). (2001). *Child well-being, child poverty and child policy in modern nations: What do we know?* Bristol, UK: Policy Press.

Waldorf, D., Reinarman, C., & Murphy, S. (1991). *Cocaine changes: The experience of using and quitting.* Philadelphia: Temple University Press.

Walker, S. (1994). *Sense and nonsense about crime and drugs.* Belmont, CA: Wadsworth.

Walker, S., & Kreisel, B. W. (1996). Varieties of citizen review: The implications of organizational features of complaint review procedures for accountability of the police. *American Journal of the Police, 15,* 65-88.

Walker, S., Spohn, C., & DeLone, M. (1996). *The color of justice: Race, ethnicity and crime in America.* Belmont, CA: Wadsworth.

Walklate, S. (1991). Victims, crime prevention and social control. In R. Reiner & M. Cross (Eds.), *Beyond law and order: Criminal justice policy and politics into the 1990s.* Hampshire, CT: Macmillan Academic and Professional.

Wallman, J. (1997, Fall). Disarming youth. *The HFG Review, 2.*

Walters, J. P. (2002, July 19). Don't legalize drugs (Commentary). *Washington Post*. Retrieved May 15, 2003, from http://www.whitehousedrugpolicy.gov/news/oped02/071902.html

Warr, M. (1995). Poll trends: Public opinion on crime and punishment. *Public Opinion Quarterly, 59*, 296-310.

Washington case is a test for "3 strikes" law. (1994, June 21). *Boston Globe*.

Weed, F. (1995). *Certainty of justice*. Hawthorne, NY: Aldine.

Weintraub, B. (2002, April 3). Police show has humans, not heroes. *New York Times*, p. B1.

Western, B., & Beckett, K. (1999). How unregulated is the U.S. labor market? The dynamics of jobs and jails, 1980-1995. *American Journal of Sociology, 104*, 1030-1060.

Whitaker, M. (1995, October 16). Decision and division: Whites v. blacks. *Newsweek*, p. 24.

Whitney, C. D., Fritzer, M., Jones, S., Mazzarella, S., & Rakow, L. (1989). Source and geographic bias in television news 1982-4. *Journal of Electronic Broadcasting and Electronic Media, 33*, 159-174.

Wilgoren, J. (2003, January 12). Citing issues of fairness, governor clears out death row in Illinois. *New York Times*, p. 1.

Wilkinson, D., & Fagan, J. (1996). The role of firearms in violence "scripts": The dynamics of gun events among adolescent males. *Law and Contemporary Problems, 59*, 000-000.

Williams, A. K. (1995). Community mobilization against urban crime: Guiding orientations and strategic choices in grassroots politics. *Urban Affairs Review, 30*, 407-431.

Wilson, J. Q. (1993). Against the legalization of drugs. In R. Goldberg (Ed.), *Taking sides: Clashing views on controversial issues in drugs and society*. Guildford, CT: Dushkin.

Wilson, J. Q., & Kelling, G. (1982, March). Broken windows: The police and neighborhood safety. *Atlantic Monthly*, pp. 29-38.

Wilson, W. J. (1987). *The truly disadvantaged*. Chicago: University of Chicago Press.

Wilson, W. J. (1996). *When work disappears: The world of the new urban poor*. New York: Knopf.

Windelsham, D. J. G. H. (Lord). (1998). *Politics, punishment, and populism*. New York: Oxford University Press.

Wintemute, G. (2000). Guns and gun violence. In A. Blumstein & J. Wallman (Eds.), *The crime drop in America*. New York: Cambridge University Press.

Wolff, E. N. (1998, Summer). Recent trends in the size distribution of household wealth. *Journal of Economic Perspectives, 12*, 131-150.

Wolff, E. N. (2000, April). *Recent trends in wealth ownership, 1983-1998* (Levy Institute Working Paper No. 300). Annandale-on-Hudson, NY: Levy Economics Institute.

Wortley, S., Macmillan, R., & Hagan, J. (1997). Just des(s)serts? The racial polarization of perceptions of criminal injustice. *Law and Society Review, 31,* 637-676.

Wright, J., & Rossi, P. (1994). *Armed and considered dangerous: A survey of felons and their firearms.* Hawthorne, NY: Aldine de Gruyter.

Wright, K. (1985). *The great American crime myth.* Westport, CT: Greenwood.

Yardley, J. (1999, March 18). One precinct, 2 very different murder cases. *New York Times,* pp. A1, A23.

Zillmann, D., & Wakshlag, J. (1985). Fear of victimization and the appeal of crime drama. In D. Zillmann & J. Bryant (Eds.), *Selective exposure to communication.* Hillsdale, NJ: Lawrence Erlbaum.

Zimmer, L., & Morgan, J. P. (1995). *Exposing marijuana myths: An objective review of the scientific literature.* New York: Lindesmith Center.

Zimring, F. (1968). Is gun control likely to reduce violent killings? *University of Chicago Law Review, 35,* 721-737.

Zimring, F., & Hawkins, G. (1992). *Search for rational drug control policy.* New York: Cambridge University Press.

Zimring, F., & Hawkins, G. (1995). *The scale of imprisonment.* Chicago: University of Chicago Press.

Zimring, F., & Hawkins, G. (1997). *Crime is not the problem: Lethal violence in America.* New York: Oxford University Press.

Index

About the Authors

Katherine Beckett, Ph.D., is Associate Professor in the Department of Sociology and in the Law, Societies & Justice Program at the University of Washington in Seattle. She teaches courses on law, culture, drugs, social control, and terrorism. She is the author of *Making Crime Pay: Law and Order in Contemporary American Politics* (1997), as well as numerous articles and chapters.

Theodore Sasson, Ph.D., is Associate Professor in the Department of Sociology and Anthropology at Middlebury College in Vermont. He teaches courses in criminology, political sociology, and social theory. He is the author of *Crime Talk: How Citizens Construct a Social Problem* (1995), as well as numerous journal articles and book chapters.